THE ṚGVEDA

MAṆḌALA III

A CRITICAL STUDY OF THE SĀYAṆA BHĀṢYA
AND
OTHER INTERPRETATIONS OF THE ṚGVEDA
(3.1.1 to 3.7.3)

THE ṚGVEDA

MAṆḌALA III

A Critical Study of the Sāyaṇa Bhāṣya
and
Other Interpretations of the Ṛgveda
(3.1.1 to 3.7.3)

BY
DR. SIDDH NATH SHUKLA

EDITED WITH AN INTRODUCTION
BY
DR. VIJAY SHANKAR SHUKLA
RESEARCH OFFICER
INDIRA GANDHI NATIONAL CENTRE FOR THE ARTS
NEW DELHI

SHARADA

Sharada Publishing House
Delhi-110 035
2001

First Published 2001

ISBN: 81-85616-73-6

Published by
SHARADA PUBLISHING HOUSE
(Publishers on India's Past and Present)
40, Anand Nagar, Inderlok, Delhi - 110035
Phone 511-7390

Typeset by Neographics, 1800 Gyani Bazar, New Delhi - 110003
and
Printed at Santosh Offset, Delhi-110035

CONTENTS

* * *

PREFACE

After the sad demise of my late lamented father Dr. Siddh Nath Shukla on November 6th, 1984, I collected all his works which were in different stages of preparation. At that time I was studying in the Allahabad University. Keeping these works in mind and also great affection to our culture and heritage, I opted for the Veda group in my M.A. final classes and ultimately completed the research on the Ṛgveda with a D. Phil degree. But after a long journey of fifteen years, I am not sure about my academic performance. I still recall the words of my late father that the whole life is not sufficient for the study of and research in the Ṛgveda. He had also quoted the line of Prof. E.V. Arnold that 'The Rigveda is not a book, but rather a library and a literature'. I got inspiration with these texts and decided to start with this onerous task knowing my limitations and the responsibility involved, only in the spirit of fulfilling my sacred duty to carry out the wishes of my father whose affection has always been an abiding source of inspiration and encouragement to me.

I would like to acknowledge my indebtedness to Prof. Baidya Nath Saraswati, UNESCO Prefessor in the Indira Gandhi National Centre for the Arts, (IGNCA) New Delhi and Pandit Satkari Mukhopadhyaya, Coordinator, Kalākośa Division of the IGNCA for their inspiration and invaluable help to publish this book. In fact publication of this volume has become possible only due to Pandit Mukhopadhyaya ji. I am fortunate enough to work with both the scholars at the Centre.

I sincerely thank Shri B.L. Bansal, proprietor of the Sharada Publishing House and M/s Neographics for their promptness in publishing this book.

Buddha Pūrṇimā
18th May, 2000
New Delhi - 110001

VIJAY SHANKAR SHUKLA

SYSTEM OF TRANSLITERATION

Vowels and Diphthongs

अ	a
आ	ā
इ	i
ई	ī
उ	u
ऊ	ū
ऋ	ṛ
ॠ	ṝ
ऌ	ḷ
ए	e
ऐ	ai
ओ	o
औ	au

Consonants Gutteral

क	Ka
ख	kha
ग	ga
घ	gha
ङ	ṅa

Palatals

च	Ca
छ	cha
ज	Ja
झ	jha
ञ	ña

Cerebrals

ट	ṭa
ठ	ṭha
ड	ḍa
ढ	ḍha
ण	ṇa

Dental

त	ta
थ	tha
द	da
ध	dha
न	na

Labials

प	pa
फ	pha
ब	ba
भ	bha
म	ma

Semi vowels

य	ya
र	ra
ल	la
ळ	ḷa
व	va

Sibilants

श	Śa
ष	ṣa
स	sa

Aspirants

ह	H

Anusvāra

ं	ṃ

Ānanunasika,

ँ	ṁ

Visarga

:	ḥ

Jihvāmūlīya

)(	ẖ

LIST OF ABBREVIATIONS

AA	=	Aitareya Āraṇyaka
AB	=	Aitareya Brāhmaṇa
Abl.	=	Ablative Case
ABORI	=	Annals of Bhandarkar Oriental Research Institute
Acc.	=	Accusative Case
Adj.	=	Adjective
Altind Gram	=	Altindische Grammatik
AV	=	Atharvaveda Saṁhitā
Bahu.	=	Bahuvrīhi-Samāsa
BSOAS	=	Bulletin of the School of Oriental and African Studies, London
BSOS	=	Bulletin of the School of Oriental Studies
Comp.	=	Compound
Dat.	=	Dative Case
Dhāt. P.	=	Dhātu Pāṭha
Der RV.	=	Der Ṛgveda
EVP.	=	Études Védques Et Pāṇinéennes
Gen.	=	Genitive Case
GK	=	Greek
HJAS	=	Harvard Journal of Asiatic studies
Indo-Ger.	=	Indo-Germanic
Inst.	=	Instrumental
JAOS	=	Journal of the American Oriental Society
JRAS	=	Journal of the Royal Asiatic Society
KS	=	Kāṭhaka Saṁhitā
Loc	=	Locative Case
Masc.	=	Masculine Gender

MS	=	Maitrāyiṇī Saṁhitā
MŚYS	=	Mādhyandina Śukla Yajurveda Saṁhitā
Nom.	=	Noṁinative Case
Neu.	=	Neuter Geuder
Nigh.	=	Nighaṇṭu
Nir.	=	Nirukta
Pā	=	Pāṇini Aṣṭādhyāyī Sūtrapāṭha
Pl.	=	Plural
PP.	=	Pages
RV	=	Ṛgveda Saṁhitā
RV.M. II	=	Ṛgveda Maṇḍala II
RV. M. III	=	Ṛgveda Maṇḍala III
RV. Bh.	=	Rgveda Bhāṣya
ŚB	=	Śatapatha-brāhmaṇa
SBE	=	Sacred Books of the East
Sg.	=	Singular
TS	=	Taittirīya Saṁhitā
Un. Ṣ	=	Uṇādi Sūtra
VS	=	Vājasaneyi Saṁhitā
Wackern-Debru	=	Wackernagel-Debrunner
Wörtb	=	Wörterbuch Zum Ṛgveda
Yu	=	Yajurveda
ZDMG	=	Zeit Scrift der Deutschen Morgenländischen Gesellschaft
WZKM	=	Wiener Zeitschrft für die Kunde des Mogen Landes

INTRODUCTION

INTERPRETATION OF THE ṚGVEDA : RETROSPECT AND PROSPECT

The language of the RV is archaic and contains such grammatical devices and linguistic forms which are beyond the reach of common mind. This has never been the language of the common pariance. During the Saṁhitā Period, perhaps, those who were well-versed in this archaic form of language could understand the real meaning of the hymns, but even in those days most of the people must have been unaware of the inherent and sublime meanings of many hymns which are even now difficult to explore. Rigidity in the ritual contexts forced the poets to introduce many new devices to give a poetic bent to the language. Among the devices are mystic illusions, configuration of similar sounds and words, metaphors, incongruous grammatical formations, unsequential syntactical relations and Word-Economy; and these create a sort of sacred quiz, which causes ambiguity and taxes the ingenuity of even the most learned one. The sublimity in the conceptual arena as well as the structural phenomena of the archaic language necessitated the origin of the interpretation.

Most of the verses of the RV were either composed for the purpose of sacrificial settings, or were traditionally employed after the composition. While employing the verses priests must have pondered over the meanings also but sometimes they must have had difficulty in comprehending them or in explaining them to their less qualified associates. This apparently gave birth to the explicatory process which is met in the *Brāhmaṇas*. This can be exemplified by some of the *Brāhmaṇas* where innumerable verses are cited. For example a verse from the RV 10.71.10 has been cited in the AB 3.2 :

'sarve nandanti yaśasā gatena' yaśo vai somo rājā, sarvo ha vā etena krīyamāṇena nandati yaśca yajñe lapsyamāno bhavati yaśca na iti.

Here the words of pāda *'sarve .... gatena'* have been paraphrased in the *Brāhmaṇa* in order to interpret the *ṛk*. The explication of *yaśaḥ* 'fame' *yaśo vai somo rājā* elucidates the style of interpretation with the help of the identificatory process which is a common phenomenon in the *Brāhmaṇas*. It also indicates the sublimity of the Vedic language and thought.

By the time of the *Brāhmaṇas* people started being sceptical about the authenticity of the meaning as well as the utility of the Veda. However, those engaged in the dissemination of thought did not stop themselves in propagating and explaining the Vedic lores through the oral tradition which may be cited here in the words of Yāska—

sākṣātkṛta-dharmāṇa ṛṣayo babhūvuḥ, te'varebhyo' sākṣātkṛta-dharmabhya upadeśena mantrān samprāduḥ

— Nir. 1-20.

"Seers had direct intuitive insight into duty. They by oral instruction, handed down the hymns to later generations who were destitutes of the direct intuitive insight."[1]

However, this tradition created difficulties for the commoners who were inadequate in grasping the flowing currents of the Vedic thought. This gave rise to suspicious minds. Kautsa, cited in the Nirukta, is a case in point. Kautsa pleads for the futility of the etymological attempts saying that if the etymology is meant to serve the purpose of explication of the *mantras*, it is useless, because *mantras* do not contain any meaning, and hence it should be discarded.[2] This provoked Yāska to refute the criticism of people like Kautsa. He said:

naiṣa sthāṇoraparādho yadenamandho na paśyati, puruṣāparādhaḥ sa bhavati. — *Nir. 1.5.8.*
"It is not the fault of the pillar if the blind man does not perceive it, that is the fault of the man himself."
And he added with the same fervour —

sthāṇurayaṁ bhārahāraḥ kilābhūd
adhītya vedaṃ na vijānāti yo'rtham /
yo'rthajña it sakalaṃ bhadramaśnute
nākameti jñānavidhūtapāpmā// — Nir. 1.6.8

"He is the bearer of a burden only, — the blockhead who, having studied, does not know the meaning of the Veda. But he who knows the meaning obtains all good fortune and, with his sins purged off by knowledge, attains heaven."[3]

This indicates the importance of the knowledge of meaning and interpretation of the Veda. The person who recites the Veda without perceiving the meaning cannot attain the real good. He is just muttering the words uselessly, as Yāska says —

yad gṛhītamavijñātam nigadenaiva śabdyate
anagnāviva śuṣkaidho na tajjvalati karhicit // — Nir. 1.6

"Whatever is learnt without being understood is called mere cramming; like dry logs of wood or an extinguished fire, it can never illuminate."[4]

This illustrates the importance and utility of the meaning and proper understanding of the Veda, as was carried on through the tradition. The first systematic attempt at interpretation was made by those who collected and compiled all the ambiguous and difficult words of doubtful origin, and arranged them properly putting all words together which had similar connotations. This arrangement was knows as *Nighaṇṭu.*

Perhaps there were many *Nighaṇṭus* before Yāska, but with the passage of time only one survived which is generally ascribed to Yāska and is commonly attached with the Nirukta. It contains useful material, in its five chapters, for Ṛgvedic interpretation.

In the history of the Vedic interpretation Nirukta is the first treatise which offers some systematic method towards interpreting the RV. Besides the derivation and etymology of words it gives complete or partial explanations of about six hundred verses of the RV. But the explanation found there is so much obsessed with the etymological problems that often it misses the main theme of the hymns and becomes an orduous exercise in futility. Yāska borrows his etymological notions from the 'popular etymologies as well as from the *Brāhmaṇas* and other sources such as tradition, folklore, grammarians and so on.[5] Hence these etymologies are 'phonologically very loose' and create laxity in the interpretation also. These preconceived notions of etymological explication of individual words do not show the light but rather lead to astray. However, the attempt made by Yāska in such a situation where no modern means and methods were available needs sympathetic evaluation and deserves proper appreciation even by the latest explorers of the Veda. Therefore, the importance of the Nirukta in the field of Vedic interpretation cannot be discarded.

Even before Yāska there were many schools of Vedic interpretation as is apparently evidenced by Nirukta. Yāska cites the names of Adhidaivata,[6] Adhyātma,[7] Ākhyanasamaya,[8] Naidāna,[9] Pūrveyājñika,[10] Yājñika,[11] Parivrājaka,[12] Vaiyākaraṇa[13] and Nairukta.[14] Besides these schools Yāska enumerates the names of sixteen[15] grammarians and etymologists who were the promoteurs of the Vedic exegesis and left an enduring impact upon the tradition of interpretation. Their treatises are no more in existence but the tradition must have been immensely enriched through their contributions. Thus a long tradition of *Nighaṇṭus* and *Niruktus* can be visualised.[16]

Tradition did not die after Yāska, but for a long period after him we do not meet with any name of exegetists. It does not mean that there were no attempts in this province of learning, but, perhaps, those contributions were not important enough to be retained by the oral tradition of the Veda. What were the reasons of this laps are not known enough to this day. But, somehow, it can be visualised and stated that due to social and political upheavals the learning of the Vedic lores suffered a lot. Besides these two reasons the literary phenomenon also seems to be accountable for this set back in learning and non-developmental activities of Vedic exegesis. The advent of Buddhism in the fifth century B.C. may be visualised as an important socio-politico-religious cause of the rearing of Vedism. By and large people were attracted towards the teachings of Buddha who admonished people to drift away from the Vedic rituals which were largely enthused with the ritualistic violence and were not supposed to be violence in the ritual norms, practices and terminology.[17] Buddha severely criticised this practice and spearheaded a new religion of non-violence. His teachings were more attuned to the common taste with all its logic and simplicity. The main philosophico-ethical contents of Buddhism were derived from Vedic religion and thoughts, yet its impact upon the people's minds came as a practical act and belief. The authority in power accepted mostly Buddhism. As Vedism and its ritual contents were largely concerned with the classes and not with the masses, there remained very little scope for the priests and scholars to play a role for the developing process of the Vedic exegesis. Rituals and sacrifices did not remain the principal religion of the day, especially in north India, hence the urgency of the Vedic lores in day-to-day life was feltless and less. Brahmanism also suffered and lacked the on going patronage of the authorities. The socio-political changes contributed largely in the development of a new type of literature. The development of *Kāvya*-literature (classical Sanskrit) during the Mauryan period attracted the new mental horizons of the day more because of its felicity and taste. The court-poetry was especially drawn from this new source of classical literature which was immensely applauded by both the classes as well as the masses. The development of the classical literature in the span of nearly one thousand years, i.e. fourth century BC to the sixth century A.D., is remarkable and cannot be ignored while tracing back the reasons of the set back of Vedism as well as the Vedic exegesis. The process of detribalization and the formation of a merchant class which, extending its influence into areas less under the dominance of Vedic orthodoxy but still within the economic context of the region, weakened the authority of the *Brāhmaṇa* caste. This all led to the non-developmental phase of Vedic exegesis for a long period in the history of interpretation.

Although the above analysis of a historical perspective indicates the set back of Vedic learning, yet it does not proclaim the end of the tradition. Tradition did not die. It continued but with a slow pace.[18] The oral tradition was deep-rooted, and none could rout it out. During the sixth century A.D.[19] the great exegetist Skandasvāmin attempted to interpret the *Ṛgveda.* He wrote his commentary on the first *aṣṭaka* of the *Ṛgveda* (RV 1.1.121), which is called *Ṛgveda-bhāṣyam* and is still in existence.[20] This is the first existing commentary on the *Ṛgveda* which throws a considerable light upon some of the obscure passages of the *Ṛgveda* . It paves the way for a proper and systematic course of Ṛgvedic interpretation. In the beginning of every hymn he mentions the name of *ṛsi*, deity and meter, and explicates every word of the verse in the same order as it occurs in the *mantra*. He supports his evidences with the help of Nirukta Grammar, internal evidence and so on. Thus, the commentary becomes very useful. Had it been possible for Skandasvāmin to render the entire *Ṛgveda*, it would have been a rare achievement in the field of Vedic interpretation.

After Skandasvāmin we hear the name of Nārāyaṇa and Udgītha who wrote the commentaries on the *Ṛgveda*. Venkaṭamādhava refers the names of all these three commentators in his *Ṛgarthadīpikā* as follows[21] —

Ṣkandasvāminārāyaṇa udgītha iti te 'kramāt cakruḥ sahaikam ṛgbhāṣyam padavākyārthagocaram /

"Skandasvāmin, Nārāyaṇa and Udgītha - all of them in a chronological order, wrote a commentary of the *Ṛgveda* together in order to explicate the words and the sentences."

This quotation indicates that they wrote the one commentary together, but we do not have any commentary written by Nārāyaṇa. The commentary which is in existence bears the name of only Skandasvāmin. This indicates a tremendous loss in the field of Ṛgvedic interpretation. From Udgītha we have a small work left which is a commentary on the tenth *maṇḍala* of the *Ṛgveda* from fourth hymn to thirtyfourth hymns second verse.[22] In between it is incomplete. It shows that Udgītha attempted to explain the last part of the *Ṛgveda*, namely tenth *Maṇḍala*. We could presume that his commentary was complete on the tenth *Maṇḍala*, which has suffered a loss during the passage of time.

The style of Udgītha's commentary is the same as found in the commentary of Skandasvāmin, which again indicates the proximity and affinity between these two commentaries. A close and comparative study of these two commentaries with other commentaries will open the new vistas in the provinces of Vedic exegesis which is still awaited.

After Udgītha's commentary we come to Mādhava-bhatta's *Ṛgveda-vyākhya* which is similar in volume and contents to that of *Skandasvāmin-bhāṣya.* Mādhavabhatta wrote his commentary on the first aṣṭaka of the *Ṛgveda,* i.e. RV. I. 1.121 hymn.

After Mādhavabhatta, Veṅkaṭamādhava's commentary, entitled *Ṛgarthadīpikā,*[23] opens a new chapter in the history of Vedic interpretation. Though brief but complete, it examplifies a profound sense of exegetical enquiry. Within a few words he tries to reveal the meaning in entirity of every verse of the *Ṛgveda.* He himself proclaimes, *Varjayan śabdavistāram śabdaih katipayair iti*[24] 'abondoning the amplitude of words, by a few words' (the meaning has been revealed). Thus he exemplifies the sense of Word-Economy already practised by the Ṛgvedic poets who have fashioned a worvellous style of telling a lot in a few words.

Veṅkanṭamādhava's style of commenting is the same as that of Skandasvāmin, Udgītha and Mādhavabhaṭṭa. He paraphrases every word in the same order as it is in the *ṛk.* Either he gives synonymous words or puts the same word which occurs in the *ṛk.* Thus a word, and not the sentence, is the unit of meaning in his commentary. But sometimes, this brevity and word-unitary style invokes the laxity and taxes the ingenuity of the reader, because in this style it becomes difficult to construe the words with each other and qualitative gap is still left between the *ṛk* and the reader. He represents the methodology of the *Yājnika* tradition mentioned in the *Nirukta,* which supports the view that Ṛgvedic verses are interlinked with the sacrificial concepts and corollaries. But this is not the whole truth. Laxman Sarup, the editor of his commentary, sums up the views regarding the commentary in these words —

"The commentary of Veṅkaṭamādhava is very brief in character. All grammatical or etymological explanation is generally eschewed. Quotations are rare. But a large number of passages from *Sātyāyana- brāhmaṇa* is preserved .... Veṅkaṭamādhava contents himself with paraphrasing the words of the original text. Almost every word of Vedic stanza is explained. If it is not explained it is repeated in the commentary."[25]

While we are dealing with the development of the interpretation of the *Ṛgveda*, we cannot ignore the contributions of Dhānuska Yajvā and Ānandatīrtha. Unfortunately the commentary of the first is not available. Ānandatīrtha's commentary entitled *Chalārī Tīkā* deals with the first forty hymns of the first Maṇḍala of the *Ṛgveda*. *Jayatīrtha* wrote his commentary on this commentary.[26] Besides them some commentators wrote their commentaries on certain individual hymns also. Among them Ātmānanda's commentary on the RV 1.164, famous with the name *Asya-vāmīya-sūkta*, is a fine example of *Ādhyātmika* tradition referred to earlier.[27] We can refer here Mudgala's contribution in the form of *Vṛtti* on the RV 5.9.1. to 6.9.7. which follows *Sāyaṇa's Bhāṣya.*[28]

The hight and the lofty ideals of interpretation are discernible through the peaks of Sāyaṇa's commentary on the *Ṛgveda*. The Indian tradition of interpretation reaches its acme in this commentary. This is the only commentary which takes the entire *Ṛgveda* in its perview and all traditional views of interpretation culminate in it.

Sāyaṇa (1315-1387 A.D.)[29] derives his materials from Yāska, Mādhava, Veṅkaṭamādhava and his other predecessors. He quotes profusely from *Brāhmaṇas, Nighaṅṭu* and *Nirukta*. Whatever help could he get in determining the meaning, he took all in his perview. Pāṇinian rules of derivation and accentuation proved a great help to him. His oceanic depth of learning and unfathomable visionary power made him supreme among all the interpreters of the *Ṛgveda.* He put *Ṛgveda* again at the pedestal of all Indian Literatures. But his overemphasis of sacrificial order in interpreting the *Ṛgveda,* sometimes mars the beauty of thoughts and strangulates the inherent sublimity of *ṛks,* which necessitates again and again to examine critically his contribution to the interpretation of the *Ṛgveda.* Sometimes he appears to deviate from the original meanings of the *ṛks* in order to justify his sacrificial points of view. Besides, he departs from the traditional views also here and there. It will be worthwhile to quote Macdonell here:

"Sāyaṇa is sometimes found to depart from Yāska, thus we arive at the dilemma either the old interpreter is wrong or the latter one does not follow the tradition. One of the defect of Sāyaṇa is, in fact, that he limits his view in most cases to the single verse he has before him."[30] But Macdonell accepts Sāyaṇa dues and says:

> "It must indeed be admitted that from a large proportion of Sāyaṇa's interpretations most material help can be derived, and that he has been of the greatest service in facilitating and accelerating the comprehension of the *Veda.*"[31]

Some occidental scholars presumed that they could interpret the *Veda* in a better way than Sāyaṇa, but judging from their works it appears that they could not move without Sāyaṇa's help and their pretentions were based on the wrong edifices. Wilson, the first full translator of the entire *Ṛgveda,* observes in this regard, "He (Sāyaṇa) undoubtedly had a knowledge of his text far beyond the pretentions of any European scholar, and must have been in possession, either through his own learning or that of his assistants, of all the interpretations which had been perpetuated by traditional teaching from the earliest times."[32]

We cannot close this discussion about Sāyaṇa without quoting the views of Max Müller, the doyen of oriental learning. He says, "If we can now walk without Sāyaṇa, we aught to bear in mind that five and twenty years ago, we could not have made even our first steps, we could never at best, have gained a firm footing without his (Sāyana's) leading strings ... let us not forget that we are standing on his shoulders."[33]

Again after Sāyaṇa there was a long lull in the field of Vedic interpretation. It was again, perhaps due to the historical reasons. Then the Muslim rule in India did not provide sufficient encouragement for the furtherance of the Vedic wisdom. But, the same historical necessity created an atmosphere of knowing the Hindu society and its basic structures through the learning of their scriptures. The interest grew more and more when many missionaries and administrators came from the West during British rule in India and got acquaintance with the wisdom of the East. They collected many manuscripts and took back with them. This created curiosities in the minds of the Western scholars. Many of them were attracted towards the East. Some of them started studying Sanskrit language and literature. The new vistas of Indological study were opened in many high institutions of learning. Here begins the new phase of Vedic studies which can appropriately be called the renaissance of the Vedic era.

Rudolph Roth (1821-1895) was the first and foremost to write on the Vedic thoughts and people. At the age of twentifive he got an old Manuscript of the *Veda* containing only seventy five hymns and out of that he could squeeze a lot to write a long essay on the *Veda*; and thus he introduced *Veda* in the West. After some time he started his work on the

Vedic lexicography in collaboration with Böhtlingk (1825-1904) and produced the famous *St. Petersberg Sanskrit Wörterbuch* in seven volumes, which still stands as a landmark in the field of Sanskrit lexicography.

When Roth started his work there was no printed edition of the *Ṛgveda*. The need was paramount. This was fulfilled by another doyen of oriental studies. This was none but Prof. Max Müller (1823-1904) who edited the *Ṛgveda*. Besides *Ṛgveda*, he edited the *Sacred Books of the East Series* running into fifty volumes without which even today a proper research cannot be carried on in the field of oriental learning. Max Müller's translation with critical annotations of the *Marut* hymns of the *Ṛgveda* was published in the same series in Vol. No. thirty two. Besides this translation his vast area of learning and erudition are exemplified in many faceted works on religion, history, language and literature. During the second half of the nineteenth century a great attempt of translation of the *Ṛgveda* and other parts of Vedic literature was going on, in which Max Müller's contribution was invaluable. Besides him H.H. Wilson's effort for the translation of entire *Ṛgveda* on the basis of Sāyaṇa's *Bhāṣya* is still commendable. Actually this translation in six volumes brought the whole *Ṛgveda* nearer the scholars. After him only R.T.H. Griffith could complete the English translation of the *Ṛgveda* in two volumes in 1889. Both these translations need a critical examination for the sake of further researches on the *Ṛgveda*, but their importance cannot be minimised.

The study of any archaic language creates the exigencies of proper lexicography. Hence attempts were made in this field also. Besides Roth and Böhtlingk, particular attempts were made for the dictionaries of the *Ṛgveda*. Grassmann's *Wörterbuch zum Ṛgveda* and Neizzer's *Ṛgveda Wörterbuch* are two important contributions in this field which gave a new inpetus to the development of interpretation.

Some studies were done in order to interpret particular sections, hymns, verses and words of the *Ṛgveda,* which created large materials for the new researches. Among such studies Geldner and Pischel's joint work *Vedische Studien,* Bergaigne's *Seventy Hymns,* Oldenberg's *Vedic Hymns* (all Agni hymns), Ludder's *Varuṇa* (in two vols), Macdonell's *Vedic Reader* are some very importants contributions in the field of interpretation. Many critical studies came into light which are still useful for researchers. Among such works Ludwig's translation of *Ṛgveda* in German and his *Kommentar zum Ṛgveda,* Geldner's *Kommentar,* Oldenberg's *Rgveda Text Kritische und Exgetische Noten* are some very important works to be mentioned here. Enumerable research papers on the interpretation of the Ṛgvedic verses and words published in WZKM, ZDMG, JA, JAOS and many other important journals of oriental studies reveal the enthusiasm and sincere efforts of the Western scholars in interpreting the Veda and furthering its knowledge, Here we can mention the names of Kaegie, Zimmermann, Benfey, Weber, Hillebrandt, Keith and many others who contributed immensely to the Vedic interpretation.

Though many studies and translations of the *Ṛgveda* in English, German, French, Italian came into light yet there was still a need of an authentic translation of the *Ṛgveda.* This need was, somehow, fulfilled by Geldner who translated in German, the entire *Ṛgveda.* This was completed in 1909, but the publication of the final volume could be possible only upto 1951, when HOS published all the three parts of *Der Rgveda Uebersetzt* with Index and Glossar.

The old guards could not be there but the Western scholarship continued. In the first quarter of the present century, Macdonell, Keith, Bloomfield, Lanman, Whiteney, Peterson and many other scholars contributed to enrich the tradition of Vedic scholarship, and they gave new dimension to the Vedic studies. This did not stop. Renou, Paul Thieme, Gonda, H.P. Schmidt and others have contributed immensely in the field of interpretation. Renou's voluminous work *Etude Vedique et Paninienen*, Thieme's *Fremdling in Ṛgveda*, Gonda's *Notes on Brahman, Epithets in the Ṛgveda, Stylistic Repetitions in the Veda. The Vision of the Vedic Poets, Loka, Dhāman, Four Studies in the Language of the Veda* and many other works, which compel us to bow down our heads before him, Schmidt's *Vedische vrata und Awestisch urvata, Bṛhaspati und Indra* and many research papers are very valuable contributions in the field.

India did not lack behind. If the western scholarship started building the road. Indian scholars cleared the bushes before it. The critical edition of the *Ṛgveda* by Vaidika Samsodhana Maṇḍala, Pune, and voluminous indices by VVRI, Hoshiarpur have been very great achievements without which Vedic studies could not have prospered as much as it is seen today. Velankar's translation and annotations of *Ṛgveda Maṇḍala* II, III and VII are important landmarks. Bhave's *Soma Hymns* in three parts have created a new phase and given some new orientations to the interpretation of the *Ṛgveda*. These are the beautiful fragrant flowers of the Vedic field which look to the prosperous future. Many research papers in this field by Vishva Bandhu, V.M. Apte, V. Subbiah, R.N. Dandekar, P.V. Kane, C.G. Kashikar, G.V. Devasthali, Ram Gopal, B.R. Sharma, M.D. Balasubrahmaniam, M.D. Pandit, K.P. Jog, G.C. Tripathi, B.B. Chaube and numerous other scholars have been enriching the field. The humble contribution of my late lamented father in the form of his Ph. D. thesis entitled *A Critical and Comparative Study of Sāyaṇa-bhāśya and other Interpretations of the RV Maṇḍala II* and published books *Ṛgveda-cayanikā, Veda* and *Avesta, Veda-Mañjarī* and *Atharva-vedīya-bhūmi-sūkta* as well as twenty research papers connected with interpretation are in a chain to fulfil the growing need of the new methodology of the Ṛgvedic Studies. The present work, hopefully, will add something new in the methods of historical interpretation.

India is a vast country of multilinear traditions where dissents from one ideology to another have been a process of change of continuity. Every tradition have been sustained in its own way. As we have seen above many schools of interpretation were in vogue during Yāska's time also, and they have maintained their continuity with certain changes in later period too. In modern period Shri Aurobindo's esoteric interpretation of the *Ṛgveda* is indicative of the old *Adhyātma* school of interpretation. His books, namely, *Hymns to the Mystic Fire, Secretes of the Veda* and so on, are important contributions to the field. This have been followed later on by many scholars like Kapali Shastri (in his *Siddhāñjana-bhāṣya* of the RV I. 1.121); M.D. Pandit and so on. *V.S.* Agaraval's two important works, namely *Sparks from the Vedic Fire* and *Thousand syllabled Speech* are extensions of the same field.

Similarly, earlier than Shri Aurbindo, Swami Dayanada Saraswati gave another dimension to this field. His spiritual approach to the *Ṛgveda* gave a new awareness to the Indian minds during the days of freedom struggle. His creation of *Ārya Samāja* movement gave new orientation of thinking to the old Vedic thoughts. The blending of the new and the old order has shown a new path to the masses. Svamiji tried to explain Veda in his own way basing his views on the sayings of *Nirukta "mahābhāgyad devatāyā eka ātmā bahudhā stūyate, ekasyātmano'nye devāḥ pratyaṅgāni bhavanti"*[34] (the one God or Ultimate Reality is invoked in many forms, other Gods are just the manifestations of the same reality), which re-minds the famous verse : *ekam sad viprā bahudhā vadanti* ...[35] He explains every verse of the *Ṛgveda* in the light of this above concept. One may differ with his methodology of the interpretation, however, his *bhāṣya* on the *Ṛgveda Maṇḍala* I to VII is an unique contribution in the field of interpretation and its importance cannot be ignored.

These two methods of interpretations have influenced the modern minds immensely, but as they are incompatible with the modern Historical Method of Interpretation it could not be possible to take them in the perview of the prsent study, however, their value is not minimized.

Now, at the last, a question arises about the exigencies of the present study. As we have observed there are many conflicting views about the meanings of the verses of the *Ṛgveda,* hence it becomes necessary to asses the previous works and evolve the suitable meanings in the various contexts of the *Ṛgveda.* Sāyaṇa himself differs on the meanings of the same words in different contexts and thus creates dilemma for the students of the *Ṛgveda.* Hence, need was felt to examine critically his *Ṛgveda-bhāṣya* with comparison to other interpretations in order to arive at certain conclusions. Upto now western scholars have mainly drawn their conclusions on the basis of Sāyaṇa, and sometimes they differ too, which again seemed problematic.

Therefore, whatever has been possible in a limited time and means, everything has been taken into account in this humble attempt. Internal and external evidences, grammar, *Nirukta,* Philology, lexicons etc. have come to much help here. Though much importance have been given to the internal evidences, yet other possible means have not been ignored. Many translations research works, commentaries and so on have been used in this work. Several books by Gonda have proved to be of immense help in understanding many inherent concepts of the *Veda.* I hope this humble but sincere effort will open some new dialogues in the field of the Ṛgvedic studies.

NOTES

1. Translation adopted from Lakshmana Sarup: *The Nighaṇṭu and the Nirukta,* Varanasi, 1962, p. 20. Translation adopted from Lakshmana Sarup, op. cit., p. 16. *Ibid.*, p. 16.
2. yadi mantrārtha pratyayāya, anarthakaṁ bhavatīti Kautsaḥ / anarthakā hi mantrāḥ, tadetenopekṣitavyam. (Nir. 1.15). "If (the object of the science) is to ascertain the meaning of Vedic stanzas, it is useless, says Kautsa, 'for the Vedic stanzas have no meaning'."
3. *Ibidem,* p. 18.
4. *Loc. cit.*
5. S. *Varma, The Etymologies of Yāska,* Hoshiarpur, 1953, pp. 8, 27.
6. Nir. 13.9.
7. *Loc. cit.*
8. *Op. cit.* 2.16.
9. *Op. cit.,* 6.9; 7.12.
10. *Op. cit.* 7.23.
11. *Op. cit.* 5.2; 7.4; 11.
12. *Op. cit.* 4.11; 29; 31; 42; 43.
13. *Op. cit.* 1.12; 9.5; 13.9.
14. *Op. cit.* 2.16.

15 (i) Āgrāyaṇa-Nir. 19.6.13.
(ii) Audumbarayaṇa - i b. 1. L.
(iii) Aupamanyava - i b. i. 1; 2.2 etc.
(iv) Aurṇavābha - i b. 2.26; 6.13 etc.
(v) Kāthakya - i b. 8.5; 6; 17; 9.41; 42.
(vi) Kautsa - i b. 1.15.
(vii) Krauṣṭuki - i b. 8.2.
(viii) Gārgya - i b. 1.3; 12; 26.
(ix) Gālava - i b. 4.3.
(x) Dharmaśiras - i b. 3.5.
(xi) Nailīki - i b. 4.3; 5.27.
(xii) Vārṣyāyaṇi - i b. 1.2.
(xiii) Śatabalākṣya Maudagalya - i b. 11.6.
(xiv) Śākatāyana - i b. 1.12.
(xv) Śakapūṇi - i b. 3.11; 13; 4.8 etc.
(xvi) Sthaulāṣṭhīvi - i b. 7.14; 10. L.

16. Visnupada Bhattacharya, *Yaska's Nirukta,* p. 33.

17. MS 1.2. 15-16 :
    na vā mriyase nota ṛṣyasi devam it eṣi pathibhiḥ śivebhiḥ/ yatra yanti sukṛto nāpi duṣkṛtaḥ tatra tva devaḥ savitā dadhātu //
    oṣadhayaḥ paśavo vṛksās tiryañca pakṣiṇastathā / yajñartham nidhanam prāptāḥ prapnuvantyucchritām gatim //
    "Neither you are dying nor being harmed; you; are ascending to the god through the blessed paths. Where only the doers of good acts go, not the sinners, may god Savitṛ place you there.
    When the plants, animals, trees, beasts and birds obtain death for the sake of sacrifice they attain lofty course (heaven)."
18. B.S. Bhattacharya, *Vedic Interpretations and Traditions* p. 11.
19. For the date of Skandasvamin, see L. Sarup, *Jha Commemmoration Volume,* Allahabad, 1937, pp. 398-410.
20. Ed. by C.K. Raja, Adyar Library and Research Institute, Madras 1939.
21. L. Sarup, *Ṛgartha-dīpikā* I, p. 1135.
22. Ed. by Vishva Bandhu, *Ṛgveda-bhāṣya of Udgīthācārya,* Lahore, 1935.
23. Ed. by L. Sarup in four volumes, Lahore, 1939.
24. *Ṛgartha-dīpikā,* vol. I.
25. Ibid. preface, p. 40 ff.
26. Baldeva Upadhyaya, *Ācārya Sāyaṇa aur Mādhava,* p. 111.
27. Ed. by C.K. Raja, Madras, 1956.
28. See Critical edition of the Ṛgveda commentaries by Vishva Bandhu, VVRI, Hoshiarpur, 1964.
29. Aufrecht, *Catalogus Catalogorum,* p. 711.
30. A.A. Macdonell, *A History of Sanskrit Litterature* p. 62.
31. *Loc. cit.*
32. H.H. Wilson, RV Trans. Vol. I, *Introduction,* p. XLVI.
33. *Preface to Ṛgveda Edition,* Vol. I, p. ix. f.
34. Nir. 7.4.
35. RV 1.164. 46.

The Ṛgveda Mandal III.1

सोमस्य मा तवसं वक्ष्यग्ने वह्निं चकर्थ विदथे यजध्यै ।
देवाँ अच्छा दीद्यद् युञ्जे अद्रिं शमाये अग्ने तन्वं जुषस्व ॥

There is considerable disagreement among the interpreters of the RV, particularly in the interpretation of individual words. The verse RV 3.1.1 becomes all the more problematic due to the word - Economy[1] practised so often by the Ṛgvedic poets. The first two pādas of the verse have been construed differently by the various exegetists. Sāyaṇa's interpretation differs much from that of his predecessor, Venkaṭamādhava.[2] Veṅkaṭamādhava paraphrases it, *he agne, somasya vegam prati mām vaha ca, voḍhāram ca kuru yajñadevān yaṣṭum. devan prati dīpyamāno'ham grāvāṇam ca yunajmi, tvām ca sukhaprāpty artham mama tavasam sevasveti.* He thus differs from Sāyaṇa's renderings of *tavasam* and *vakṣi* in the first *pāda*, and in explaining the verbal form *cakartha* in the second *pāda*. The third and the fourth *pādas* have been explicated by these two scholiasts in the same manner except in the case of *samāya*. This has been rendered by Veṅkaṭamādhava as *sukhapraptyartham*, 'for gaining pleasure or well-being', taking it as a dative infinitive while Sāyaṇa explains it as a form of the pres. first person. sg. of the root *śam*. It appears necessary here to take up and examine individually all these words to understand their exact import and significance.

Tavasam : The word *tavas* occurs frequently in the RV.[3] *Sāyaṇa* has given its alternate meanings as *bala*[4] (strength), *pravṛddhi*[5] (increase) and *vega*[6] (rapidity) or 'impetuosity'.

The first and the third meanings are attested in the Nighaṇṭu,[7] and between these two the first, i.e. 'strength', has been followed by Böhtlingk and Roth,[8] Grassmann,[9] Wilson,[10] Ludwig,[11] Griffith,[12] Oldenberg,[13] Geldner,[14] Renou[15] and Velankar.[16] To this meaning they have added 'power', vigour, 'courage' etc. connoting the same sense in accordance with the different contexts. Here Sāyaṇa explains it as *balinam,* 'strong' construing it with *mā* 'to me'. But Veṅkaṭamādhava explicates it as an abstract noun *vegam,* 'impetus' construing it directly as an object of the verbal form *vakṣi.*

The word *tavas* (mas, fem, neu) is derived from root *tu*> *tav* (class 2) 'to make strong', 'to injure', 'to go', 'to increase' etc. (*gativṛddhihimsāṣu*). The Avestan root *tav,* 'to be able', and Latin *tueri, tatus,* 'to swell', Indo. Eur. *Teu,* 'to swell', Greek *taus* 'great', are identical with Vedic root *tav.*[17] Thus the word *tavas* derived from root *tav* will mean 'to be powerful', swelled with strength, i.e. strong, vigorous, etc. In the present context its meaning 'strength' is suitable. The explanation offered by Veṅkaṭamādhava as *vegam,* 'impetus' is not up to the mark. Moreover, his rendering of *somasya mā tavasam vakṣi* as *somasya vegam prati mām vaha,* 'carry me towards the impetus of soma', also seems faulty, because again he hastens to add *voḍhāram ca kuru* (and make me carrier) showing his doubt about the real object of the verb *vakṣi.* Here mā (to me) seems to act for dative and *tavasam* for accusative, and therefore, the rendering would be "carry the vigour of Soma to me", and with it the second *pāda* may be rendered as - "and let me be the carrier of (this Soma) in the sacrificial place for worship". Thus *tavasam* should be construed with *somasya* and *vakṣi,* and not with *mā* directly. Sāyaṇa differs from this and explains the first two *pādas* together as 'agne, tvam yajñe yaṣṭum somasya vodhāram yam mām kṛtavānasi tam mām tavasvinam balinam kāmayasva, 'Agni, you have made me the carrier of *Soma* in the sacrifice to worship, so you desire me to become strong'. Thus his paraphrasing ignores the syntactical relation of *somasya* with *tavasam vakṣi* and clearly goes beyond the limit in construing *somasya* with *vahnim cakartha.* No doubt that *cakartha* is in perfect tense and could be rendered first, but in the Vedic language this is not a first instance where perfect is being treated as imperative. Sāyaṇa himself explains *cakartha* as *kuru,* 'do or make', at some places.[18] Even if *cakartha* is treated as perfect we can interpret these two *pādas* as 'as you have made me the accomplisher (carrier) of worship in the sacrificial place, desire or bear (carry) the vigour of soma to me (so that I can perform all desired duties with strength)'. Sāyaṇa explains *vakṣi* as *kāmayasva,* 'desire (for me)', which seems controversial. Due to this controversy, this *pāda* has been rendered differently by various exegetists. According to Ludwig[19] and Geldner[20] the phrase *tavasam vaksi* is a case of parenthesis. Geldner translates the first *pāda* as 'du wünschest, dass ich den starken (trank) des Soma (opfere)',[21] ('you wish that I (may) offer the strength (drink) of soma)', and elsewhere[22] he renders it with 'so hast du mich (zu) deinen Soma mschenkendenn dich getustet nach dem starken, O Agni bestellt '(O Agni, thou hast commissioned me for Soma juice which thou longest in order to be strong)'. In both these renderings *vakṣi* has been taken in the sense of 'desiring', and *tavasam* has been construed with *somasya.* This point has been clarified in his annotation also.[23] Max Müller[24] offers its translation as 'strong of Soma', i.e., 'full of Soma', which has been followed by Oldenberg[25] and Renou. But this rendering seems unnatural. Velankar[26] has followed Geldner's rendering, though it is not much different from Max Müller's translation, i.e., 'powerful (draught) of Soma'. All his annotations seem to be based on Geldner's annota-tions about this phrase. A detailed discussion on *vakṣi* will clarify the argumentations more.

Vakṣi — The accented form occurs only here and the unaccented form occurs twenty five times in the RV According to Sāyaṇa it is an imperative form of root *vas* 'to desire', and this has been followed by Wilson, Griffith, Oldenberg, Ludwig, Geldner, Velankar, etc. as has been shown above. Veṅkaṭamādhava takes it from root *vah,* 'to carry, lead, procure, conduct, bear along', (Dhāt. P. xxiii, 35) which has been followed by Renou.[27] Grassmann attests it as the form of root *vah,*[28] and renders it with 'verhilf' (procure for me)[29] which stands in conformity with Veṅkaṭamādhava's explanation. Elsewhere[30] Sāyaṇa also explains it as an imperative of root *vah* (to carry). Actually here this imperative form carries the meaning of subjunctive mood.

The meaning given by Sāyaṇa and followed by others as *Kamayasva* 'desire eagerly', does not appear convincing here. As other contexts[31] indicate, it should be interpreted in the sense of 'to carry on', 'procure', 'bring or bear' and so on. In some contexts *Agni, Indra* and *Uṣas* have been invoked to carry oblations,[32] to bring riches and happiness,[33] and here also the same sense prevails with the word *tavasam* which can be equated with *vājam, iṣam,* and *havyam,* elsewhere standing as an object to the verbal form *vakṣi.*

One thing is remarkable with this form. The majority of the usages are connected with *Agni,* and everywhere he is entreated either to carry oblation to the gods, or to bring (or to lead) the Gods themselves to the sacrificial place. Some occurrences are with *Indra*[34] and *Uṣas*[35] where it means to procure or bring riches, food and vigour for the worshippers. This variation in connotations is due to the varied functions of the Gods.

In the present context the form *vakṣi* may be taken in two senses; firstly, '*Agni* longests for the vigour of Soma' (as Sāyaṇa explains), and secondly, 'procure or carry the vigour of Soma'. Or simultaneously we can apply both the senses together and render the first *pāda* with, 'O *Agni*, procure for me that vigour of Soma for which you long yourself'.

Here we can compare RV 7.98.2 *dive dive pītim idasya vakṣi* - '(O Indra) you desire for its drink (or food) daily'.

Vahnim : The epithet *vahni* stands especially for *Agni* in the RV, but sometimes the seers drift from their normal practice of usages and employ the epithets with other divinities also as they have employed *vahni* with *Maruts* (1.6.5; 44.13), *Indra* (2.21.2), *Some* (9.20.5), *visvedevas* (1.3.9), *Uṣas* (1.48.11), *Ṛbhus* (1.20.8), *Bṛhaspati* (2.24.13), *Savitṛ* (2.38.1), *Aśvins* (7.73.4; 8.8.12) and so on. Here if we accept Sayaṇa's interpretation the invoker himself is *vahni* whom *Agni* has employed (*cakartha*) to carry on the duties of the sacrificial setting. Due to the employment of *vahni* with several deities it connotes different concepts in different contexts. When it is employed with *Agni* it is equal to *havyavāha* and thus the word *vāhas* is meant there, i.e. *Agni* is the 'carrier of the oblation or Gods message'. In such contexts *vahni* is derived from root *vah* (to carry, lead, guide, direct, conduct etc.); otherwise it carries another meaning, i.e. the concept of 'elevation' or 'carrying upward' as is indicated by its usages with Soma at RV 9.89.1; 91.1 and 9.9.6.[36] According to Grassmann[37] *vahni* stands for 'horse' in such contexts and in all the Soma hymns (where ever *vahni* occurs), according to him, only his meaning is implied. Some occurrences at the YV (35.13) and the AV (12.2.47) also bear testimony to this meaning. Neisser[38] attests the meaning of *vahni* as 'Zugthier' (traveller) and taking his clue from this meaning. Oldenberg goes further to state that *Savitṛ* (2.38.1), *Aśvins* (7.73.4; 8.8.12), *Viśvedevās*

(13.9), (compare, 1.44.13 *vahnibhiḥ sayāvabhiḥ*) also appear to be travellers. Other meanings according to Oldenberg are 'elevated, exalted, lofty' (erhabend, erhebend), 'benevolent, gracious' (buldigend) and 'praiseworthy' (betend) etc.[39]

In the present context *vahni* seems to be used for the invoker or worshipper himself and signifies the role of the 'conductor of the sacrificial acts' at the place of the worship (*vidathe*).

Vidathe : The meaning of the term *vidathe* has been a subject of controversial discussions among scholars since the yāskan period. Sāyaṇa's explanation of this as 'sacrifice' (*yajña*) is based on Yāska's Nigh.[40] where it has been attested as a synonym of *'yajña'*. Elsewhere Sāyaṇa explains it as 'knowledge, action, invocations, house' and so on but always connecting it with 'sacrifice'. Veṅkaṭamādhava and other traditional interpreters follows Yāska. Occidental vedists have been arguing about *vidatha* up to the present. M. Regnaud[41] has given *Roth's*[42] view on it as '*consell, avis, reunion on 1*' on delihere, assemblee, troupe, armee. Grassmann[43] attest its meaning as: 1. Versammlung (congregation); 2. Versammlung zum gottesdienste (congregation for divine worship); 3. Genossenschaft, Gemeinde (association) and so on, giving stress to 'assembly' and 'congregation' Ludwig[44] derives *vidatha* from root *vid* 'to be acquainted', 'to know' but gives its meaning as 'assembly', 'sacrifice'. Regnaud[45] differs on this point and traces it from root *vidh*, 'to sacrifice', and maintains that *vidhatha* would become *Vidatha*. Geldner[46] derives it from root *vid* 'to know' or in the sense of 'art', 'science', Bloomfield[47] traces it from root *vid* 'to gain' while Paul Thieme[48] proposes it as an aorist formation from root *dhā* with *vi* as prefix (*vidatha*). Bartholomae[49] puts *vidatha* with Avestan *muhrkacra* which seems an erroneous deduction.

Max Müller's[50] suggestion that "*vidatha* may have been the name of a sacred act, as *Veda* is of 'sacred knowledge' and can be best translated by assembly, particularly as assembly for sacrificial purposes" bears the testimony to the meanings gives by Grassmann.

Following Wackern-Debru[51] it can be argued safely here that *vidatha* is formed by - *atha* suffix which is acceptable even according to Sāyaṇa's explanation and can be put together with the other formations formed by the same suffix, such as *sacatha* (*sacathāya* - RV 1.156.5), *stanathā* *(stanathāḥ)* - RV 5.83.3, *Caratha (Carathāya* - RV 1.36.14; 4.18.10), *vakṣatha - (vakṣathāya* - RV 10. 99.12) *stavatha* (RV 4.21.2), *ucatha* (RV 1.73.10; 110.1;). *svasatha* (*svasathāt*- RV 8.96.7), *tvesatha* - (*tvesathāt* - RV 141.8), *ravathaḥ* (RV 1.110.13), *ravath* (*ena* - RV 9.80.1), *sapathāḥ* (RV 10.87.15) and *jīvathaḥ* (RV 6.59.1). In all these formations the suffix - *atha* - and the original roots are sufficiently clear to deduce the conclusion that nothing else is needed to form these words than the original root and the suffix - *atha* -. On the basis of these analogies as well as Avestan *Zbarava* "foot, base" we can conclude that *vidatha* is derived from the root *vid* plus - *atha* suffix.

Now the question arises about the exact meaning and accent-rules. The accent can be explained by *ādyudāttasca* (*Pā* 3.1.3), according to which the acute accent is always on the first syllable of the affix. Therefore, all the formations cited above have the acute accent on the first syllable of the suffix, i.e. on *a (atha)*; thus all are paraxytone. The other possibility of accent might arise here with the rule *thāthāghañ* - *(Pā* 6.2.144) by which we have to form *vidatha* by *upasarge Vaseḥ* (Uṇ s. 3.116) by which *vidatha* would be a compound word as has been decided by *Bailey*.[52] Thus the acute accent will fall on the first syllable of the second member of the compound. But this possibility is ruled out here on the basis of several words cited above.

The meaning can be decided on the basis of the root. As is apparent through above examples, viz. the words *stanatha, caratha, yajatha* etc. which are directly derived from root *stan,* root *car,* root *yaj* respectively, the word *vidatha* also being in the same analogical category, should be derived directly from root *vid.* This root is attested in five classes, namely, *adādi* (ii) *divadi* (iv) *tudādi* (vi) *rudhādi* (vii) and *curādi* (x) and bears various meanings, as 'to know, perceive, attain, gain, to think over, to exist, stay' and so on. Thus *vidatha* may mean wisdom, knowledge, perception, observation, a place of pleasure, attainment, existence, house, a place of pleasure-thinking etc. But all these meanings cannot be applied to the various contexts of the RV. Therefore we have to make some choice out of these meanings which can be applied meaningfully to the various contexts. At the very outset *vidatha* appears to mean 'place' which can signify 'house', 'sacrificial place' or 'place of assembly or discourse' and 'world' as is evident in several Ṛgvedic contexts such as 1.130.1; 2.1.14; 16; 3.8.5; 54.11; 56.5; 8; 4.16.3; 6.24.2; 52.17; 7.18.13; 21.2; 9.32.1; 74.6; 86.27 and so on. Three *vidathas* can be compared with three *savanas* of the day such as *tṛtīye vidathe* at 2.4.8 which may be compared with *tṛtīye savane* at 1.161.8; 3.28.5 etc. and *tṛtīye rajasi* at 9.74.6; 86.27 etc. Thus *vidatha* signifies the sacrificial place' as well as the 'act of sacrifice' which ultimately means 'sacrifice' or 'rite' itself as has been suggested by Renou[53] and Gonda.[54] But mostly it means the 'place of sacrifice' as is clear in such contexts as *'kṛtam no yajñam vidatheṣu cārum'* (7.84.3), "make our sacrifice lovable in the 'sacrificial place'" ('assemblies' - Velankar[55]). It may be put parallel to the words *astam* (house), *niṇyam* (house), *duroṇe* (house) and *sadane* (house) which occur with *vidatha* at RV I. 130.1; 4.16.3; 3.1.18; and 10.12.7 respectively.

In some contexts *vidatha* appears to mean the 'battle field' but perhaps it denotes the 'place of heated discussions'. At RV 3.8.5; 6.24.2; 7.18.13; and 7.21.2 it occurs with *samarya, vājī, mṛdhravācam (jeṣma)* and *dudhravācaḥ* respectively with *vidatha* which signify the argumentations in a heated atmosphere with the learned people. Therefore the seers seek the help of the Gods to overcome these people at *vidatha,* i.e. the 'place of assembly'.

In some places it denotes 'knowledge' which is again connected with the 'sacrificial knowledge'. Such contexts are RV 1.164.21; 3.1.2; 4.38.4; 6.8.1; 11.2; and 8.39.9. It is strange that in all these contexts the form is *vidathā* which stands for *vidathāni.*

Thus it is clear that *vidatha* is a derivative of root *vid* either in the sense of 'attainment or knowledge'. When it denotes 'place' it signifies the root meaning 'to attain', and in the sense of 'knowledge' it is derived from root *vid* 'to know'. In the present contexts the meaning 'sacrificial place' or 'sacrificial assembly' is more suitable than any one else.

The last two *pādas* are to be divided into four distinct clauses in which *yunje adrim samāye* appears to be a parenthetical statement. Thus we can observe that (i) *devān acchā dīdyat,* (ii) *yunje adrim,* (iii) *samāye (aham)* and (iv) *agne tanvam juṣasva* are four clauses which indicate the four dimensional actions of Agni and the invoker. Among these clauses the first has been explicated in two ways by the exegetists. Veṅkaṭamādhava and Sāyaṇa explain it as 'shining (myself) towards the Gods', (*devān abhi dīpyamāno'ham).* This explication has been followed by Grassmann, Oldenberg, and Renou with certain alterations. There is a difference of opinion about the meaning of *dīdyat* only. They render it in the sense of 'thinking' (guiding luminous thought' -Renou) which is not much different from 'shining', because 'shining' also connotes the same sense. Ludwig renders it in favour of Agni as 'thou shinest towards the Gods' (du den gottern herbei beuchtet) which has been followed by Griffith, Geldner, and Velankar. But Velankar construes it with Agni as well as with the invoker, and gives in support of his view the arrangement that the poet suddenly thinks of himself as a consecrated *vahni* (b) and as such *devān acchā dīdyat* by way of its justification; so he parenthetically adds *yuñje adrim samāye.*[56] This view is certainly based on Oldenberg's[57] critical annotation on this part of the verse. Both of them quote the same passages from the *Ṛgveda* to justify their stand. The passages quoted are RV 6.20.13 *dīdayadit tubhyam Somebhiḥ sunvan dabhītiridhmabṛtiḥ:* 1.59.4 *kavayaḥ sudītayaḥ*; 8.97.12 *sudītayo* and so on. Oldenberg goes even beyond this, and on the basis of Roth[58] he suggests that the reading *dīdyat* is actually corrupt, and it should be *dīdhyat* as is found at RV. 3.4.3 *dīdhitiḥ*, 3.55.3 *sami - dīdye* and so on. Accordingly all the forms should be interpreted in the sense of 'thinkings' But this opinion of Roth and Oldenberg seems unconvincing, because the *di* (to shine) is frequently used in the RV as well as in later Vedic literature. Besides, *dīdyat* has been used with Agni everywhere in the RV All the occurrences can be quoted here to substantiate the arguments.

RV 1.143.4: *indhāno akro vidatheṣu dīdyat*
(inflamed and keen, refulgent in the assemblies).

RV 2.9.2 : *agne .... dīdyad bodhi gopā.*
(O Agni, be the unfailing and refulgent defender).

RV 7.10.1 : *uso na jāraḥ ...... dīdyat sosucānaḥ*
(like the lover of the Uṣas blaxing and shining Agni).

RV 10.118.1 : *agne .... dīdyat martyeṣu ā sve ksaye*
(O Agne, - refulgent among men - in your abode).

RV 10.118.8 ; *sa tvam agne .... urukṣayeṣu dīdyat*
(that you Agni shining in wide regions).

RV 10.122.6 ; *agne .... tri ṛtāni dīdyat*
(Agni, lighting the three worlds.)

RV. 3.27.15: *agne dīdyatam bṛhat*
(O Agni, shining mightily.)

On the basis of these occurrences we can say that *dīdyat* stands for Agni and not for the Priest, and the last two *pādas* should be interpreted as "O Agni, while I join the pressing stone and make it active, shining towards the Gods you willingly assume your own form".

III. 1.2

प्राञ्चं यज्ञं चकृम वर्धतां गीः समिद्भिरग्निं नमसा दुवस्यन् ।
दिवः शशासुर्विदथा कवीनां गृत्साय चित् तवसे गातुमीषुः ॥

This verse presents four-fold activity of the sacrificial assembly, i.e. (i) the sacrifice is being advanced, (ii) the priest asks to elaborate the speech performing oblation-offering acts for Agni, (iii) the Gods are supposed to come from heaven to govern and protect the sacrificial assemblies of the poets and finally (iv) the priests appear to have cleared the way for exalted Agni (in order) to attain vigour. In order to clarify the meaning, the entire verse can be divided into five clauses which are interlinked with each other. The clauses are —

(i) *prāñcam yajñam cakṛam,* (ii) *vardhatām gīḥ,* (iii) *samidhbir agnim namasā duvasyan,* (iv) *divaḥ śaśāsur vidathā kavīnām* and finally (v) *gṛtsāya cit tavase gātumīṣuḥ.*

Prāñcam : In the first *pāda* of the verse the word *prāñam* has been assigned two meanings by the exegetists of the RV.

Veṅkaṭamādhava[2] explicates the phrase *prāñcam cakṛma* as *karma pravṛddham,* 'advanced by acts', Sāyaṇa explains *prāñcam* as *prakarṣeṇa gacchantam,* 'going effectively', and he analyses it elsewhere[59] as *pra + añca;* from √*añca* 'to go', and correlates it with 'facing towards east or front side' (*prāñmukhañcan-āḥ gacchantaḥ*) which has given some clue to the modern interpreters to interpret *prāñcam* in the sense of 'eastwards' or 'front'. Ludwig, Griffith, Oldenberg, and Renou follow the meaning 'eastward', 'front' or 'before'. Grassmann, Geldner and Velankar render it in the sense of 'advancing' or 'bringing (the sacrifice) to the front' which seems ultimately in confirming to Sāyaṇa's explication of *prakarṣeṇa gacchantam akārṣma,* 'made it advance'.

Following Bergaigne,[60] Oldenberg[61] remarks, "Many sacrificial rites are performed from west to east", as is found with ıegards to *barhiṣ* 188.4; 10. 110.4; with regard to the sacrificial ladle, III.6.1; V.28.1; to the *havirdhānas,* Vāj. S. 5.17 Thus the whole sacrifice is spoken of as proceeding in an eastward direction. He substantiates his view by examplifying RV X. 66.12 *prāñcam no yajñam pra ñayata;* 10.87.9 *yajñam prāñcam ... praṇaya.*

Padapāṭhakāra has not analysed the word *prañca* - and therefore, there is some doubt whether it is *pra + añcà* or something else. But some similar forms like *ṛju-añcaḥ* (RV 4.6.9.), *sadhryañca* (RV 1.108.3), *sadhryañcaḥ* (RV 4.4.12; 5.60.3), *svañcaḥ,* (RV 4.6.9; 7.56.16; 9.73.7); *ud añcakaḥ* (RV 5.44.13), *ni añcanam* (RV 8.27.18); *parāñcaḥ* (RV 1.64.19) etc. indicate that though unanalysed, *añca* - is a separate entity, and should be regarded as a derivative of either √*ac* or √*añca.* This root has its cognates in Indo-germ and Indo-Iran languages also. Indo-germ *oqu* and *GK-ov* as well as Iran. *anc* are identical with *añca.* The Indo-germ word *proti-esq,* 'to what way moving' and *proti-qu,* 'where looking' may be put together with *pratyañca* and *pratyak.*[62] Avestan *anc* -

'turned' or 'directed' is similar to *añca,*[63] and thus it can be surmised that *añca* has its individual identity and the prefixed word *pra -, su, dadhi, ṛju* and so on are quite different from it. Thus the meaning given by Sāyaṇa can be justified, and those who have interpreted it in the sense of east can be put aside. Thus the clause first can be rendered as 'we have advanced the sacrifice' or 'made it go ahead' as has been rendered by Geldner (wir haben des opfer vorgeführt) and followed by Velankar.

The phrase ***vardhatām gīḥ*** just after this clause, first gives an indication towards the existing phenomenon in sacrificial acts regarding the loud incantations. The invocations are made loudly and therefore, the *ṛtvik* priest orders the accompanying priests to make the speech *gīḥ* (invocations, *stutiḥ* - Sāyaṇa) loud. But Sāyaṇa construes it with Agni who has been entreated to increase the hymn. As there is no mention of Agni, it should be construed with priests who have been asked to serve Agni with homage (*namasā*). *Namasā* - Sāyaṇa has explained this word as *haviṣā* 'with oblation' which is similar to Veṅkaṭamādhava's rendering *annena,* 'with food'. Both of them have followed the meaning of this word attested in the Nigh.[64] But at the same time both of them have explained it as 'invocation' or 'benediction' at many places in the RV[65] The present context can be compared with RV 1.1.7 *namo bharanta emasi* where Sāyaṇa explains *namo bharantaḥ, 'namaskāram sampādayanataḥ',* 'offering the homage' or 'completing the benediction or reverence'. The same may be applied here with *namasā duvasyan* also, and therefore, it can be rendered as 'prayer' or 'reverance'.

Duvasyan : There is some difference of opinion regarding the form and meaning of *duvasyan* which appears at 3.1.13 also. Once the accented form *duvasyan* also occurs (1.167.6). Veṅkaṭamādhava and Sāyaṇa both take it in the sense of 'serving' (paricaran) and barring a few occurrences,[66] they have everywhere explained it in the same sense which explains their predilection for accepting the meaning attested by Nigh.[67] where *duvasyati* has been enumerated with other forms in the sense of 'service' (......... *namasyati duvasyati .... paricaranakarmā)*. But at RV 1.112.15 and 21 Sāyaṇa explicates *duvasyathaḥ* as *rakṣathaḥ*, 'you two protect', and at RV 1.119.10 he explains it as *dattavantau*, 'you two gave'. This indicates that Sāyaṇa had some doubt about the exact meaning of the *duv-*, and he took the traditional point of view for granted with regard to this verb. At a few places[68] he explains *duvas* as *dhanam*, 'wealth', where he seems to derive it from *duv*, 'to give', which appears to give it some support as a collateral form to give, as *gu* to *gā*, *pu* to *pā*, *sthu* to *sthā* and so on which are met with *agregu (guvaḥ)* VS 1.12; TS 1.1.5.1; MS 1.1.4; 4.4), *adhriguḥ* (RV 6.45.20; 8.70.1; 93.11), *agrepu (puvaḥ)* (MŚYV. 1.12; TS 1.1.5.1) and *sthaviraḥ* (RV 1.171.5; 10.103.5). Grassmann[69] also suggest the same formation and meaning. According to him *duvas* means 'a gift' either *from* or *to* the Gods, and thus it may be taken as an equivalent to sacrifice which is *paricaraṇa* in the words of traditional commentators. This meaning can be extended in the sense of 'worship', 'reverence', 'oblation', 'friendship', 'favour' etc.[70] Root *duv* can be identified with Indo-Eur. *due* or *dou*, 'to revere, favour, bless'.[71]

III. 1.3

मयों दधे मेधिंरः पूतदंक्षो दिवः सुबन्धुंर्जनुषां पृथिव्याः ।
अविंन्दन्नु दर्शतमप्स्व १ंन्तर्देवासों अग्निमपसि स्वसृंणाम् ॥

Agni's relation with Heaven and Earth has been described in this verse. Nothing seems very controversial here for a detailed discussion, only the meanings of *mayah* and *apasi* need a fresh look.

Mayaḥ : Sāyaṇa explains *mayaḥ* as *sukham,* "pleasure". He derives it from the √*min* "to injure" and explicates it *hinasti duhkhamiti sukham mayaḥ* (see RV 1.13.9). He quotes traditional view *yad vai sukham tanmayaḥ* (RV 1.31.7) also. Veṅkaṭamādhava, followed by Grassmann, Oldenberg, Geldner etc. also assign the same meaning with some extensions like 'vigour, refreshment, delight, restoration' etc.

The etymology and derivation proposed by Sāyaṇa do not appear convincing, because the root *mīn* connotes altogether different and rather negative concept. Therefore, we have to derive this word from a root which is directly connected with it. The radical form *mayante* occurs in the RV 10.40.10: *jīvam rudanti vi mayante adhvare* which is followed by the nominal form *mayaḥ* also:, *mayaḥ patibhyo janayaḥ pariṣvaje.* Sāyaṇa explains *mayante* as *niveśayanti,* "make (them) to enter". This gives a clue to explain the root *may* in the sense of 'entering, approaching, reaching" and such similar meanings. The word *mayaḥ* can be identified with the Avestan *mayaḥ* "coition, lust, cohabitation".[72] Thus it comes near the word *retas* which is commonly combined with the root *dhā* in the RV. (RV 3.56.3; 5.69.2; 7.101.6; 9.86.39; 10.129.5) and which can be compared with *mayaḥ dadhe* in the present context as well as with the RV. 8.39.4; 10.40.10. The original meaning of *maya* - appears to be "approach, affinity, embrace or coitus-pleasure" which was later on developed into "pleasure, well-being, happiness" and so on, and it can be placed with *sumnam.*

Apasi : The locative sg. of the substantive *apas* - creates a problem of ellipsis here, and can be supplied with *dakṣa* - or *sarga* which occur with it at 1.2.9 and 10.89.2 respectively.

Veṅkaṭamādhava explains it *vege, vasthitam,* "residing in the flow". Sāyaṇa takes it in the sense of "activity" (*yajña-*

vahanarūpe karmani nimitte). As it is directly connected with *svasṛṇām* it has to be interpreted in the sense of "activity". *Svasṛṇām* may be interpreted in two ways, namely, in favour of the "waters" and secondly in favour of the "ten fingers" who are active in the performance of the sacrifice.

The comp. *putadakṣaḥ* has been explained by Sāyaṇa as *Śuddhabalaḥ,* which according to this explanation seems *tatpuruṣa.* But as the accent on the first member indicates it is a bahuvrīhi corup. and it should be rendered with "whose dexterity is purified", or "one who possesses the purified dexterity".

III. 1.4

अवंर्धयन् त्सुभगं सप्त यह्वीः श्वेतं जंज्ञानमंरुषं मंहित्वा ।
शिशुं न जातमभ्यांरूरश्वां देवासों अग्निं जनिंमन् वपुष्यन् ॥

The phrase *sapta yahvīḥ* refers to the "seven streams" which are closely connected with Apām Napāt, another form of Agni. This can be compared with RV 2.35.9 cd:

> *tasya jyeṣṭham mahimānam vahantīḥ hiraṇyavarṇāḥ pariyanti yahvīḥ*

"The gold-coloured maidens, carrying his highest greatness, surround him".[73]

Sāyaṇa explains *sapta* as *sarpaṇaśīlāḥ,* "flowing, moving, creeping", which seems doubtful because the number 'seven' is a very common usage in the Ṛgvedic phraseology. Hence the meaning "seven" is more probable as Venkaṭamādhava[74] thinks.

Sapta yahvīḥ can be compared with *sapta mātaraḥ* at RV 9.86.36, which also refers to the rivers. *sapta yahvīḥ* are the close associates or wives of Agni, as Oldenberg[75] has pointed out. This can be compared with RV 3.1.9 below.

Abhi āruḥ : This verbal form, pf. of √ṛ "to go" with the prefix *abhi,* is to be construed with *asvāḥ* as well as with *yahvīḥ.* Both of them reach Agni swiftly.

Vapuṣyan : This is an unaugmented impf., which is the denominative form of *vapus.*[76]

III. 1.5

शुक्रेभिरङ्गै रजं आततन्वान् क्रतुं पुनानः कविभिः पवित्रैः ।
शोचिर्वसानः पर्यायुरपां श्रियो मिमीते बृहतीरनूनाः ॥

Sāyaṇa's explanation of *ātatanvān* as *ātanvan vyāpnuvan,* 'pervading' differs from Veṅkaṭamādhava's rendering *vistārayan,* 'spreading' which is more literal. If we accept the meaning of *rajaḥ* as *antarikṣam,* 'mid-region' as given by Sāyaṇa and Veṅkaṭamādhava[77] both, the explanation given by Sāyaṇa seems more suitable. But the meaning of *rajaḥ* is doubtful.

Rājas : The word *rajas* occurs frequently in the RV (149 times). It has been attested in the *Brāhmaṇas*[78] as the Synonym of *loka,* "world".[79] This has led Yāska to give its etymology and meanings as *'rajo rajateḥ jyoti raja ucyate, udakam raja ucyate; lokā rajānsi ucyante asrgahanī rajasī ucyete'.*[80]

These meanings have been followed by the subsequent exegetists invariably without going into pros and cons. Upon a closer examination of the contexts of the RV where the word *rajas* occurs it seems that the original meaning of this word is "way, road, route", and not the "world". Only by implication later on, it developed into several facets which became vogue in the later literature.

Here in the present context the meaning "way" is more suitable. Sāyaṇa has also accepted this meaning elsewhere.[81]

Western scholars have identified it with *goth. rigis* "darkness". GK. *esepos* "world of the darkness", Avestan. *razaḥ* "a long way".[82] But these words do not go well with *rajas* so far as the meaning is concerned. Therefore, we have to rely on the internal evidences only in order to get the real sense of the individual context.

Thus in the light of above discussion the first *pāda* can be rendered as: "(Agni) widening his path (*rajas*) by his lusturous body (limbs)".

Kratum means 'activity' according to Sāyaṇa and Veṅkaṭamādhava. But modern exegetists have offered new meanings, i.e. 'vigour, strength, power' and so on. The word *kratu* - is identical with Avestan. *xratus* "power", GK *xratos, xretos* 'strength' and *khot, grata* "understanding". Thus the meaning may be extended as "power of thinking", "vigourous activity", 'will power' and so on. Here *kratum* has been construed by Sāyaṇa with the sacrificer, but it appears to be related directly with Agni, Therefore, *kratu* should be taken in the sense of 'visionary power' of Agni which he himself purifies with his thoughts (*kavibhiḥ*).

III. 1.6

व॒व्राजा॑ सी॒मन॑दती॒रद॑ब्धा दि॒वो य॒ह्वीरव॑साना॒ अन॑ग्नाः ।
सना॒ अत्र॑ युव॒तय॒ः सयो॑नी॒रेकं॒ गर्भं॑ दधिरे स॒प्त वाणीः॑ ॥

This *ṛk* has some semblance with the fourth *ṛk* discussed earlier where seven heavenly streams have been described as encompassing Agni after he is born. In this *ṛk* those same seven maidens arising from heaven have been mentioned as the bearer of the embryo, i.e. Agni. The verbal form *vavrāja* indicates the 'continued' activity of Agni towards the maidens, and the verb stands without the *agentis causa*. *ekam garbham* stands for Agni as an object of *dadhire*. Thus there are two actions and notions involved simultaneously creating *virodhābhāsa*. Besides, *anadatīḥ-adabdhāḥ* 'do not eat but are uninjured' and *avasānaḥ - anagnāḥ* "do not wear but are not - naked" also produce the sublimity of *virodhābhāsa*.

Anadatīḥ creates some doubt, because it can be interpreted either as *anadatīḥ* (a + nadatiḥ) 'not making any sound' (*sabdam akurvatīḥ*) as Venkaṭamādhava has done, or it can be *anḥ adatīḥ* 'without eating' (*abhakṣayantīḥ*) as Sāyaṇa has explained. But, the form being *hapax legomenon* it is quite difficult to arrive at a certain conclusion. So far as the accent is concerned both the roots, i.e. √*ad* and √*nad* take the *sap*, and thus being *pit* the accent remains on the original root *anudāttau suppitau* (Pā 3.1.6), and which has again been shifted to the *nan* comp. governed by Pā 6.2.1. Therefore, accentuation-rule cannot help to decide the meaning. However, the contexts indicates the notion of *virodhābhāsa* in which the meaning 'even without taking food remains uninjured' seems more suitable. Hence, preference should be given to Sāyaṇa's explanation. Geldner[84] and Renou[85] also follow Sāyaṇa.

Sapta vāṇīḥ: According to Sāyaṇa and Venkaṭamādhava it refers to the seven rivers, which are taken as 'celestial rivers' by Lüders RV 3.7.1. This is confirmed by such references as *pra āvan vāṇīḥ puruhūtam dhamantīḥ* RV 3.30.10.

Vāṇīḥ refer to 'waters' as well as to 'speech'. The adjective *'sapta'* is also attached with both of them. *sapta vāṇīḥ* stands in the sense of 'seven speeches' (seven metres) also in the RV e.g., *abhi vaṇīr ṛsīṇām sapta nūṣata* RV 9.103.3. However, here we have to relate it only with the 'celestial rivers' as is evident from the *divaḥ yahvīḥ* in p.

III. 1.7

स्तीर्णा अस्य संहतो विश्वरूपा घृतस्य योनौ स्रवथे मधूनाम् ।
अस्थुरत्र धेनवः पिन्वमाना मही दस्मस्य मातरा समीची ॥

Saṅhataḥ refers to the 'flames' of Agni which are 'clasped together', or have a 'compact-form'. But at the same time they appear to assume varied forms' (*viṣvarūpaḥ*) also due to their different colours.

Dhenavaḥ refer to the 'waters'. This context has its relation with most of the following *ṛks* where Agni is called the embryo of 'waters'.

III. 1.8

वभ्राणः सूंनो सहसो व्यंद्यौद् दधांनः शुक्रा रंभसा वपूंषि ।
श्चोतंन्ति धारा मधुंनो घृतस्य वृषा यत्रं वावृधे काव्येंन ॥

Agni has been called here ***'sūno sahasaḥ'***, "son of conquering power". The exegetists Venkaṭamādhava and Sāyaṇa do not explain here the phrase *sūno sahasaḥ* which relates to a special concept of 'power' in the RV Agni and some other gods are closely related with 'power' which are termed as *sahas, savas* and so on. *sahas* conveys the notion of "victorious or conquering power (ueberlegenheit), irrestibility, prepondering power, overwhelming force, that particular strength, power or ability by which its bearer can vanquish his enemies".[86] Thus *sūno sahasaḥ, sahasasputra, savasasputra* etc. are the indicatives of Agni's overwhelming force by which he eliminates his rivals and vanquishes his enemies.

III. 1.9

पितुश्चिदूधंर्जनुषां विवेद व्यंस्य धारां असृजद् वि धेनांः ।
गुहा चरंन्तं सखिंभिः शिवेभिंर्दिवो यह्वीभिर्न गुहां बभूव ॥

Sāyaṇa explains ***dhenāḥ*** as *mādhyamikā vācaḥ*, 'the mid-region speeches', which seems doubtful because in the preceding contexts *yahvīḥ, dhenavaḥ* etc. refer to the 'rivers' and have no relation with 'speech'. Hence here also *dhenāḥ* cannot be taken for 'speech' because there is no change of context. Veṅkaṭamādhava also explains it erroneously as *prīṇayitrīr oṣadhīśca dhenāḥ* has nothing to do with the 'plants'. *dhārāḥ* and *dhenāḥ* refer to the same object and thus *dhenāḥ* can be taken as the adjective of *dhārāḥ* here, and together they connote the sense of 'nursing streams',[87] which are relieved by Agni from the udder of the sky, the father of Agni. Though it seems paradoxical to relate 'udder' (*ūdhaḥ*) with the father, yet in the language of the Veda all mystifying concepts can be found and explained as is well-known that "in order to remove the monotony of a rigidly ritual context the poets enter into various devices to introduce novelty such as word-play, mystic ellusions, metaphors, irregular grammatical forms and constructions and the whole becomes a sort of sacred quiz".[88] Water comes from the mid-region, 'sky', which has been referred to as the father of Agni. *Ūdhaḥ* "udder" is just a symbolical expression here.

The phrase *guhā carantam sakhibhiḥ,* "moving invisible with friends (waters)" indicates "lightning" which is invisible before it manifests its form. Sāyaṇa explicates *sakhibhiḥ* as *vāyubhiḥ.* "with winds but it seems doubtful because wind has no relation with Agni in the present context. Venkaṭamādhava interprets it as *anyain agnibhiḥ,* 'with other Agnis', which is also open to objection. If any one else, except 'waters', can be associated here that has some relation with Agni they are only 'Gods' who are associated with Agni in the following *ṛk.* But this also seems improbable. Oldenberg thinks that cd stands as an anakoluthic construction, because *carantam* is here object standing for Agni, while in d Agni becomes the subject. This statement has been followed by Velankar[89] in verbatim. But it seems rather doubtful. *carantam* should not be taken as an object, rather the use of accussative is just for the sake of retaining the rhythm as the proper form *caran* could not fulfil the urgency of the metre.

III. 1.10

पितुश्च गर्भं जनितुश्चं बभ्रे पूर्वीरेकों अधयत् पीप्यांनाः ।
वृष्णों सपत्नी शुचंये सबंन्धू उभे अस्मै मनुष्येइं नि पांहि ॥

There appears some doubt over the interpretation of ***adhyat*** explained by Sāyaṇa as *dhayati bhakṣayati*, "eats, devours". This becomes more doubtful when he explicates *pūrvīḥ pīpyānāḥ* as *vṛddhim prāptā oṣadhīḥ*, "grown plants". The entire context from the very beginning of the hymn refers to the "celestial waters" as the moṭhers of Agni who germinates and manifests himself in them, and finally becomes their co-mate also. Here also *pūrvīḥ pīpyānāḥ* refer to the "waters", and not to the plants. Therefore *adhayat* should be interpreted in the sense of "sucking, drinking". Being the son of waters Agni sucks (or soaks up the oozing (*pīpyānāḥ*) mothers.[90]

Pitus'ca-babhre : The first pada of the *ṛk* appears quite obscure. Sāyaṇa, following Venkaṭamādhava, explicates it as "Agni bears the embryo of the father, i.e. sky, in the form of rain-water, and of the *brahman* in the form of plants". Venkaṭamādhava explicates *janituḥ* as *pṛthivyāḥ* "of the earth" which has no bearing over the present context. Oldenberg and subsequent scholars, felt that it is quite obscure, as is clear from the remark made by Oldenberg that the exact meaning of this verse is very difficult.[91] But a comparison of the similar contexts facilitates the position to unravel the mysteries of this *ṛk*. The embryo is, here and elsewhere, Agni, who manifests himself in waters, sky, mid-region plants, and so to say, in every particle of the universe. He himself is germ, and germinates as well as causes to germinate in the entire world. The Vedic cosmology is based upon this principle that Agni being the germ himself causes the manifestation of the entire universe. The same cosmic principle has been garbed into mystic language.

pituḥ stands for Heaven or Sky who produces the world, and *janituḥ* for the Ultimate-Reality. Or, both may be related with *Dakṣa* and *Tvaṣṭṛ* who have been related with *Prajāpati* later on. To examplify this point we may quote here —

i. *bhūtānām garbhamā dadhe dakṣasya pitaram tanā/* RV 3.27.9.

ii. *daśemaṁ tvaṣṭurjanayanta garbham* / RV 1.95.2.

(1) "I have established him who is the embryo of the creatures as well as the father, and the son of Dakṣa".

(2) "The ten directions have produced this embryo of *Tvaṣṭṛ*".

The second *pāda* may be compared with the RV 2.35.13 where Apām Napāt is said to be generating embryo in the waters :

sa īṁ vṛṣājanayat tāsu garbhaṃ
sa īṁ śisurdhayati taṁ rihanti /

"The powerful one, i.e. Agni, has generated embryo in them; the child (Agni) sucks them indeed and they lick him (as mothers)". This explains the entire range of relationship between Agni and waters. He is the male, the progenitor as well as the child himself. Waters bear him as their child but at the same time they become the object of having pregeny through him. Thus the cosmic male and female principles are woven together and this blending of the relations creates and justifies the Vedic concept of the cosmic evolution of the universe.

Sapatnī and ***Sabandhu*** refer to the sky and the earth which are protecting and binding each other, *vṛṣṇe* is to be construed directly with *sapatnī* because it indicates the sublimity of generative power which has close resemblance with *vṛṣa,* the seminal power of Agni. *sapatnī* refers to the creative ability of the sky and the earth. Sky or heaven sheds the rain and the Earth enjoins it with procreation. Agni being the heat acts for the semen which makes him *vṛṣṇa*. Thus all these three have close relationship with each other, hence the earlier two, i.e. Heaven and Earth, are called *sabandhu*, "bound together". Or *sabandhu* is to be construed with *sucaye* only. *sucaye* symbolizes the brilliance of Agni which resides in the Heaven and the Earth, hence the latters are called *sabandhu* 'close relatives, brothers, closely connected, correlatives of the first. Sāyaṇa explicates *sapatnī* as *samāna ekaḥ sūryaḥ patir yayoste* which seems to be a confused concept of explication, because the sun has no relevance here. Further he construes *asmai* with *vṛṣṇe* which again seems doubtful, because *asmai* should go directly with *manuṣye* which stands for the invoker who prays for his protection. Syntactically *ubhe ..... pahi* is a complete unit, therefore, it has to be interpreted separately.

The form ***manuṣye*** occurs only here in the RV According to *padapāṭha* it appears to be acc. du. and stands with *ubhe*. Sāyaṇa follows this implication of *padapāṭha* and explains it as *manuṣyebhyohite* (*ubhe*). But syntactically to be connected with *asmai*, and thus it should be a dative singular form. As the regular formation *manuṣyāya* could not be used here due to metrical exigency, the irregular form *manuṣye* came into existence on the analogy of *avase* and other similar formations. Veṅkaṭamādhava seems right in explaining it as (*asmai*) *manuṣyāya*, "for this man".

III. 1.11

उरौ महाँ अंनिबाधे वंवर्धाऽऽपों अग्निं यशसः सं हि पूर्वीः ।
ऋतस्य योनांवशयद् दमूंना जामीनामग्निरपसि स्वसृंणाम् ॥

The implied meanings of some words in this verse is more important. Firstly the verse identifies Apām Napāt with the sacrificial fire. The word ***urau*** suggests the wide region as well as the wide *vedi. pūrvīḥ apaḥ* are the cellestial waters as well as the water used in the sacrifice. The form *yaśasaḥ* plays dual role of nom. pl. as well as of gen. sg. Firstly it refers to the glorious waters, and then to the worshippers whom the sacrificial waters belong. Similarly *ṛtasya yonau* also refers to the mid-region as well as to the sacrificial altar where homely Agni resides. *jamīnām svasṛṇām* are the inter-related sisters refering to the rivers and fingers simultaneously. *apasi* may be interpreted for the deep water as well as for the activity of the fingers.

According to Geldner[92] the phrase *yaśasaḥ sam hi pūrvīḥ* is a proberbial location which occurs at RV 10.46.10 also. Oldenberg[93] follows it partially and suggests to supply the verb *gam* with it in order to get the meaning: "Many superior (wives) are wont to assemble". But these notions seem erroneous; because *sam* has the direct connection with the verbal form *vavardha* which has to be construed with it by the way of Word Economy. Some may argue here that *vavardha* is a sg. form and cannot be used with *apaḥ*, the plural. But this can be answered that in the RV the usage of the singular forms with the plural, or vice-versa, is a common phenomenon.

III. 1.12

अक्रो न बभ्रिः संमिथे महीनां दिदृक्षेयः सूनवे भाऋजीकः ।
उदुस्रिया जनिता यो जजानाऽपां गर्भो नृतमो यह्वो अग्निः ॥

The verse depicts Agni as the warrior in the battle. The word *akraḥ* appears doubtful. Yāska traces it from *akramaṇa (akraḥ akramaṇāt,* Nir. 6.17) on the basis of which Sāyaṇa explicates it as *pareṣāṁ ākramita parair anākramaṇīyo vā,* "one who attacks others or who cannot be attached by others". Veṅkaṭamādhava quotes Yāska. But this derivation as well as explication needs verification.

The word ***Akra*** - occurs five times in the RV (1.143.7; 189.7; 3.1.12; 4.6.3; 10.77.2). Traditionally it has been derived from √*kram* with either *nañ* or *an* prefix plus *ḍa*- suffix. Thus the accent on the final syllable can be explained either by Pā. 6.2.139 (*gatikarakopapadatkṛt*), or by Pa. 6.2.172 (*nañsubhyām*). Thus it is a *bahuvrīhi* according to the accent. There is another form *akrau* also at RV. 1.120.2 which has been taken by Sāyaṇa as nom. du. of *akra* -, but as it occurs just after *marte*, the loc. sg. form, it can be a loc. sg. of *akri* and not nom. du. of *akra.*[94]

If we take *akra*-as a bahuvṛ. comp. formed by *nañ* it will add some negative meanings like "not attacking, not going, inactive,[95] unattacked" and so on, which are not compatible with *babhriḥ*, "the carrier, sustainer". Here *akraḥ* stands in complete consonance with *babhriḥ* which is explicit by the use of *na* here which has been taken by Sāyaṇa as a *pādapūranaḥ* erroneously. It stands here as an *avyaya* giving the sense of *iva* "similar, like", as has been suggested by Veṅkaṭamādhava, Skandasvāmin[96] and Durgāchārya. This fact can be corroborated by the other occurrences of *akra* where *na* occurs invariably in the sense of simple. Thus *akró nā babhrīḥ*, means "sustainer like *akra*". Thus *akrā*- and *babhrī* - are parallel to each other, and they connote the similar concepts. Therefore, *akra* - cannot be regarded as an "attacker" here. Hence we have to trace some other derivation and the meaning of this term.

The only other concrete suggestion can be made on the analogy of *śukra* which is derived from the √*suc*, "to shine". Similarly *akra* - can be derived from the √*ak*, "to go". Suffix - *ra* - is common with many words like *śukrā, śubhrā, - citrā* - , *mandrā* -, *tamrā* - and so on,[97] and in every case there is an accute accent on the last syllable. Thus, according to this derivation *akra* will be an agent noun meaning "one who goes or is active". For Agni this is a befitting appelative and at the same time it conveys the idea of the doer, sustainer, carrier also, like *babhrīḥ*. Geldner[98] has given its meaning "like horse (who carries the prize)" which has been adopted by Oldenberg,[99] Renou[100] and Velankar.[101] But the meaning of *babhrīḥ* with it as "who carries the prize" is open to objection, because if *akraḥ* connotes the meaning "horse" it is only the "goer" or who carries the warrior in the battle. *samithe* connotes dual sense here. The foremost meaning is "battle", and the secondly it conveys the sense of "sacrifice" in which Agni is the active sustainer and protector (*babhrīḥ*) of the worshipper (*sunave*). So the first meaning is connected with the simple of the horse who protects the hero on the battle field, and the second sense is attributed to Agni in the sacrifice. Thus, by the way of the Word Economy every word in the first *pāda* conveys double meanings.

Usriyāḥ, according to Sāyaṇa, means "waters". Veṅkaṭamādhava renders it with *paśūn* "cattle". But both of these interpretations here should be discarded, because *urriyāḥ* here refers to uṣas and not to the "waters" or "cows". It can be derived from the √*vas* > *uṣ* "to shine" in favour of *Uṣas* *usriyāḥ* should be construed twice here with *yaḥ*, thus *yaḥ usriyāḥ janitā* "who is the creator of the Uṣas" (Agni as the Sun) and *usriyāḥ* yaḥ *jajāna* "who created the Uṣas". Thus *usriyāḥ* stands firstly as acc. pl. and secondly as gen. sg., both refering to the Uṣas. In the first case it refers to the Uṣas in general and in the second the Uṣas in particular, i.e. daily-Dawn. Sāyaṇa's way of construing these words here seems faulty. First and second *pādas* should be construed together making a proper syntactical unit, and the third and the fourth *pādas* make one complete unit referring to the greatness of Agni.

Bhārjīka: The camp *bhārjīka*- occurs four times in the RV (3.1.12; 14; 1.44.3;). Sāyaṇa explicates it as *svadīptyā prakāśamānaḥ* "shining through own light". Veṅkaṭamādhava quotes Yāska who explains it as *prasiddhabhāḥ* (Nir. 6.4). But these scholiasts as well as Western exegetists appear to be at a loss in assigning its exact meaning. Oldenberg says that "the meaning of *bhāḥ-ṛjīka* is quite uncertain"[102] and in the same breath he adds that *dhūmaketum bhāhṛjīkam* would be exactly parallel. If they are parallel the meaning also should be parallel, but this is not the case. Unless we do not decide the derivational meaning of *ṛjīka* - the exact meaning of *bhāhṛjīkam* cannot be ascertained. *ṛjīka*- can be derived from √*ṛj* - (*ṛja gatisthānārjanoparjaneṣu*) with - *ika* - (*kīkan* suffix, - Un. S. 4.462) on the analogy of *mṛdīka, dṛsīka* and so on.[103] Accent will fall either on the initial or the final syllable as they are formed by such a suffix which contains an indicatory *k* and *n*. Thus by *kitaḥ* (Pā - 6.1.165) there will be *ādyudatta*, and by *ñnityādirnityam* (Pā. 6.1.197) there will be barytone. But in the case of *bhāḥṛjīkaḥ* accent remains on *bhāh* which indicates that it is a *bahvṛ* comp., and thus the acute accent on the initial syllable can be explained by Pā 6.2.1 *ābhuvrihau prakṛtyā pūrvapadam.*

√*ṛj* or *ṛji* has several meanings among which "to go, to take place" seem more plausible in the case of Agni. Thus *bhāṛjīka* can be interpreted in two ways, namely "one who goes through the brilliance" or "one who assumes his place or position in the brilliance". Both these interpretations goes very well with Agni. Roth's[104] translation "licht glänzend" and Bergaigne[105] "fleche" are not up to the mark. Geldner's[106] rendering "glanzverschönt" and Renou's[107] "ayant la lumiére pour marque-éminente" also can be refered to, in the light of the above discussion. Velankar's[108] translation "whose strength consists of light" is based upon the wrong premises of *góṛjīka* and *āvīhṛjīka* - which can be explained in an entirely new configuration of meanings.

āvīḥ ṛjīkaḥ at RV 4.38.4 may be explained as "whose course (*gati*) or place (*sthāna*) is clear (*āviḥ*) or who goes brilliantly" in favour of *Dadhikra,* who having his course cleared, observes fully the places of sacrifice or congregation - (*āvīrjīko vidathā micikyat*).

górjīkam is an appelative for Soma-juice at 3.58.4; 6.23.7 and 7.21.1. Cows milk is mixed with Soma-juice, and thus symbolically it means that Soma gets or obtains the cows. Here √*ṛj* can be taken in the sense of *arjana,* 'obtain', and thus *górjīka-* means 'obtaining cow (cow's milk)'. Velankar's rendering of *gorjīkam* as "which is strengthened by cow's milk" is not upto the mark. He quotes *āvīḥ-ṛjīkaḥ* but does not explain it which indicates his doubt.[109]

III. 1.13

अपां गर्भं दर्शतमोषधीनां वना जजान सुभगा विरूपम् ।
देवासश्चिन्मनसा सं हि जग्मुः पनिष्ठं जातं तवसं दुवस्यन् ॥

There is nothing controversial in this verse except the meaning of *duvasyan* which has been traditionally explained as *paricaran* "sarving",[110] but the comparison of all the occurrences of the word *duva-* indicates that it means either "reaching" or "moving fast" towards some one which by implication may mean "serving" some one.[111]

III. 1.14

बृहन्त इद् भानवो भाऋजीकमग्निं सचन्त विद्युतो न शुक्राः ।
गुहेव वृद्धं सदसि स्वे अन्तरपार ऊर्वे अमृतं दुहानाः ॥

Bhārjīkam again refers to Agni's course in this verse. The first two *pādas* present a simile here. As brilliant rays go together with the sun so the great lusture accompanies Agni. *amṛtam duhānāḥ* refers to the concept of universal vitality or generative power which is supposed to be contained in the heaven. The Sun and Agni both bring forth it to the earth in order to produce generative power in the universe. The same concept has been initiated here in this verse.

Sāyaṇa explains it as *udakam kṣarantaḥ* "sprinkling water" which does not clarify the inherent concept of *amṛta* "not subject to death".[112] *amṛta* is said to reside in the waters (1.23.19).

III. 1.15

ईळे॑ च त्वा॒ यज॑मानो ह॒विर्भि॒रीळे॑ सखि॒त्वं सु॑म॒तिं निका॑मः ।
दे॒वैरवो॑ मिमीहि॒ सं ज॑रि॒त्रे रक्षा॑ च नो॒ दम्ये॑भि॒रनी॑कैः ॥

The form ***dāmyebhiḥ*** explained by Sāyaṇa as *damanīyair niyantavyaiḥ,* "worthy of control" actually stands in constrast with *divya* "pertaining to heaven, or heavenly". Thus *damya* can be related with *dama-* "house", and so it means "homely" and not "worthy of control" *dāmyebhiḥ ānikaiḥ* implicity indicate the brilliance of "sacrificial fire which are manifested here on the earth in his own home".[113]

III. 1.16

उ॒प॒क्षे॒ता॒रस्तव॑ सुप्रणी॒तेऽग्ने॒ विश्वा॑नि॒ धन्या॒ दधा॑नाः ।
सुरे॑तसा॒ श्रव॑सा॒ तुञ्ज॑माना अ॒भि ष्या॑म पृतना॒यूँरदे॑वान् ॥

The word ***upakṣetāraḥ***, explained by Sāyaṇa, as *upagantāraḥ,* "those who go near (Agni)" seems to be parallel to *upavrata* or *upavāsakartā,* "observer of the vow of Agni" as Veṅkaṭamādhava has explained. Here the worshipper is meant to place all his riches in the service of Agni in order to gain power over his enemies, and reside himself near Agni (in his service). *kṣetṛ* is to be derived from √*kṣi,* 'to dwell'.[114]

Tuñjamānāḥ, according to Sāyaṇa means "offering the oblations" (*havīṅsi prayacchantaḥ vāyam*) but it seems to refer to something else. Sāyaṇa construes it separately, though syntactically it appears to be related directly with *suretasā śravasā (tūñjamānāḥ).* As other two occurrence of *tuñjamānāḥ* indicate it seems that √*tuī tuñj* has been used in the sense of 'vitalizing, strengthening, making effective' and so on. Thus the last two *pādas* can be rendered with: "May we be able to overpower our antagonists itching for battle being strengthened by good vigour and fame".

Or *tuñjamānāḥ* may be derived from the *tuj* 'to injure' and thus we can render these *pādas* as: "injuring through good vigour and fame we may overpower our godless enemies itching for battle".

Oldenberg's[115] rendering of *tuñjamānāḥ* "pressing onward", followed by Velankar,[116] and Renou's[117] "implantons" do not seem up to the mark. Geldner's[118] translation "fortpflanzend" is nearer the sense.

III. 1.17

आ देवानांमभवः केतुरंग्ने मन्द्रो विस्वांनि काव्यांनि विद्वान् ।
प्रति मर्ताँ अवासयो दमूंना अनुं देवान् रंथिरो यांसि साधंन् ॥

Mandrāḥ and ***sādhan*** need here re-interpretation. According to Sāyaṇa *mandrāḥ* means *stutyaḥ* "praiseworthy". But the analysis of the occurrences and etymological enquiries reveal that it means "lusturous, beautiful, brilliant" and so on. These meanings go very well with Agni as well as other deities in all the contexts of the RV.[119]

sādhan here means "making effective the activities of the Gods whom Agni follows".

III. 1.18

नि दुंरोणे अमृतो मर्त्यांनां राजां ससाद विदथांनि साधंन् ।
घृतप्रंतीक उर्विया व्यंद्यौदग्निर्विश्वांनि काव्यांनि विद्वान् ॥

Amṛtaḥ stands in contrast to the *martyānām*. Agni, being "immortal" has taken his seat in the home of the "mortals", and being their king he makes effective all their sacrificial activities.

III. 1.19

आ नो गहि सख्येभिः शिवेभिर्महान् महीभिरूतिभिः सरण्यन् ।
अस्मे रयिं बहुलं संतरुत्रं सुवाचं भागं यशसं कृधी नः ॥

The word ***Saraṇyan*** has been explained by Sāyaṇa as *sarvatra saraṇam gamanam icchan*, "desiring to move everywhere", but the context indicates that it means "moving" (with your great protections) come to us, with thy favourable friendship, O the great one!", and it should be construed directly with *mahībhiḥ ūtībhiḥ (saraṇyan)*. Sāyaṇa construes it with *mahān* directly.

III. 1.20

एता ते अग्ने जनिमा सनानि प्र पूर्व्याय नूतनानि वोचम् ।
महान्ति वृष्णे सवना कृतेमा जन्मंजन्मन् निहितो जातवेदाः ॥

Sanāni and ***nūtanāni*** refer to the two-fold aspects of Agni's birth, who has been said 'twice-born' (*dvijanmā* - RV 1.60.1; 140.2; 149.4; 5). By *sanāni* Agni is all pervading and omnipresent i.e., he is immortal; and *nūtanāni* implies his manifestations in different forms and places. The invoker seeks to eulogize both the aspects of Agni's birth.

The phrase *janman janman nikitaḥ jātavedāḥ* refers to Agni as omnipresent and omniscient. The same expression has been repeated in the following verse also.

III. 1.21

जन्मंजन्मन् निहितो जातवेदा विश्वामित्रेभिरिध्यते अजस्रः ।
तस्य वयं सुमतौ यज्ञियस्यापि भद्रे सौमनसे स्याम ॥

The word ***Ajasraḥ*** has been explained by Veṅkaṭamādhava and Sāyaṇa as *anavaratam* "perpetual", but it needs re-interpretation and etymological explanation. Sāyaṇa does not give its etymological explanation, however, he derives *jasamānam* from √*jas*, 'to injure' which provides a base for the derivation of *ajasra* also. *jas* can be identified with GK *Obevvuui*, "loschen", (exhaust), Indg. *Zaes*-original ancient Iranian *jjas* and Avestan *fra-zah*, "extinguish, be lost, disappear".[120] Thus the original meaning of √*jas* appears to be "to exhaust, extinguish, be lost" and so on, and this furnishes the clue to explain *ajasra* (*a+jas+ra-*) in the sense of "not exhausted, which cannot be extinguished, so, perpetual". In the present context *idhyate ajasraḥ* means - "the unextinguished or unexhausted (Agni) is kindled". These same meanings, i.e. "unexhausted, not lost" etc. were developed in the sense of "perpetual, continued" and so on.

III. 1.22

इमं यज्ञं संहसावन् त्वं नों देवत्रा धेंहि सुक्रतो ररांणः ।
प्र यंसि होतर्बृहतीरिषो नो ऽग्ने महि द्रविंणमा यंजस्व ॥

The formation of ***sahasāvan*** seems doubtful. Agni is said to be the son of *sahas* (*sūnuḥ sahasaḥ*), "strength, vigour, power". Thus here *sahasāvan* is related to *sahas*, and may be formed by *sahaḥ* + *vatup* in which the insertion and lengthening of *a* is *chandas* (*sahaḥ sabdat matupa chandasa akāropajanaḥ* - Sāyaṇa on RV 1.91.23). The only other formation of this type is *Śavasāvan* which bears the same meaning and leads to presume that in both the cases, perhaps, instr. Form *sahasā* and *śavasā* have been used to form *sahasāvan* and *śavasāvan* with the help of the possessive suffix *vant.*[121] According to Velankar[122] "this looks like a double possessive with the affix *vat* placed after a case-form, with the final consonant dropped".

III. 1.23

इळांमग्ने पुरुदंसं सनिं गोः शंश्वत्तमं हवंमानाय साध ।
स्यान्नंः सूनुस्तनंयो विजावा ऽग्ने सा तें सुमतिर्भूत्वस्मे ॥

Sāyaṇa construes ***īlām*** and ***goḥ*** separately which seems unjustified because both these words indicate the same principle of sustenance and nourishment. Therefore, they should be construed together with *purudaṁsam sanim.* Similarly, *śaśvattamam* also should be construed with *sanim.* Here it is not an indeclinable as understood by Sāyaṇa. He construes it with *sadhaya* and explains it as *cirakālam yathā bhavati tathā,* "for a long time as it may be, "but this explanation does not hold good. As is clear by the occurrence of *śaśvattama* (RV 10.39.1) etc. *śaśvattamam* stands here as an adj. to the acc. sg. of *sanī.* Therefore, it has to be construed with *purudāṅsam sanim* generating the sense "perpetual or undecaying nourishment of manifold vigour".

goḥ refers to the "earth" here who provides all kinds of food, vigour and nourishment, *ilā* also connotes the same meanings, but here it stands specifically as an adj. to *goḥ* implying the sense "nourishing earth". Agni has been entreated to "make effective the perpetual nourishment of manifold vigour provided by the nourishing mother earth for the invoker".

Sūnuḥ and ***Tanayaḥ.*** are synonimous, but here *tānayaḥ* stands a good chance of being adj. to *sūnūḥ*; and thus *tānayaḥ sūnūḥ* together imply the sense the son who causes the furtherence of the progeny or coming generation", or *tānayaḥ sūnūḥ* may be 'one's own son' (progenited from one's own body)[123] as Velankar[124] thinks. Such type of son has been desired to be, *vijāvā.* The term *vijāvā* is nearer to *prajāvān*[125] and can be derived from *vi* + √*jan* + *vant*; the *n* of the root and the affix being dropped and *a* in both lengthened. This word occurs only in the verse which has been repeated at 3.5.11; 6.11; 7.11; 15.7. and 3.22.5. *vijā́vā* signifies the sense of "being born again and again, and thus creating a chain of progeny, i.e. the continuance of the generation". This indicates the Vedic concept of the continued family tradition.

NOTES

1. H.D. Velankar, '*Word Economy in the Ṛgvedic Interpretation*, ABORI, (Poona 1965), p. 1 ff.
2. Ṛgveda with the commentaries of Skandasvamin, Udgītha, Veṅkaṭamādhava and Mudgala, Part III, ed. by Vishva Bandhu (VVRI, Hoshiarpur, 1963), p. 1282.
3. RV. 1.138.1; 3.1.1; 13; 32.9; 5.58.2; 60.4; 6.18.4 etc.
4. RV Bh. 3.1.1; 32.9; 5.58.2 etc.
5. Ibid. 1.51.15; 57.1; 64.12; 114.1 etc.
6. Ibid., 9.97.46.
7. Nigh. 2.9.4
8. *Sanskrit Wörterbuch*
9. *Wortb.*, 531; *RV. Ubersetzt* I, p. 55.
10. *RV. Trans.* Vol. II. p. 193.
11. *Der RV Hymn.* Brah., I, p. 328.
12. *Hymns RV Vol. I,* p. 315.
13. SBE, 46, p. 219.
14. *Der. RV Ubersetzt,* I, p. 332.
15. *EVP,* XII, p. 48.
16. *RV.Maṇḍala III,* p. 1.
17. See *Wackernagel, Altind Gram,* I, p. 83. S. Varma, *Ety. of Yaska,* p. 45.
18. RV 3.30.17.
19. *Op. cit.,* p. 326.
20. Pischel und Geldner, *Vedische Studien,* 1, p. 157.
21. *Der RV. ubersetzt,* I, p. 332.
22. Pischel und Geldner, *Vedische Studien,* I, p. 157.
23. *Übers,* fn. p. 332.
24. *op. cit.,* p. 223.
25. *Loc. cit.*
26. *Loc. cit.*
27. *Loc. cit.*
28. *Wört, RV,* p. 1243.
29. *RV Ubers.* p. 55.
30. RV 1.188.3.
31. RV 1.188.3; 2.3.11; 36.4; 3.7.1; 7.9; 17.2; 15.5. etc.
32. RV 5.I.11; 7.4; 9.1; 6.15.18; 21.12; 47.9; 7.78.1
33. RV 3.15.5; 6.21.12; 47.9; 7.98.2; 8.54.6.

34. RV 6.21.12; 47.9; 7.98.2; 8.54.6.
35. RV 7.78.1.
36. At RV 9.9.6 Bhave interprets *vahni* as 'carrier', but *vāhniḥ vā vahiḥ* may be interpreted as 'elevater of the elevated one, i.e. drink', See S.S. Bhawe, *Soma Hymns,* I, p. 50.
37. *Wörterbuch Zum Ṛgveda,* P. 1245
38. W. Neisser, *Zum Worter des RV.*
39. ZDMG, 50., p. 423.
40. Nigh. 3.27
41. *Revue de 1' on History des Religion,* 1890.
42. *Sanskrit Wörterbuch*
43. *Wört erbuch zum Ṛgveda,* P. 1278.
44. Der Hymns Brah. I, p. 328.
45. *Etudes Vediques* l' hymne III, 1 du Ṛigveda.
46. *Vedische Studien* I, p. 147; II. p. 149; Glossars.
47. JAOS 48, p. 200 f
48. P. Thieme, *Untersuchungen.* p. 36 f.
49. *Abtiranische Forschungen* 2, 49 f.
50. SBE 32, p. 350.
51. *Altind, Gram.* II. 2, p. 172 f.
52. H.W. Bailey, *JRAS* 1965, Pt I & II; p. 56 f.
53. *EVP,* III, p. 36.
54. Vision, p. 91.
55. *RV Maṇḍala III.* P. 1.
    For the usage and meaning of *kṛ* (*kṛtam* here) See S. Varma, VI J ix, Pt. I, 1971, pp. 34-37.
56. *Loc. cit.* fn
57. *Ṛgveda Textkritische und exegetische Noten,* p. 224.
58. ZDMG 48, p. 108 (quoted by Oldenberg).
59. RV 1.18.8. Here he explains the accent of *añca*- by Pā. 6.2.52 *aniganto'ñcatau vapratyaye,* according to which the acute accent remains on the *gati,* i.e. prefix.
60. A. Bergaigne, *Religion de Vedique* I, p. 109.
61. SBE 46, p. 224.
62. See Wackernagel, *Altind Gram.* II, 2, p. 15 cf.
63. See Brugmann, *Comp. Gram* II, p. 292; Whitney, *Sans. Gram.* 407 ff; Bartholomae, *Handbuch* S. 192; J. Damesteter, *'La suffix-ac-en Iranien', Meme de la soc. de la Ling.* III 202 ff.
64. Nigh. 2.7
65. RV 1.57.3; 62.11; 2.23.13; 30.8 etc.

66. RV 1.112.15; 21; 119.10.
67. Nigh 3.5.5.
68. RV 1.30.15; 36.14.
69. Grassmann, *Worterb.*, p. 617. See Bhave, *Soma Hymns* III. p. 85.
70. M. Mayrhofer, *Ety. Sanskrit Dict.* I. p. 778.
71. See. Walde Poklorny, *Comp. Dict.* I, p. 778; Wackernagel, *Altind Gram* 112, p. 233; III. p. 81. K. Gunther, 269, p. 239 ff; Havers, *Sommer-Festschrift*, p. 70f.
72. See Mayrhofer op. cit. II, p. 586 f; Gershevitch, *Avestan Hymns to Mithra*, p. 205 f.
73. See Velankar, RV Maṅḍala II, p. 96.
74. RV. comment. Pt. III, p. 1282.
75. SBE 46, 224.
76. See Velankar, RV Maṅḍala III, p. 2 fn.
77. *Loc. cit.*
78. *rajo loko bhavati rajater gatyarthāt* - AB 1.25; see also SB. 6.7.4.5.
79. For details on *loka* see Gonda, *Loka*, Amsterdam, 1966, pp. 110 ff.
80. Nir. 4.19.
81. RVBh. 2.31.3.
82. See Brugmann, *Comp. Grammar* I, 47, Wackern-Debru, *Altind. Gram*, 112, p. 220, 934; T. Burrow, BSOS 12, 645 ff.
83. See Neisser, *Wort.* RV. 2, p. 66 f, Wackern. *op. cit.* II, 2, p. 474; Walde Poklorny I. p. 354; Mayrhofer, M Kurz *Wört.* I, p. 276.
84. *op. cit.*, p. 333.
85. *op. cit.*, p. 4-9.
86. For details see Gonda *'Gods and Powers in the Veda'* (S. Gravanhage 1957), p. 15 ff.
87. For the etymology and literature on *dhenā* see Mayrhofer, M. kurz, *Ety. Wörtb* II, p. 113.
88. S.S. Bhawe, *Soma Hymns* II, p. 103.
89. See H.D. Velankar, *RV Maṅḍala III*, p. 3.
90. See also Geldner, *Vedische Studien* I, 166; Oldenberg, *Noten* I, 225; SBE 46, 225 f; Renou, Études Vediques et Paṇinienne, XII, 49.
91. Hermann Oldenberg, *Textkritische und Exegetische Noten*, I. 225.

92. Vedische Studien I, 166.
93. *Noten* I, 225; SBE 46, p. 226.
94. See also *Vaidic Padanukrama Kosa* Vol. III, Pt. I, p. 9.
95. See Wackern Debr., *Altin, Gram.* II. I, p. 80, 215; II. 2, 73; Mayrhofer, Kurz. *Ety. Word.* I, p. 15.
96. Comm. on Nir. 6.1.7.
97. See Warkern-Debr, *op. cit.* II. 2, 8508.
98. *Vedische Studien* I, 168.
99. *SBE* 46, 220.
100. *EVP.* XII, 49, 114.
101. *RV Maṅḍala* III, 4.
102. SBE 46, 40.
103. Uṇ. Sū 4.463
104. ZDMG. 48,118.
105. *Religion Vedique,* Vol. I, 206.
106. *RV Ulbersetz.* I, 334.
107. *Loc. cit.*
108. *Loc. cit.*
109. *RV Maṅḍala* VII, p. 58.
110. *namasyati duvasyati .. paricaranakarmā* - Nigh. 3.5.5.
111. For details see *infra* 3.2.6.
112. See J. Gonda, *Change and Continuity in Indian Religion* (The Hague, 1965), p. 60 ff.
113. See Renou, *op. cit.,* p. 114; Cf. RV 1.73.3; 3.55.21; 10.125.4.
115. *op. cit.,* p. 221.
116. *Loc. cit.*
117. *op. cit.,* p. 50.
118. *Loc. cit.*
119. For details see *infra,* 3.2.4 *mandrasya*; and author's paper on *mandrá* in Prācya Prajña, Aligarḥ Muslim University, 1977, pp. 25 ff.
120. See Wackern, *Alt. Gram* I, p. 273, Renou, *EVP.* XII, p. 114.
121. See Wackern *op. cit.,* 112, p. 885.
122. *RV Maṅḍala* VII. p. 4 fn. 5 (7.1.5).
123. Cf. *aṅgādaṅgād sam bhavasi hṛdayād adhi jāyase /*
ātmā nāma vai putro'si atho jīva śarīdaḥ śatam //
- As. Gr. Sutra.
124. *RV M. III,* p. 7.
125. RV 3.30.18; 54.18; 56.3; 4.25.

The Ṛgveda Maṇḍal III.2

वै॒श्वा॒न॒राय॑ धि॒षणा॑मृता॒वृधे॑ घृ॒तं न पू॒तम॒ग्नये॑ जनामसि ।
द्वि॒ता होता॑रं॒ मनु॑षश्च वा॒घतो॑ धि॒या रथं॒ न कुलि॑शः॒ समृ॑ण्वति ॥

After the critical examination of Sāyaṇa's commentary on this verse it seems that he is not sure with regard to the meanings of *Vaiśvānarāya* and *ṛtāvṛdhe.* Also his interpretations of *dhiṣaṇā dvitā* and *vāghataḥ* are doubtful. Therefore, a detailed discussion of the interpretations of these terms will be useful. *vaiśvānarāya* - The epithet *vaiśvānara*- occurs Sixty one times in the RV[1] and generally it is attributed to Agni. Once it occurs in plural form for Viśvedevās (RV 8.30.4). The etymology of this word has always been controversial, Sāyaṇa, following Yāska, explicates it thus - *viśveṣām narāṇām lokāntaram prati netṛtayā sa nibandhi vaiśvānaraḥ "vaiśvānara putraḥ pitre lokakṛt jātavedo vahemam sukṛtam yatra lokāḥ"* iti. *Yadvā viśve sarve narā evam agnim yajñādau prīṇayanti iti tat sambandhad vaiśvānaraḥ yadvā viśvān sarvān prāṇinaḥ prasṛto gacchataḥ iti, viśvānarau madhyamottamau. 'ṛ gatau' ityasmāt pacādy aca. lugamāvaś' chāndasaḥ tābhyām utpannatyād yamognir vaiśvānaraḥ vaidyuto agnir hi madhyam sakāśāt jāyate. aśani patanānantaram eva pārthivo agniḥ sampadyate. āditya sakāśād api gharmakāle sūryakāntādi naṇiṣv agner utpattiḥ prasiddhā. tasmān nāmanirvacanānurodhena ayam eva agnir vaiśvānara ityetad upapannam.*[2]

Even before Yāska, there was some controversy about the original meaning of *Vaiśvānara.* In relation to *Vaiśvānara* Yāska cites the views of his predecessors. According to some of them, Vayu or Indra, presiding over the mid-region was Vaiśvānara. Some of them are of the opinion that the Sun presiding over the sky was called *Vaiśvānara.* But Yāska does not agree with these views and, according to him, only Agni deserves the epithet of *Vaiśvānara.*[3]

Vaiśvānara originally meant "related to him who possesses the total amount of vital strength".[4] Kuiper identifies it with GK nwpotic xaxwl.[5] A wish is expressed to win *vāja* at RV. 6.8.6. through *Vaiśvānara's* help - *vājam jayema .... vaiśvānara - vājam agne tavotibhiḥ*; in the third verse of the same hymn he is said to possess the strength of a bull; and in RV 6.7.7 he is 'a protector of life' (*amṛtasya rakṣitā*); at RV 6.9.7 he himself is 'immortal' (*vaiśvānaro amartyāḥ*); at RV 6.8.7 he is invoked in order to promote longivity and at RV 1.59.4 he is "most manly" (*nṛtama);* RV 1.98.2 describes him as entering the vegetations. Thus he assumes numerous forms. ***Vaiśvānara*** has been identified with the "tree of life".[6] and this fact can be corroborated with the ŚB where he has been identified with 'semen'.[7] On the basis of this statement Kuiper gives the original meaning of *Vaiśvānara* - as 'related to him' etc. as mentioned above.

The frequent occurrences of *Vaiśvānara* - in the RV as well as in the other *Saṁhitās* - evidently indicate that it has always been associated with Agni. But some peculiar epithets attributed to *Vaiśvānara* show that it must have been something different from Agni, the God presiding over the earthly region. Agni is said to reside in heaven as well as on the earth. In the first form he can be identified with the Sun. According to the Ṛgvedic sources Agni was brought to the earth by *Mātariśvan.*[8] Here *Mātariśvan* is identified with Vāyu, but in the most of the verses where Mātariśvan occurs, it is associated with Agni and *Vaiśvānara.*[9] Thus it indicates the fact that *Mātariśvan* and *Vaiśvānara* are the same principles which govern the activities of Agni.

The picture which emerges through the study of various epithets used with *Mātariśvan* and *Vaiśvānara* indicates the identity of Savitṛ, the Sun with them. For instance, *Mātariśvan Vaiśvānara* goes through the sky - *mūrdhānam divaḥ aratim pṛthivyāh vaiśvānaram agnim.* "Das Haupt des Himmels, den Lenker der Erde, den Agni *Vaiśvanara,* den zum rechten (Zeit) Gebornen" (Geld. II, p. 29). Thus, one who travels through the sky can be none here but the Sun. This same Vaiśvānara was brought from the heaven by Mātariśvan (RV 6.8.4). In another context it is said that Soma 'Pavamāna created the great light like brilliant thunder belonging to all men' (RV 9.61.16).

The comp. word *viśvacarṣaṇi* can be placed with *vaiśvānara. viśvacarṣaṇi* is also applied to Savitṛ, Indra, Agni etc. and means 'belonging to all men'. These two words are almost synonymous.[11] Another word in this category is *Viśvānara* which has been attributed twice to Savitṛ (RV 1.168.1; 7.76.1) out of its four occurrences in the RV, and like *viśvacarṣaṇi* and *vaiśvānara* it can be rendered as "belonging to all men". The epithets *amṛta-vicetas* and *nṛtama* indicate the all pervasiveness and omnipresence of *vaiśvānara-.*[12] Thus it can be concluded that *Vaiśvānara* presents the life-force of Agni, through which he pervades all creatures of the universe, and remains immortal. Here in this *ṛk* he is said to be *ṛtāvṛdha,* i.e. who is full of truth, and this can be compared with other contexts such as RV 1.59.4.

Its derivation is doubtful. Sāyaṇa derives it from *viśvenaraḥ* + *taddhita* suffix *a* (*n*) with the meaning 'belonging to all men'. 'The lengthening of -*va*- (in *vaiśvānara*-) is explained by Paṇini' as *nare saṁjñāyām,* (Pā 6.3.129), but here the exact meaning of *smjñā* is not clear. Grassmann[13] while rendering *Vaiśvānara* with 'der genzen Menschheit angehörig' (belonging to all men), follows the traditional way of interpretation, and derives it from *Vaiśvānara,* as does Sāyaṇa Geldner leaves it as it is.

Dhiṣaṇā - The acc. sg. form of *dhiṣaṇā* - occurs thrice in the RV.[14] It is a much discussed word among the Vedists. Here Sāyaṇa explains it as *stutim* "praise" but elsewhere he renders it with such alternative meanings as 'wisdom' (*buddhiḥ*-3.32.14), 'goddess of speech' (*Vāgdevatā*-4.34.1), 'speech' (*vāk*-1.109.4; 5.41.8) and so on. At one place[15] he renders *dhiṣaṇābhyaḥ* with *grāvabhyaḥ* (with two stones). Veṅkaṭamādhava gives its meaning as *stutim* 'prayer'.[16] Their predecessor Yāska explicates it as 'speech' (*vāk*) but derives it from √*dhiṣ* in the sense of √*dhā* to sustain'.[17] Uvaṭa and Mahīdhara, the commentators of VS,[18] also follow Yāska's interpretation.

Modern exegetists differ invariably on the exact meaning of *dhiṣaṇā*. According to Johanson *dhiṣaṇā* is a 'goddess' the personification of suckling and nutritive power' (gottin und Personifizierung der Saugung und Nahrungsmacht).[19] Jan de Vries also follows the same meaning. Hillebrandt and Pischel also tried to solve the meaning - problem of this word. According to Hillebrandt *dhiṣaṇā* signifies the Earth (in the dual Heaven and Earth, in plural Heaven, Air and Earth), and sometimes *Vedi* - 'altar'.[21] Pischel follows this explanation but adds that *dhiṣaṇā*. in sg, signifies a proper name, i.e. the name of the 'goddess of wealth and prosperity. But in dual it means 'Heaven and Earth. He remarks that *dhiṣaṇā* is closely related to, or identical with, Aditi, whom he thinks to be a personification of mother earth.[22] Oldenberg does not agree with the scholars and thinks that *dhiṣaṇā* was originally 'an implement used at the sacrifice, more especially at the Soma sacrifice'. He cites references from RV I.109.3; VS. vi. 35; ŚB. 3.9.4.18. But he holds the view that *dhiṣaṇā* in dual means 'Heaven and Earth'.[23] This view of Oldenberg, namely, to take *dhiṣāṇā* in the sense of 'implement' seems unconvincing, because the sacrificial sense, which he attaches here, must have originated only through symbolic expression in a later period of Vedic literature. At another place Oldenberg relates *dhiṣaṇā* with *dadhāti*, and thinks that it signifies the 'power of sustenance' ('Potenz des Setgens').[24] According to Geldner[25] here *dhiṣaṇā* signifies 'action' ("work"), which can be extended as the 'action or work of the priest' (RV 3.2.1; 4.36.8; 9.59.2)'.'act, desire for activity or power or action of the Gods (RV 1.102.1), then as the personification of a goddess who governs the sacrifice (RV 1.22.10; VS 6.26; RV 196.1; 10.20.6; 4.34.1; 1.109.4; 10.17.12); then as inspiration of the singer (RV 3.32.14; 6.11.3) and again as the goddess of activity (RV 1.102.7; 3.31.13). In dual it means 'Heaven and Earth' (RV 1.160.1; 6.50.3; 10.44.18). Thus it appears that Geldner has accepted all the meanings given by his predecessors except in a few cases with slight differences in contexts. Thus it is difficult to arrive at a certain conclusion on the basis of the varied meanings attested by exegetists.

According to Wackernagel its etymology is quite uncertain. He identifies it with its cognate GK word *Vis, Vinos.*[26]

Discussing *dhiṣaṇā* Renou suggests that it indicates the 'poetic inspiration', "une personification de l'inspiration poètique",[27] and he adds that *dhiṣaṇā* is identical with or contiguous to *dhi* "poem" as in RV 1.102.1 "je l'apporte ce poeme une fois que la *dho* etc' ointe", *imām te dhiyām ... dhiṣaṇā yat ta ānaje.*[28] Gonda follows this same interpretation while elaborating his thesis on the interpretation of *dhiḥ* in the RV.[29]

Thus the latest researches tend to accept the meanings of *dhiṣaṇā* as 'inspiration, poetic vision, godly insight or wisdom' which are not much different from Sāyaṇa's interpretation. The only difficulty with Sāyaṇa appears to be that of his overchanging views in different contexts. His interpretation at RV 1.102.1; 3.32.14 and TB 2.7.13.4 as *buddhiḥ* 'wisdom' can be identified with '1' inspiration poetique and simultaneously can be extended to all other contexts of the RV related with *dhiṣaṇā*.

Ṛtāvṛdhe - The comp. word *ṛtāvṛdhe,* the Dat. sg. of the comp. ending in the root noun *vṛdh* -, and not in the derivative-*vṛdha* as the accent indicates, occurs only here in the RV Other forms of the comp. *ṛtāvṛdha* - occur at several places in the RV They are *ṛtāvṛdhaḥ* (RV 1.13.6; 14.7; 44.14; 142.4; 5.44.4; 6.15.18 etc.); *ṛtāvṛdhā* (RV 1.106.3; 159.1; 5.65.2.9.3); *ṛtāvṛdhā* (RV 1.47.1; 3; 5; 2.41.4.3.62.18 etc.); *ṛtāvṛdham* (RV 10.65.3); *ṛtāvṛdhau* (RV 1.23.5) and *ṛtāvṛdhau* (RV 1.2.8). The accented form of this comp. can be equated with other similar comps. like *tamahvṛdhaḥ* (RV 7.104.1), *payahūṛdhaḥ* (RV 1.64.11), *rayivṛdhaḥ* (RV 7.91.3), *vayahvṛdhaḥ* (RV 5.54.2) etc.

Sāyaṇa, renders *ṛtāvṛdhe* with *tasyodakasya yajñasya vā vardhayitre* (for the augmenter of the water or the sacrifice). The meaning of *ṛta* as 'water' has already been attested by his predecessors such as Yāska[30] and Veṅkaṭamādhava.[31] The alternative meanings such as 'sacrifice' and 'truth' are also found in all the subsequent commentaries. The western exegetists given its meaning as 'ordinance' and 'truth' with some variations. Starting from Ludwig[32] to Geldner[33] we find the same meanings. Lüders[34] and Schmidt[35] advocate 'truth' by identifying *ṛta* with Avestan *aṣa.* But their predilection for only this meaning seems unjustifiable, because *ṛta* indicates the various shades of Ultimate Reality as seen, observed and experienced by Vedic seers. Even if we accept the meaning 'truth' it is not something new, because it has already been attested by the Niruktakāra Yāska.[36] Gonda[37] accepts the meaning of *ṛtāvṛdha* as given by Lüders,[38] 'who increases by truth but in elaborating it he gives the meaning of *ṛta* elsewhere as the universal and fundamental order, hormony and structural unity, of the ultimate "truth" on which the world and the ritual is founded'.[39] This meaning covers all the fundamental aspects of *ṛta,* but here the compounded word creates some difficulty. *ṛtāvṛdha* - can be interpreted in two ways: *ṛta* can be taken here either as an instrumental sg. or as occusative sg. In the first case the comp. means 'one who is augmented or increased by the *'ṛta'* as has been explicated by Lüders and Gonda. Secondly it means 'one who increases or protects or prospers the truth'. But the first meaning seems more plausible if *ṛta* is taken to mean the truth'. 'sacrificial order' and so on. In comparison with *tamovṛdhaḥ* (those that grow powerful in darkness),[40] *vayovṛdhaḥ* (those who increase food),[41] *payovṛdhaḥ* (those who increase water, or grow in water),[42] and *rayivṛdhaḥ* (who increase their riches)[43] both of the above meanings can be accepted. Thus Agni is here the 'increaser of *ṛta*' as well as he grows or increases his power with 'ṛta'.

Dvitā - Here this word stands for Agni. Sāyaṇa explains it as *dvidhā garhapatyāhavanīya rūpābhyām yuktam,* 'Agni in the form of *gārhōpatya* "master of the house" as well as *āhavanīya,* worthy of invoking in the sacrifice'. Sāyaṇa's explication is similar to Venkaṭamādhava's interpretation. *dvita* not only signifies the forms of Agni, but also here it can be connected with the verbal form *samrnvati* 'brings', and thus it can be equated with the other contexts like RV 2.4.2 B; 8.71.11c; 84.2bc where Agni is either brought by gods, or remains himself in two places, i.e. in the heaven (*divi*) or on the earth. Or, it may be connected with *hotāram* as an objective, and in this case it may be regarded as relating Agni with the other gods as well as with the men. Moving between heaven and earth (cf. 4.7.8) or between gods and men (cf. 4.2.2) he conveys the sacrifice (cf. 1.72.7; 1.188.1; 3.11.2) and visits all abodes (cf. 4.1.8), and by virtue of this fact he is attributed with the adjective *dvitạ.*[44]

Vāghataḥ - This form of the word *vāghat* occurs ten times in the RV[45] Other forms which occur in the RV are *vāghat* (9.103.5), *vāghataḥ* (3.60.4), *vāghatam* (3.3.4; 8; 10.33.47). *Vighate* (1.31.14; 40.4; 4.2.13), *vāghadvhiḥ* (1.36.13; 3.8.10; 8.5.16; 9.103.5). This word has been attested in the Nigh'.[46] as the synonym of *ṛtvik* 'priest'; and Sāyaṇa as well as other traditional exegetists followed this same meaning invariably. Sāyaṇa derives it from √*vah* 'to carry, to receive' etc. and attaches the root-meaning to the word with its explication as 'one who carries either oblation, or something else; and thus he explains *vāghataḥ* in most of the contexts as '*ṛtvik* the priest'. At three places[47] he construes this word with the sacrificer himself, and in one context[48] he explains it as *viśvedevās,* 'all the gods' and the Aṅgirasas who carry on the sacrificial acts. But this context is certainly similar to the other contexts and thus it is indicated that this explication has been offered by someone other than by Sāyaṇa.

Among the modern interpreters Roth[49] derives it from √*vah,* and identifies it with *vahni* as well as with GK word *Ev'xouai.* This same interpretation was followed by Neisser,[50] Oldenberg[51] and Grassmann[52] attest several other meanings to this word, i.e. 'betend' (prayer), 'ofpfernd' (offering), 'beter' (worshipper), 'ofpferer' (ofpferer), 'Veranstalter des ofpfers' (organizer of the offering). All these meanings suggest only the traditional way of interpretation. Geldner and Renou[53] has follow the commentery of Sāyaṇa.

Geldner construes *manuṣaḥ* and *vāghataḥ* separately. He construes *manuṣaḥ* with *hotāram* and explains it as 'der Hotr such des Manu'. But the use of *ca* with *manuṣaḥ* suggests explicitly that *ca* should go with vāghataḥ also, and thus *manuṣaḥ ca vāghataḥ* (ca)[54] should go together signifying the role of the priest as well as that of the sacrificer.

Keeping in view all the contexts of the RV it can be observed that *vāghat* stands for the priest who bears or carries the oblations. Some parallel context can be compared here, e.g. *uśijam ca vāghatam* (3.3.8); *vayunam ca vāghatam* (3.3.4); *uśijam bhṛgūṇam* (3.2.4); *yantāraṁ dhīnām* (3.3.8). All these contexts against that *vāghat*- is employed with the person who possesses *dhī*- 'vision', and they are none other but poet priest. Therefore, it can be surmised that *vāghat* is employed only for the 'priest' and not for the sacrificer.

The word *vāghat* can be formed with root √*vah* 'to carry, to receive' plus the suffix *a*. The accent remains on the suffix by the rule *pratyayaḥ* (Pans. 3.1.3). It can also be explicated by *'phiso'nts udāttaḥ* (*Phits.* 1).

Dhiyā - Here the word *dhiyā* instr. sg. of *dhī* 'vision, wisdom, skill' etc., has been construed by Sāyaṇa only with *manuṣaḥ* and *vāghataḥ* with its explanation as 'by action' (*Karmana*). But it would have been better to construe it with the *upameya vāghata*. with its *upamana kuliśaḥ* standing for the wielder because, as the wielder of the kuliśa, 'thunderbold' sends forth the chariot, the poet sends his calls (prayers) to Agni, or he calls ahead to Agni through his skill or visionary power. Geldner and Velankar follow the same pattern.

Samṛṇvati - This is the third sg. form of *ṛṇu* with the prefix *sam*. It should be construed with *hotāram*, the *upameya*, as well as with *ratham* the *upamāna*. The priest brings forth Agni as the hatchet sets forth the chariot.

RV. III. 2.2

स रोचयज्जनुषा रोदसी उभे स मात्रोरभवत् पुत्र ईड्यः ।
हव्यवाळग्निरजरश्चनोहितो दूळभो विशामतिथिर्विभावसुः ॥

Sāyaṇa's commentary on this verse seems genuine except his rendering of the meanings of a few individual words. Some doubts can be raised on the meanings of the words *canohitaḥ* and *dūlabaḥ*. They have been explained differently by the various exegetists. Their renderings need justification by critical examination.

Canohitaḥ - This compounded word occurs five times in the RV (3.2.2; 7; 11.2; 9.75.1; 4), and the form *canaḥ* occurs at twelve places separately (1.3.6; 26.10; 107.3; 2.31.6; 35.1; 6.4.2; 10.6; 10.6; 49.14; 7.38.3; 8.10.11; 32.6; 10; 116.8). Sāyaṇa derives *cana* - from *iay* by *cayater anne hrasvasca* (Un 5.4.639). According to this rule after *ca* there will be elizion of y and insertion of *n* (*nud*) with the suffix *asun.* Due to elizion of *n asun* there will be an acute accent on the first syllable by the rule *ñnityādirnityam* (Pan. 6.1.197). Veṅkaṭa-mādhava[55] also gives the same meaning.

Modern interpreters differ invariably with Sāyaṇa's explanation of this word. Oldenberg[56] translates it as 'with satisfied mind' which bears the testimony of Ludwig's[57] rendering as 'Zur freunde geschaffen'. Grassmann[58] attests its meaning as 'holdgestimmt' (Pleasing, gracious); and this meaning has been followed by Griffith[59] also. Geldner's[60] rendering also comes closer to this meaning. He gives its meaning a 'beliebt' (favourite, popular). Renou[61] agrees partly with Ludwig while translating it as '*mis en place, pour la satisfaction (des homes)*', (Placed wall for the satisfaction of the man). Here Gonda's[62] rendering of this word as 'inclined to do anything' appears unjustifiable, because it has no etymological base.

Thus, judging all the above interpretations it is clear that the controversy is here only with regard to *cana* and *hitaḥ* is taken for granted as a pp. of the *dha* 'to place'. The etymology of the word *cana* given by Sāyaṇa[63] from the √*cay* raises doubts because linguistically it does not seem valid to derive *cana* from √*cay* where the elision of - *ay* - has no basis. Rather we can derive it from the Vedic root *can kan* which is analogous to *kā* in *kāyamanaḥ* (RV 3.9.2) and *hapax legomenon,* and *Avestan canah* and *cinah* (desire, ask for) derived from *can.*[64] The formations of *caniṣṭam* (RV 7.70.4) 'take pleasure', (*caniṣṭham* 5.77.4), 'most delightful', *caniṣṭha* 'most delightful',[65] (favour), '*caniṣṭhayā*' (9.9.2), 'most pleasing enjoyment', *canasyatam* (1.3.1), 'desire for',[66] etc, indicate that *cana*- cannot be derived from √*cay*, but rather it is a derivative of √*can* which could originally be *kan* as found in *Kanya* 'young girl'. The meaning of *canaḥ* developed later on as 'grain' or 'food because it was sought for, or was delightful. Thus the compounded word *canohitaḥ* may be explained as 'established or placed for the enjoyment or satisfaction' (of the worshipper). Sāyaṇa, explicates it as a Bahuvrīhi comp. and on this basis he explains its accent on the initial syllable. But even if it is not a Bahuvrīhi comp. its accent can be explained otherwise on the basis of Pans. 6.2.1., by which rule the accent will remain on the first member of the comp., and thus there will be oxytone on the initial syllable by the rule Pā 6.1.197.

Dūlabhāt - This form of Non. sg. of the word *dūlabha* occurs thrice in the RV (3.2.2; 4.9.2; 8). Other forms *dūlabha* (RV 2.28.8; 7.86.4), *dūlabham* (RV 1.15.6) and *dūlabhāsaḥ* (3.56.8; 7.60.6) also occur in the RV. Here Sāyaṇa relates this word with *hiṁsitumaśakyaḥ* 'impossible to be injured'. Elsewhere he attaches the same meaning with slight variations. The modern exegetists explain it as 'undeceivable', 'difficult to deceive'; and they appear to derive it from the *dobh*, 'to deceive', 'to seize' with the prefix *dus.*[67] But the *dobh* has other connotations also 'to injure, destroy, kill, hurt' etc. Therefore, Sāyaṇa's rendering such as be seen to be justified on this ground.

RV. III. 2.3

क्रत्वा॒ दक्ष॑स्य॒ तरु॑षो॒ विध॑र्मणि दे॒वासो॑ अ॒ग्निं ज॑नयन्त॒ चित्ति॑भिः ।
रु॒रु॒चा॒नं भा॒नुना॒ ज्योति॑षा म॒हामत्य॒ं न वाज॑ं स॒निष्यन्नुप॑ ब्रुवे ॥

The interpretation of the first pada of the *ṛk* appears to be problematic. The explication offered by Sāyaṇa does not seem convincing, and especially the renderings of the words *kratvā na vājaṁ*, which occurs frequently in the RV, also needs a fresh rendering. The interpretation of the above words offered by Sāyaṇa in full conformity with the traditional interpretations given by Yāska, Veṅkaṭamādhava, Mādhava, Udgītha etc. But when compared with the meanings attested by modern exegetists they need a critical examination.

Kratvā : We have already discussed the form *Kratum*[68] (occus. sing. of *kratu*) 'power' and GK zgatos 'strength'. Therefore, we can take the same meaning here and can interpret *kratvā dakṣasya* as 'by the power of *dakṣa*'. Geldner[69] has translated it here as 'with the intelligence (mit der klugheit), and Renou[70] as 'spiritual power' (Avee le pouvoir - spirituel). Velankar[71] has followed Geldner.

Dakṣasya : The word *dakṣa* occurs frequently in the RV. The form *dakṣasya* occurs twenty four times in the RV.[72] The phrase *kratvā dakṣasya* occurs thrice (RV 3.2.3; 5.10.2; 9.16.7) and *kratve dakṣāya* eight times in the RV (1.111.2; 4.37.2; 5.43.5; 9.36.3; 100.5; 109.2; 10; 10.57.4), which indicate close relationship between these two words. *Kratu* is somewhat abstract, and so signifying the 'power of intellect or mind, and *dakṣa* appears to be the 'physical power', Sāyaṇa derives it from *dakṣa* 'to increase', grow (Dhat. Pa. 16.7), 'to go quickly' (Dh. Pa. 19.8) with *ghañ.*[73] But he explains its oxytone accent here on the basis of Pa. 6.1.197 *ñnityādirnityam.* though it should have been barytone according to the rule *karṣātvato ghañoant uddātaḥ* (Pa. 6.1.159)'. But here the rule *Pūrvatrā siddham* (Pa. 8.2.1) may be applied even out of its scope.

The phrase *kratvā dakṣasya* has been explained by Sāyaṇa as 'by the act of strength' (*balasya karmaṇā*), Venkaṭamādhava does not explain *dakṣasya* here, but elsewhere he renders the phrase *'kratye dakṣaya'* with *'prajñānāya balāya ca'* 'for the vision and power', which indicates clearly that there is no difference of opinion between these two scholiasts. But Veṅkaṭamādhava's rendering of *Kratvā* is remarkable up to the work, which has been followed by modern exegetists also. Geldner's rendering as 'mit der klugheit des Verstandes[74] and Renou's[75] as 'ave le pouvoir-spirituel de la pensee - agissante' (by the spiritual power of the efficient wisdom' are nearer to Veṅkaṭamādhava's above interpretation. Velankar[76] and Bhave[77] have also followed the same interpretation. But Velankar construes *dakṣasya* with *kratvā* and *taruṣaḥ* both, while *taruṣaḥ* has been taken by Sāyaṇa as an adj. to *dakṣasya.* Sāyaṇa's explanation of the complete phrase, i.e. *kratvā dakṣasya taruṣaḥ* differences all other interpretations, because where *taruṣaḥ* is here to be construed with *dakṣasya* as being gen. sing. of *taruṣ* needs minute observation which has not been explained by any one of these exegetists. Even Sāyaṇa has not explained the etymology and formation of *taruṣ*. Therefore, before we venture to give any meaning *taruṣaḥ* would be better to look into all the aspects of.

Taruṣaḥ: This form occurs four times in the RV (1.122.13; 3.2.3; 6.15;3.10.115.5). Other forms, namely, *taruṣasa* (1.129.10), *taruṣi* (6.25.4) also occur. The verbal forms connected with *taruṣ* also occur, as *taruṣanta* (1.132.5), *taruṣante* (5.59.1), *taruṣema* (7.48.2) and *taruṣyataḥ* (8.99.5). The word *taruṣ* has not been analysed by Sāyaṇa and others as stated above. The formation of this word can be explained on the basis of some similar words such as *janus, manus, yajus, arus, vapus* etc. All of them are formed with original roots plus *us* suffix, by *janerusih* (Un. 5.2.115), and by *arti partitapibhyo* nit (Un. 4.1.117). They will be taken as *nit* to explain their oxytone. Being *nit* they will be governed by general rule *ñnityādirnityam* (Pa. 6.1.197). The word *taruṣ* also will be formed similarly, viz *tar US.*, *tarus*, by the role *behulam anyatrapi nit* (Un. 5.2.117), will be taken by *anuvṛtti*; and thus the word *tarus* will have the oxytone. But the declension of this word is irregular as is the case with other similar Vedic words.[78] The form *taruṣaḥ*, according to this declension, will be in N. pl., acc. pl. and gen. sing. For example RV 1.122.13 it is N. pl. with *īśānāsaḥ.*, but in all other occurrences (RV 3.2.3; 6.15.3; 10.115.5) it is gen. sing. The inster. sing. *taruṣasa* (1.129.10) is irregular, while loc. sing. *taruṣi* (6.25.4) is regular. These two forms indicate that the word *taruṣ* is used as an adj. signifying both masc. and neut. The original root in the word is *tṛ.* 'to cross, conquer, sieze' etc. and therefore, the forms *taruṣanta* etc. are denominatives.

After this detailed study of the word *taruṣ* we can discuss its meaning. Here Sāyaṇa renders it with *'vyasanebhyas-tārakasya'* (his, who liberates from vices') and thinks it to be a qualifying word for *dakṣasya*. RV 1.122.13 he explains it as *śatrūṇām tārkān*, ('to them who cross over the enemies'), taking it as occ. pl. form with *īśānāsaḥ*. Here (at RV 1.122.13) Geldner takes *taruṣaḥ* for the singers.[79] which can be applied in the present context also because *taruṣaḥ* appears to be related with *vidharmaṇi* here which signifies the sacrifice or the sacrificial place or act. Therefore, Sāyaṇa's paraphrasing of *taruṣaḥ* and *dakṣasya* together is not convincing; and the same may be said about Velankar's statement that *taruṣaḥ* should be construed with *dakṣasya*.[80]

The meaning given by Sāyaṇa is also not convincing. The root *tṛ* originally has the meaning 'to cross' but it has other meanings also, as 'to conquer', 'over power', 'over-come', 'subdue'[81] etc. which can be applied with *taruṣaḥ* here; and thus *taruṣaḥ* means here 'of the conquerer' or 'of him who wishes to cross over or conquer'; and thus *taruṣaḥ* will be construed with *Vidharmaṇi.* Oldenberg[82] has translated[83] *taruṣaḥ* as 'superior strength' which is similar to Griffith's rendering of it as 'surpassing power'. Geldner[84] has followed this sense in his translation, 'um ihre macht auszubreiten', indicates. He rightly construes *'taruṣo vidharmaṇi'* together. Following Geldner and Renou also renders the phrase *taruṣo vidharmaṇi* with 'dans Í extension de (leur) force -triomphante.[85] 'Velankar's translation of this phrase as 'for the sake of upholding their overpowering wisdom' appears far from the mark. All the interpretations offered by modern exegetists from Griffith to Velankar are in the same line with minor differentiations. They are led by the same notion that *taruṣaḥ vidharmaṇi* is connected with the gods who generate Agni. But it would be certainly better to separate this phrase from the gods and connect it with the singers or worshippers in whose domain of activity Agni is generated by the gods. This will be clear through the contexts of *Vidharmaṇi* which appears to be polisemic here.

Vidharmaṇi : The form *vidharmaṇi* occurs eight times in the (RV 1.164.36; 3.2.3; 6.71.1; 9.4.9; 86.29; 30; 100.7). Another Loc. sing. form *vidharman* also occurs thrice in the (RV 9.97.40; 109.6; 10.123.8). *vidharmaṇa* (10.46.6) Instru. Sing., *Vidharmaṇe* (RV 8.7.5) dat. sing. and *vidharman* (RV 5.17.2) voc. sing. also occur unnecessary in the RV Sāyaṇa. has offered many explanations for it, as 'having many duties, viz. the singer of hymns', 'sacrifice in which many priest perform several duties', 'mid region', etc. Some of these meanings have been followed by Grassmann who attests these meaning as (1) 'Vertheilung' (spreading), 'Ausbreitung' (extension), (2) die weite Ausdehnung, 'der weite Umfang' (expansion, elongation, dimension, range of activity), (3) 'Himmel' (heaven, sky); (4) 'die Somaseihe' (*pavitram*) and so on.[86] Wilson[87] has followed Sāyaṇa in rendering it as 'in the multiform rite'. Ludwig,[88] Griffith[89] and Geldner[90] follow one of the meanings given by Grassmann, i.e. 'range or domain of activity' (macht gebiete). Geldner and Renou have accepted the meaning 'extension' attested by Grassmann but Geldner appears to take it as a loc. infinitive as it explicit by his translation of the phrase *taruṣo vidharmaṇi* as'um ihre Macht auszubreiten' (in order to widen their power). Velankar like Geldner, thinks that *Vidharmaṇi* is a loc. infinitive and compares it with *ṛtasya dhartari* RV 2.23.17; and in accordance with this argument he translates *taruṣoḥ vidharmaṇi* as 'for the sake of upholding their overpowering wisdom'. But the forms *vidharmaṇa* (Instr. sing.), *Vidharmaṇe* (Dat. sing.) etc. stand against the fallcy that *vidharmaṇi* has been used here as Loc. infinitive. Rather it should be taken Loc. sing. as the form indicates; and thus the phrase *taruṣaḥ vidharmaṇi* should be translated as 'in the domain of the conquerer' or 'in the sphere of the powerful one'. Thus *taruṣaḥ* stands here for the singer or worshipper or sacrificer who desires victory over his enemies and invokes gods in the sacrificial act to generate Agni, and gods do that with their vision and deep thoughts which are indicated here by the words *kratvā* and *cittibhiḥ*.

Matyam na vājam saniṣyan : The phrase *atyam na vajam* occurs frequently in one way or another in the RV. Some times *vājīnam* is used in the place of *vājam* which makes very little difference in the set meaning. Here Sāyaṇa explains the phrase as *'bharasahamaśvmiva vājam annam lipsamano'ham'* (desirous of food I eulogize Agni as a vigorous horse). Veṅkaṭamādhava renders it alike were except he explained *vājamas 'sanvaman* conflict'. Most of the modern interpreters differ on the meaning of *vājam* as well as in explaining the fourth Pāda as a whole. Griffith[91] translates *Vājam* as 'strength', Oldenberg thinks that *vājam saniṣyan* refers to the worshipper who desires to obtain vāja (quick strength and the booty or prize obtained by it, Oldenberg), in comparison to the owner of a race-horse, who desires to win the race.[92] Many stanzas related to this phrase may stand in the justification of Oldenberg's statement, but the statement itself is not conclusively convincing. He is followed by Geldner who renders the fourth *pāda* of the present *ṛk* as 'rede ich zu wie dem Rennpferd der, der den siegpreis gewinnen will'.[93] Oldenberg's predecessor Ludwig[94] translated *vājam* as 'kräftijung' (strengthening). Renou[95] translates prix-de-victoire (ś adresse) au coursier' (I address to him alike the man who addresses his steed, desiring to gain the prize of victory. This rendering is entirely in conformity with Geldner's translation given above, and does not indicate any improvement over the preceding translations. Velankar[96] has also followed the same. Here the main controversy arises out of the exact meaning of *Vājaḥ* which has been translated in other contexts by Geldner as "Sieg" (1.27.11). "Gewinn" (1.27.8) "Siegerprieis" (1.27.9), "Lohn" (1.110.6), " Belohnung" (1.63.9), "Ehrenpreis" (1.48.12), etc. which are not very felicitous. Renou has remarked elsewhere that *vāja* basically means 'prize', and especially the reward bestowed by the divinity, but in some other contexts it may mean 'booty' for certain groups or prize for some participants in a tournament.[97] This remark of Renou may be partially true but is difficult to rules crib to it. Oldenberg and Gonda have rendered it with 'energy'.[98] But Gonda has elaborated his points in many places and explained *vāja* as "generative power believed to reside in vegetation, cattle, etc. and by which new food and new life are obtained" and qualified by attributes such *assravasyaḥ* "praise-worthy".[99]

RV. III. 2.4

आ मन्द्रस्यं सनिष्यन्तो वरैण्यं वृणीमहे अह्रयं वाजमृग्मियंम् ।
रातिं भृगूंणामुशिजं कविक्रंतुमग्निं राजंन्तं दिव्येनं शोचिषां ॥

The syntactic structure of the verse is affected when Sāyaṇa construes the words *ahrayaṁ* and *ṛgmiyam* with *vājam* while Veṅkaṭamādhava[100] construes them with *agnim* which also changes the meaning. Besides, they explicate *mandrasya* differently. The meanings of *ahrayam, ṛgmiyam* and *mandrasya* needs a full discussion here.

Mandrasya - The form *mandrasya,* gen. sg. of *mandra.,* occurs four times in the RV (3.2.4; 6.7; 6.39.1; 9.68.6). Other forms also occur frequently. This word stands mostly as an epithet to *Agni.* In a few occurrences it is employed with soma (9.96.7; 65.29; 67.1; 68.6; 109.8; 10.61.20), Indra (6.48.4; 10.73.1), Maruts (1.166.11) horses of Indra (perhaps Maruts 3.45.1), Vāk (8.100.11; 10.101.2; 7.18.3), streams (9.6.1; 107.8), Bṛhaspati (4.50.1), Naktoṣasā (1.142.8) and Viśvedevāḥ (10.93.4). Agni has been ascribed with the epithet *mandrajihvā* - (1.19.7; 4.11.5; 5.25.2). Once Savitṛ also enjoys this epithet at RV 6.71.4 where it seems to suggest the 'charming rays' of the sun. Once (RV 4.6.5) *madhuvacā* follows *mandraḥ* with Agni which signifies the close identity of these two words. Besides, *priya (puru priya* - 8.43.31) also seems to be a parallel to *mandra* - A close observation of all the occurrences of this word indicates that originally this epithet belonged to Agni but later on with the development of the Ṛgvedic poetry it was also applied to other gods to signify their pleasing qualities.

Sāyaṇa has offered two alternate meanings throughout his commentary on the RV, i.e., 'delightful' (*madanīya, maīdavitā*) and 'laudable or 'praiseworthy' (*stutyaḥ*). These same meanings have been extended in various ways in various contexts as 'exhilerating, intoxicating skillful in praise' etc. But in the majority of the contexts Sāyaṇa[101] appears to prefer the meaning 'delightful or delighted'; and this fact indicates that he has followed Yāskas' rendering of *mandrajihvam, modamajihvam iti va* (Nir. 6.23). How he could render *mandraḥ* with *stutyaḥ* (Praiseworthy) is yet to be explored. Perhaps in such contexts where he offers this meaning he derives *mandra* from *mand* or *mad* 'to praise'. In other contexts *Sāyaṇa* explains the derivation of *mandra.* from *mad* with the Uṇādi suffix *rak* governed by the rule *sphayi tanci vanci* (Un S. 5.2.13) with insertion of *num* (*idito numdhātoḥ* - Pā. 7.1.58). Accordingly the accent will remain on the suffix, i.e. on the last syllable.

Roth[102] and Grassmann[103] have followed Sāyaṇa in attesting the meaning of *mandra* as 'erfreuend' (delightful), 'angenehm' (pleasant), 'lieblich' (lovely). They derive it from *mand.* Ludwig[104] renders it with 'freudigen' (joyous, glad) which indicates his inclination to derive it from *mad* 'to be happy' following almost his predecessors. Griffith's[105] rendering as 'friendly' is also as follow up, but cannot be reckoned with as an exact one. Oldenberg's[106] translation as 'joy giver' may be compared with Ludwig's who renders it as 'joyous' and thus it is clear that Oldenberg has not contributed any thing new here. Max Müller[107] has translated *mandraḥ* as 'sweet-toned' (Maruts) deriving it from *mand* 'to please, to make rejoice'.[108] But his translation appears here streched just to suit the context of Maruts, who may be otherwise also. If we apply the same meaning here, it will not be suitable, because Agni cannot be called in this context 'sweet toned'. This same translation appears to be followed by Geldner[109] who renders *mandrasya* here as 'des wholredenden' (Agni) with good eloquence or sweet-toned; but elsewhere he himself translates it as 'ergotzenden',[110] (delightful) and 'erfreudent' (delightful)[111] in the context of Soma who has been ascribed with the epithets *Vahni* and *Kavi* like Agni. Thus it appears that in some places he follows Max Müller and in others Grassmann and Roth. Renou[112] renders it with 'réjouissant' (cheering) which resembles Ludwig's and others renderings. Thus it appears that all these western scholars are in harmony with one anothers and all of them derive the word *mandra* from the *mand*, 'to rejoice' etc.

Velankar[113] has followed the meaning 'delightful'. Bhawe has offered almost a fresh interpretation of the word *mandra*. To quote him verbatim; *mandraḥ* (= *madayitāram*", according to Sāyaṇa) can better be derived from *man+ra* with the development of a voice unspirate infix, *viz.* - *d* - *in* between, meaning 'the thoughtful of songful one".[114] He hastens to add that this insertion between *mantra* is 'a phenomenon which is common to the gndo European languages'.[115] But here the insertion of - *d* - appears unnecessary because with a host of the original vedic roots this *ra* suffix has been applied invariably without adding any infix to them. For examples we can take the words like *citra* (*citra*), Avestan *Civra, kṣip+ra,* Avestan *kaudra xsiwra* (swift); *kṣudra*- (*kṣud+ra*) Avestan *'Kasudra,* Semen (virile); *gradhra* (greedy) Avestan *garora-candra* shining (*scand*-), lat. *candere,* and GK (coal); *namra* (*nami* ....., Pan 3.2.167), *Avestan mra; bhadra*- (*bhand*), Avestan. *badra; Vipra* - (*vip* -) Avestan *vifra* (clever); *sukra* (*sud*), Avestan *'suxra'* (shining); *tandra* (*tand*), *tugra* (*tuj*), *mathra*[116] (*math*-), *radhra* (*radh*-), *rudra* (*rud*-); *mitra*- (*mit*); *vadhra* (*vadh*-), *sakra*- (*sac*-); *sidhra*- (*sidh*-) and so on.[117] All these words clearly indicate that the suffix - *ra* does not require any insertion before it. Not only this but the verbal forms like *mandatu* (RV 6.17.3; 7.22.1), *mandantu* (RV 1.134.2; 2.11.11), *mandaya* (RV 3.30.20; 50.4), *mandayadhyai* (RV 4.29.3), *mandayan* (RV 9.67.16),[118] *mandase* (RV 1.51.12; 8.12.16; 17.54.2), *mandamahe* (RV 1.122.13) and so on clearly exemplify that the root *mand* was very much in existence in the Ṛgvedic time, and therefore, a derivative of it like *mandra* was not out of orderly usage.

The several meanings which are given to *mand* are 'to rejoice, be glad, to be delighted, to praise; to intoxicate, exhilerate, gladen, inflame, inspirit.[119] Only these meanings have been taken into consideration by the interpreters while explaining *mandra* in the RV. Nighantu[120] attests some more important meanings which have not attracted the attention of any interpreter. They are 'to be splendid or beautiful, shine'. These meanings could have been applied safely by the interpreters in the contexts of Agni as well as the other gods. Only recently Gonda[121] has translated *mandra* as "charming" and that also without any explication. But the meanings 'resplendant, beautiful, charming and shining can be applied in the context of *mandra* without any hesitation. These meanings must have been prevalent before Nighaṇṭu was collected and restored to the posterity. Thus Agni and Soma as *mandra*[122] *mandrajihva*,[123] *mandratama*[124] and Poets as *mandrayu*[125] (desiring to be resplendant) exhibit the meanings as shining, beautiful, resplendant and charming.

Ahrayam : The form *ahrayam* occurs six times in the RV (3.2.4; 5.79.5; 7.67.6; 8.54.8; 56.1; 60.16). Other forms, *ahrayaḥ* (RV 1.74.8; 8.70.13; 9.54.1; 10.93.9), *ahraya* (RV. 5.79.6; 8.8.13) and *ahraye* (RV 10.147.3) also occur in the RV. Thus it is clear that the word *ahraya* - was not much in usage in the Ṛgvedic time. Sāyaṇa paraphrases here ahrayam as *alajjavaham*, 'exempt from shame'. Veṅkaṭamādhava also explains in the same way. Grassmann and all other subsequent interpreters have followed this meaning. Oldenberg's[126] 'glorious' and Griffith[127] 'confident' also display the same trait, though not accurately.

Somehow, the interpretation *alajjavaham* or *alijjamanam* (Venkaṭamādhava) does not appear quite convincing here since 'shameful' or 'not shameful' has nothing to do with *vājam* 'the procreative power'. Therefore, we have to trace some other 'meaning' of *ahrayam* which can suit all the contexts of the RV. The contexts like *rādhoahrayaḥ* (RV

5.79.5), *reto ahrayam* (RV 7.67.6), *rādho ahrayam* (RV 8.54.8), *vāji ahrayaḥ* (RV 1.74.8), *suriryo ahrayaḥ* (Indraḥ) (RV 8.70.13), *kṛdhī no ahrayo deva savitaḥ* (RV 10.93.9) clearly exemplify that the meaning *'not ashamed'* does not suit there contexts, but rather the explanation given by Sāyaṇa as '*akṣiṇam*' ('not perishing') in RV 8.60.16 can be applied very well in these contexts also without tampering the original sense of the *ṛks*. The only contexts where the meaning 'unashamed' or 'bold' fits is RV 7.80.2 where Uṣas has been called *ahrayāṇā* (*agra eti yuvatirahrayāṇā*), but here also the first pada of the same *ṛk* says *'eṣā sya navyamayurdadhana* (this well known Uṣas generating new life), which shows that *yuvati* Uṣas bears always new life. At the same time she is described as *ajra amṛta*[128] and *ajuryaḥ*[129] in many places in the RV which can be identified here with *ahrayāṇā*[130] giving the sense of 'undecaying'. Though its etymology seems difficult to explain, because the only root for derived by all the interpreters is *hri* 'to be ashamed, bashful'. and this would give the meaning to *ahraya* as assigned by the interpreters of the RV. As Bhawe mentions 'the word *ahri* can be a nañ-tat. i.e. *a* + *hri*, the latter being a root-noun with shortened final vowel (without the *t* -ending) from *hri* 'to feel shamed'. [131] But this presumption, i.e. from *hri* does not hold good, because from along root there is no possibility of root noun *hri*, and at the same time the word is mostly as (*a*) *hraya* -, not-hri-as taken by Bhawe. His assertion that *ahrayaḥ* is noun pl. confirmed by *duduhre* (RV 9.54.18)[132] is untenable because the actual base appear to be a *hri* + *asun* = ahrayan (Neut. 7). This may be explained on the analogy of *jrayaḥ* (RV 1.95.9; 101.7; 140.9; 4.52.5; 5.44.6; 8.86.1-6; 9.68.2; 10.92.5).[133] As *jrayaḥ* is from jri, so *hrayaḥ* may be from *hri*. In both of them the suffix *asun* will be added which will be governed by the accent-role '*ñnityadirnityam* (Pa 6.1.197), accent falling on the first syllable; but this will be debarred by the rule '*tatpuruṣe* (Pa. 6.2.2), *ahrayaḥ* being *nan tatp.* here and therefore there will be oxytone on the indeclinable *a hray* (not attested anywhere) which may be a similar form of *hary* meaning 'to threaten'.[134] As the form *harya* occurs in the RV it is difficult to accept *hray*- but it is evident that the form *harva* occuring in the RV does not bear the meaning 'to threaten' but rather they have common root meanings such as 'to go, like, delight' etc. Therefore, '*hary*' and '*hray*' cannot be identical. But, Nighaṇṭu know the use of *hary*: 'to threaten' otherwise there was no possibility of his attesting it here. On this basis we can say that this *hary* was originally *hray* which was not in much use even in Ṛgvedic times because the word *ahray*- was used only in the Ṛgvedic verses, and the usages which are found in later literature, viz. Yajurveda ete.[135] are mere repetitions of the Ṛgvedic phrases. Thus we may presume that *hray* is basically *hary* - 'to threaten'; and this root meaning can be applied in the RV also. For example we can quote here some of the phrases where *ahraya* - occurs.

1. *tvoto vajyahrayos, bhi purvasmadaparaḥ* [RV 1.74.8]
   (Agni, the man helped by you stands unthreatend before others)[136]
2. *upastutim bhojaḥ suriryo ahrayaḥ* [RV 8.70.13]
   (Pray) Indra who is liberal, princely and unthreatened)[137]
3. *asya pratnamanu dyutaṁ sukraṁ duduhre ahrayaḥ* [RV 9.54.1]
   (The unthreatened (poets) have milked his old (ripe), shining and brilliant (sap).[138]
4. *kṛdhī no ahrayo deva savitaḥ* [RV 10.93.9]
   (O God Savitṛ, make us unthreatened).[139]
5. *pari cid vaṣṭayo dadhurdadato rādho ahrayaṁ sujate aśvasūnṛte* [RV 5.79.5]
   (thou nobly bar none delightful with they steads).[140]

(Uṣas, while giving the unthreatened riches thy worshippers have girded around us in order to accomplish their desires).[141]

In the above verse, i.e. RV 5.79.5 *rādhoahrayaḥ* occurs where it has been explained by Sāyaṇa as *akṣīṇaṁ* 'undecaying' (riches), and this seems identical with *vājam ahrayam* in the present context. The meaning 'unthreatened' can be extended to 'undecaying' easily. Therefore, these meanings, i.e., 'unthreatened' and 'undecaying', can be applied suitably with the contexts of *ahraya* - in the RV.

Thus we can render the first two padas with, "we desire to choose the beautiful (worthy to choice) excellent and undecaying generative power[142] of the resplendant Agni".

Here the word ṛgmiyam explained by Sāyaṇa as *'praśasya'* 'excellent' needs detailed discussion as follows.

Ṛgmiyam - The word *ṛgmiya* - occurs eleven times in the RV. The form *'ṛgmiyaḥ* (Nom. sg. of *ṛgmiya*) occurs twice (RV 8.23.3; 9.74.3) and *ṛgmiyāya* once (RV 1.62.1) while *ṛgmiyam* eight times (RV 1.9.9; 51.1; 3.2.4; 6.8.4; 8.39.1; 40.10; 9.68.6). Other cognate forms *ṛgmiṇaḥ* (RV 9.86.45); *ṛgmibhiḥ* (RV 1.100.4) and *ṛgmī* (RV 1.100.4) also occur. *ṛgmiya* is here and at RV 6.8.4; 8.23.3; 39.1 an epithet for Agni. Elsewhere (except in RV 9.63.6; 74.3 for Soma) it stands for Indra. Sāyaṇa explicates *ṛgmiyam* here as *'praśasyam'*, 'praiseworthy', 'excellent', taking it as an adjective of *vājam*. But from Veṅkaṭamādhava's paraphrase, *ṛgarham agnim*, 'agni, worthy of hymns', it seems that *ṛgmiyam* stands here as an epithet for Agni; and this becomes more evident from the above statement about its occurrences as an epithet for Agni and mother gods in other contexts. The verbal form *vṛṇīmahe* has to be applied with *agnim* in the third *pāda* also and therefore, *ahrayam vājam ṛgmiyam ... agnim* are to be construed together according to Veṅkaṭamādhava's interpretation. But the syntactical relation of *ahrayam vājam ṛgmiyam* goes with *mandrasy* and *vṛṇīmahe.* For the sake of economy of words we have to construe again *vṛṇīmahe* with the third and fourth pādās, otherwise the first and second pādās are to be interpreted independently and thus, here *ahrayam* and *ṛgmiyam* should be construed with *vājam.* Oldenberg[143] etc. have followed Sāyaṇa. So far as its derivation is concerned Sāyaṇa under RV 1.9.9. analyses it into *re+mi,* root noun from *ma,* 'to measure', change of *a* in *i* being explained by Pā 6.4.66; *ghumasthāgāpajahātisāṁ hali* and attested in *manyumīḥ,* RV 1.100.6; 2.23.4; in this case *ṛgmiyam* is acc. sg. of *ṛgmiya.* But this derivation with root-noun *mu* or *ma* is doubtful. The word may be analysed into *ṛc + mi + ya, or ṛc + ma + iya.* The suffix *mi* has been used by Sāyaṇa in the analysis of *tuvikūrmin* RV 3.30.3, and *ma* in *iṣmiṇo* RV 1.87.6, governed by Un. 5.1.145. The suffix *mi* is the product of *'gmiḥ'* (*vāco gminiḥ* - Pa. 5.2.124) where it suits well; but in the analysis of *ṛgmiyam* it does not suit properly, because *ṛgmiyam* seems the product of *ṛgms,* not of *ṛgmi*: because formations in *min* according to *Wacker-Debru,*[144] are not inherited from older times; only two such forms noted by Pāṇini (5.2.114 and 124), viz. *gomin,* and *vagmin* are known to Sanskrit. Though the above noted forms *tuvikūrmin* - and *iṣmin* - are found in the RV, are not sure whether they represent the formations in - min or in - *in.* Sāyaṇa has derived them by Un. suffix *mak,* changed into - *min.* The word *ṛgme* has been used in the AB[145] which testifies that the original word had been *ṛgma,* not *ṛgmin;* and only from *ṛgma* - the word *ṛgmiya* - was derived. We have a sound parallel for it in the word *yajanīya*[146] (worthy of worship) derived from *yajña.* The forms *ṛgmibhiḥ, ṛgmiyaḥ, ṛgmiyam* and *ṛgmiyāya* can compared with *yajñiyebhiḥ* (RV 10.14.5.88.3), *yajñiyaḥ* (RV 1.142.3), *yajñiyam* (RV 1.6.4) and *yajñiyāya* (RV 1.27.10) respectively. The paroxytone accent is visible on both the words. Therefore, on the basic of *vājñiya* we can analyse *ṛgmiyam* thus; first from *ṛc + mak=ṛgma* (on the basis of *iṣmin* by Un.s. 1.1.145). From *ṛgma* it may be *ṛgmin* also. Now as *Yajñiya* is formal with suffix *gha,* in the sense of "deserving", by the rule *yajñartvigbhāyaṁ, ghakhañau* (Pa. 5.1.71), we can form *ṛgmiya*-also with *gha* suffix in the sense of 'deserving the performance of *ṛgma.* 'possessed of songs' (*tatkarmārha-tītyupasaṁkhyanam-Vart.* on Pa. 5.1.71). *gha* is changed into *iya* by the rule *'āyaneyīnīyiyaḥ phadhakhachaghāṁ pratyayādinam* (Pa. 7.1.2) and thus accent will fall on *i* of the suffix *-iya-* by *ādyādāttaḥ* (Pa. 3.1.3).

Now we can render *ṛgmiyam* as 'deserving the song of the performance of the singer when applied with Agni or any other god, but in the present context the meaning can be extended as *'praiseworthy,* virtuous' and so on. *ṛigma* as a primary derivation will mean 'song' or 'a group of songs' as is found in the AB 5.9, not 'finger' as presumed by Bhawe[147] because in the sense of 'singer' which can be compared with *ismin* (RV 1.87.6). In the sense of deity *'ṛgmī'* will be used. In RV 1.100.4 *ṛgmibhirṛgmī* indicates 'singers' by *ṛgmibhir,* and deity, i.e. Indra, by *ṛgmi,* which can be equated by the parallelism *aṅgirābhiḥ aṅgirastamoḥ, vṛsa virsabhiḥ* and *pakhibhi sakha.* The word *ṛgma* does not mean *'both* the singer-devotee as well as the deity' as Bhawe thinks, but it means only 'possessor of song'. Further since the word *ṛgma* means only 'a group of songs' or 'song', the form *ṛgmiya* will mean only 'one who deserves songs or excellent praises' and not 'full of (excellent) praises' as Bhawe[148] thinks. Ludwig[149] compares *ṛgmiyam* with *ṛṇajmi* which is found nowhere in the Vedic literature, and his comparison with GK is unconvincing.

Finally a few words may be added about the phrase *'ratim bhṛgūṇām uāśjam kavīkratum* which occurs in other places also.

RV. III. 2.5

अग्निं सुम्नायं दधिरे पुरो जना वाजंश्रवसमिह वृक्तबंर्हिषः ।
यतस्त्रुंचः सुरुचं विश्वदैंव्यं रुद्रं यज्ञानां साधंदिष्टिमपसांम् ॥

This *ṛk* has been repeated in the VS[150] also, where the commentator Uvvaṭa explains *agnim* as *'anyadevatā nivṛttyārtho'gni sabdaḥ (agni* is used here to word of other deities). Veṅkaṭamādhava[151] construes *dadhire puraḥ* together explaining the phrase as *'āhavanīyam kurvanti* (make him worthy of call). Uvvaṭa and Mahīdhara go ahead and explicate it as *'āhavanīya rūpeṇa pura agrataḥ purābhāge sthāpetavantaḥ* (they, the priest have placed him at the front portion in the form of *Āhavaniya*). Literally *dadhire* connotes 'established', but Sāyaṇa explains it as 'eulogized by the priests', and this explanation has been followed by the modern exegetists like Wilson,[152] Griffith,[153] Grassmann,[154] Geldner[155] etc. There appears a general agreement on the meaning of the whole verse.

The word *sumnāya*, in the *ṛk*, has been rendered with 'pleasure', (*sukham*) by all the exegetists but its derivation and formation needs a discussion here.

Sumnāya - The word *sumna*- (neut.) occurs frequently in the RV (nearly thirtyfive times). It has been attested in the Nigh.[156] among the synonyms of *sukha* - 'pleasure', happiness', and this meaning has been followed by the commentators invariably with some additions. Roth[157] and Grassmann[158] have attested its meanings as 'wohlwollend, hold, gesinnt des Göttern', (goodwill, kindness benevolence of the gods, etc.) Aufrecht[159] made attempt to establish its meaning as 'favour'. *sumnam* - occurs in the Ārṣeyabrahmaṇa as a name of a particular *saman.*

RV. III. 2.6; 2.7

पाव॑कशोचे॒ तव॒ हि क्षयं॒ परि॒ होत॑र्य॒ज्ञेषु॑ वृ॒क्तब॑र्हिषो॒ नर॑ः ।
अग्ने॒ दुव॑ इ॒च्छमा॑नास॒ आप्य॒मुपा॑सते॒ द्रवि॑णं धेहि॒ तेभ्य॑ः ॥
आ रोद॑सी अपृ॒णदा स्व॑र्म॒हज्जा॒तं यदे॑नम॒पसो॒ अधा॑रयन् ।
सो अ॑ध्व॒राय॒ परि॑ णीयते क॒विरत्यो॒ न वाज॑सातये॒ चनो॑हितः ॥

There does not appear any basic difference between Sāyaṇa and Veṅkaṭamādhava on the general meanings of the above two *ṛks* except on the compound ***vājasātaye*** which has been paraphrased by Veṅkaṭamādhava as *saṅgrāmāya* "for battle" and explicated by Sāyaṇa as *annasya kīrter vā lābhāya* "for the gain of food or fame". Another thing which marks the difference is the phrase *atya na* which has been construed by Veṅkaṭamādhava with *vājasātaya* while Sāyaṇa does not care it due to his predelection for the sacrificial contexts. Ignoring the fact that *atyo na vājam* (or *vājasātaye*) is a common phrase in the vedic poetry, he construes *atyo na* with *kaviḥ* only. In this *ṛk* there are two parallel statements, i.e. *adhavarāya pariṇīyate kaviḥ* and *atyaḥ* (*pariṇīyate*) *vājasātaye.* This parallelism creates an occasion for the Word-Economy which is enjoyed with *pariṇīyate.* This verbal form has to be construed with *kaviḥ* as well as with *atyaḥ.* Similarly *vājasātaya* also stands with *kaviḥ* as well as with *atyaḥ.* This *adhvarāya* and *vājasātaye* stand parallel to each other. The last two *pādās* can be rendered with - "he, the possessor of vision, the well satisfied (agni) is being carried around the sacrifice for the gain of the generative power as a well fed horse (is carried around) for the gain of the power". This statement reminds the few popular practices of the *Aśvamedha* in which the victorious horse was driven around the kingdom as the symbol of full fledged victory over the rival kings.

This verse occurs in the VS[160] also where Uvvata construes *vājasātaye* with *canohitaḥ atyo na,* but Mahīdhara follows Sāyaṇa's line and construes *canohitaḥ* with *kaviḥ* (*agniḥ*). His explanation *yathasvo annalābhāya sarvato nīyate* "as the horse is driven around for the gain of food" is in tune with Sāyaṇa's explanation and gives a better understanding of the simile.[161] But his interpretation of *vājasātaye* cannot be accepted. This coup. means "for the gain of the generative power"[162] which ultimately tend to signify the victory in the battle.

Grassmann[163] thinks that this verse stands in isolation in this hymn, and therefore, he leaves it untranslated. Ludwig, commenting upon *pari ṇīyate,* observes that *pari* does not always mean "round" (herun) but it means "near, up to" (heran) also, and thus it indicates towards the *agni parikirya* performed by the *Agnīdhra* priest who brings *agni* near the sacrifice as a race-horse is brought near the race-course.[164] This statement appears convincing leaving the meaning of *vājasātaye* as 'race-course'. Oldenberg[165] follows Ludwig, Griffith has nearly misinterpreted the phrase *vājasātaye* constitute while translating it as "graciously inclined that he may win us strength". Geldner[166] renders it with "zur Preisgewinnung, der Beliebte" (for winning the prize, the favourite one). But this rendering is not sound. Like Ludwig he also explains *pari ṇīyate* as *paryāgnikaraṇa.* Leaving *canohitaḥ,* Renou[167] follows Geldner. He explains *canohitaḥ* as "installé pour la satisfaction (des hommes)". Velankar[168] is a hit ahead in translating *vājasātaye* as "for the acquisition of the prize". He renders *canohitaḥ* with "delighted" which may be improved as "satisfied", because "delighted horse" does not suit the context.

RV. III. 2.8

नमस्यतं हव्यदांतिं स्वध्वरं दुंवस्यत दम्यं जातवेंदसम् ।
रथीर्ऋतस्यं बृहतो विचंर्षणिरग्निर्देवानांमभवत् पुरोहिंतः ॥

Sāyaṇa[169] explicates *havyadātiṁ* as *haviṣāṁa dātārum* in favour of Agni, which is different from Venkaṭamādhava's rendering. Veṅkaṭamādhava[170] takes *havyadātim* for the sacrificer and quotes SB[171] to substanate his view. Similarly he takes the first and the second pādās as two distinct clauses while Sāyaṇa does not separate them and construes all of them as one unit. Syntactically they are two clauses, but the appealatives used here for Agni may be construed to other and thus *namasyata* and *duvasyata* also may be put together to give more stress to the worship. The stylistic parallelism of two clauses necessitates to put these two verbal forms in the beginning of the two pādās so that the rhythmic weightage could be maintained.

Havyadātim- When we look to the appelatives *svadhvaram, damyam* and *jātavedasam, havyadātim* obviously appears as a parallel word to them used for Agni. Though all of its occurrences in the RV[172] (except on at 6.48.2) indicate that it has been used either for 'giving or distributing the offering' or for 'the distributor himself', yet as Agni is the carrier of the oblations to the gods by virtue of his name *vahniḥ* here also he may be called *'havyadāti'*. But the explanation given by Sāyaṇa and others as 'the giver of the offering' may be altered as 'distributor of offering', because the word *dati* may be a derivative of either *da* 'to give' or of *da* 'to cut or distribute' *(dap lavane)* as attested by Sāyaṇa in RV Bh. 1.65.4 Geldner[173] also confirms it. His rendering 'opferausteiler' (distributor of offering), followed by Velankar,[174] appears more convincing. Grassmann's renderings "opfergüsse in Empfang nehmend"[175] (pouring out the offering in reception) and "Speis' empfangt"[176] (food-receiver) do not seem correct. Max Müller[177] translation "offering" followed by Ludwig[178] (*havya* darbringung) seems to indicate the 'act of offering' based on Sāyaṇa's explication there[179] as *yajñaṁ*. Griffith's[180] rendering 'oblation bearer' appears to correspond with *'havyavoḍh-'* rather than *havyad-ti-*, hence should be rejected. Renou's[181] rendering "donne l'affrande' conveys the act of offering.

Thus there are two views with regard to *havyadāti*, namely, (i) it is anattrihutire word for Agni; (ii) it indicates the act of offering'. As *damyam* is to be construed with *jātavedasam* in the second *pāda* standing for Agni, so *havyadātim* is to be construed with *svadhvaram* in the first pāda. The form *svadhvaram* occurs ten times in the RV,[182] and out of these ten occurrences seven stand for Agni excluding the present context. At two places it stands for chariot (RV 4.46.4) and Indra (RV 8.40.11) according to Sāyaṇa's explication, but there also it can be interpreted in favour of Agni. Therefore, on the analogy of other parallel contexts it may be surmised here that *svadhvaram* as well as *havyadātim* stand for Agni and not for anything else.

Damyam - see *damyebhiḥ* above RV 3.1.15.

rathīrṛtasya bṛhataḥ vicarṣaṇiḥ - Sāyaṇa construes *brāhataḥ* with *ṛtasya* as an adjective to *ṛtasya*, and explains *vicarṣaṇiḥ* as a separate entity. Thus, according to him Agni is the 'leader (*rathīḥ*) of the great sacrifice and seer'. Veṅkaṭamādhava construes *rathīḥ* with *ṛtasya*, and *bṛhataḥ* with *vicarṣaṇiḥ*, and to substantiate the first construction he quotes SB 1.4.2.11 *rathīraddhvarāṇam iti. raths ha va esa bhūtvā devebhys yajñam vahati.* Some of the parallel occurrences like *divo bṛahataḥ* (RV 1.54.4; 59.5; 71.2 etc.), *bṛahataḥ divaḥ* (RV 6.2.4), *bṛhataḥ ṛasya* (RV 6.13.27), *rathi ṛtasya bṛhataḥ* (RV 4.10.2), *yajñasya bṛhataḥ* (*agram yajñasya bṛhataḥ nayantīḥ* - RV 6.65.2), *brhataḥ adhvarasya* (RV 7.11.4) *sūryasya bṛhataḥ* (RV 9.74.1), *Satyam ugrasya bṛhataḥ* (RV 9.113.5), *ṛsvasya bṛhataḥ* (RV 1.25.9; 52.13) and so on confirm that *bṛhataḥ* should be taken as a qualifying word for *ṛtasya* here, and not with *vicarṣaṇiḥ* which stands in none sg. Griffith, Oldenberg, Geldner, Renou, Velankar have followed Sāyaṇa.

There is some difference of opinion about the meaning of ***vicarṣaṇiḥ*** among the scholars. Venkaṭamādhava and Sāyaṇa render it with *vi drasṭa* and *drasṭa* (seer) respectively. Oldenberg translated "he who dvells among manifold tribes", perhaps taking it as a synonym of *kṛṣṭīḥ* 'people', But this meaning is not acceptable to others. Grassmann attests it meanings 'sehr regsam' (very active), 'rüstig' (vigourous) which have been followed by Griffith and Velankar. Ludwig renders it with 'ausgezeichnete' (excellent) which has been followed by Geldner. Renou translates 'circulant au lion' (encircling the lion, i.e. hold). Bhawe gives its meaning 'one moving diversely'.

RV. III. 2.9

तिस्रो यह्वस्यं समिधः परिंज्मनो ऽग्नेरंपुनन्नुशिजो अमृंत्यवः ।
तासामेकामदंधुर्मर्त्ये भुजंमु लोकमु द्वे उपं जामिमीयतुः ॥

There is no basic difference between the two important commentaries of Veṅkaṭamādhava[183] and Sāyaṇa on the interpretation of this *ṛk*. Both of them explicate it with much imaginative material inserted in. Modern scholars have, more or less, followed Sāyaṇa's explication in which much remains doubtful, because the *ṛk* remains somewhat of a different character, not because of some difficult words like *Parijman, Yahvasya, bhujam, jāmim* etc. but because of the concepts underlying these words. Therefore, to get some clear concepts, obviously they need to be explained in detail.

Tisraḥ samidhaḥ - According to Veṅkaṭamādhava 'three *samidhās* constitute 'three different forms of Agni's body', '*Agneḥ tisraḥ samīdhikāḥ tanuḥ*'. Sāyaṇa, following this explication, names the 'three bodies' as the manifestations of Agni in earthly fire, lightening and the Sun - *'Pārthiva-*

vaidyutasūryarūpastisrastanūḥ'. But none of the Ṛgvedic contexts, except one, confirms this explication of three forms. Only in RV 3.20.2 *'tisra'u te tanvo devavātāḥ'* the 'three bodies' of Agni have been mentioned before which *'tisraste jihva'* precedes; and here Sāyaṇa explains *'tisraḥ tanvaḥ'* as *'Savamanapavakasucyātmakāni trini śarīrāṇi'* following here too Veṅkaṭamādhava's renderings in these contexts *incognits*.

The numerals used in the Veda signify nothing but the ritual symbolism and cosmogonic speculations. Sometimes they stand only as the attributive adjectives, and sometimes they emphasise that such entities belong together or form unity, or that all of them are the components of certain entities undergoing a common experience.[184] The word *tisraḥ* is used here just to enumerate the of said *samiādhās* being either "three" or seven, as far example in RV 10.90.15 *triḥsapta samidhāḥ kṛtaḥ*; 1.154.2 *gayatrasya sanudhas tisra ahuḥ*; KS 101:10 *triḥ sapta samidhāḥ kṛtaḥ*. At the same time it may be compared with other parallel phrases like *tisro divaḥ* RV 2.3.2; 27.8; 53.5; *tisraḥ bhūmiḥ* RV 2.27.8; 1.102.8; *tisraḥ pṛihivīḥ* RV 1.34.8; 4.53.5 *tisro mahiḥ* RV 3.56.2 and so on. These usages of numeral 'three' actually refer to three combinations of the three world or lokās.[185] Hence three *samidhās* here symbolically denote three worlds in which Agni is supposed to reside.[186]

Among modern interpreters Grassmann[187] renders it (*tisraḥ samidhaḥ*) with "drei Flammen" (three flames) which agrees with Wilson's[188] rendering "three rediances" followed by Griffith[189] as "three splendours". Ludwig[190] gives its meaning as "drei hölzer" (three firewood or twigs) which has been followed by Oldenberg[191] "three logs" and Geldner's[192] "drei Brenhölzer" (three burning twigs) renderings. Oldenberg adds a fool note to it, saying that "Agni is stated here to have one terrestrial and two celestial forms;

the fire belonging is men, and, it seems sun and lightening".[193] His statement is in consonance with Max Müller's[194] and Bergaigne's[195] views. He himself holds the same opinion elsewhere.[196] Renou[197] also renders it alike as "trois bûches' (en les faisant flambar)" (three twigs for burning). Velankar[198] renders it with "three samidhās" with annotation that "the *samidha* is kindling material"; corresponding to the three forms of Agni, terrestrial, aerial and celestial, viz. (Agni, Apāṁnapāt and Sūrya). The ancient priests like Aṅgirasās, devised three kinds of fuel, viz. wood, water and light. Thus, from all these renderings and annotations it is evident that they have nothing to say more than the traditional exegetists.

Yahvasya - This (gen. Sg of *Yahva* -) form occurs here and once in other context of Agni (RV 3.28.4). Traditionally it has been interpreted as 'great, young' which has been followed by subsequently by all the interpreters of the RV. In consonance with Oldenberg's[199] statement 'the meaning of *yahva* cannot be determined with full certainty' (For details see above 3.1.12 *yahvaḥ,* and 3.1.4 *yahviḥ*).

Parijmanaḥ - This gen. Sg. form of *Parijman* occurs only here. Other forms *Parijmane* (RV 4.36), *Parijmanoḥ* (RV 1.46.14), *Parijma* (RV 1.79.3; 112.4; 4.45.1 etc.), *Parijmanaḥ* (RV 5.10.5), *Parijmānam* (RV 1.20.3; 8.72.10; 10.40.1), *Parijman* (RV 1.63.8 etc.) also occur in the RV. Traditionally its meaning has been attested as 'walking around' (*Paritaḥ gantā*).

Jman and ***gmīn*** can be placed parallely, and they can be traced from the similar roots *jam* and *gam* which are identical with Avestan *jsam* (*jasaiti* - 'gses'). From the same roots *jma* (Avestan *zema*) and *gma* 'earth' are also derived. Thus the meaning of *Parijman* as 'going around' can be justified easily. Agni is called *parijman* because he goes around the world, which is suggestive of his cosmic activity.

RV. III. 2.10

वि॒शां क॒विं वि॒श्पतिं॒ मानु॑षी॒रिषः॒ सं सी॑मकृण्व॒न् त्स्वधि॑तिं॒ न तेज॑से ।
स उ॒द्वतो॑ नि॒वतो॑ याति॒ वेवि॑ष॒त् स गर्भ॑मे॒षु भुव॑नेषु दीधरत् ॥

The cosmic activity of Vaiśvānara is the main theme of this *ṛk.* The human urges have made Agni more active for the sake of his brilliance as they sharpen the hatchāt. Agni pervades the every part of the universe traversing through the high and low places. He has placed his seed in all the creatures, i.e. everything germinates due to the fiery energy of Agni. Sāyaṇa's interpretation of *eṣu bhuvaneṣu* as *araṇyaḥ* of the araṇi, 'sacrificial wood' is just a symbolical one. Actually it signifies the entire universe.

Iṣaḥ, acc. pl. of *isa*- 'food, desire, crabs, may be interpreted here variously. But 'desires' or 'urges' which are symbolically 'prayers' here, seem to be the central idea of the *ṛk.* Moreover, the verbal form *saṁ akṛnvan* indicates the 'purifying activity' which is possible only through the 'power of vision' and not with the food.

Veṅkaṭamādhava[200] and Sāyaṇa render *veviṣat* with *vyāpnuvan* 'pervading'. Western exegetists translate it with 'busied' (geshaftig)[201] and 'working repeatedly' (mitquifer wirkend, arheitend),[202] Velankar[203] has also followed the same meaning. But the study of the *viś* in the RV proves that the meaning 'pervade' is more plausible.[204]

Tejase is a trifunctional term which refers to the three-fold virtues of Agni, namely, sharpness, intense heat and brilliance.[205]

RV. III. 2.11

स जि॑न्वते ज॒ठरे॑षु प्रजज्ञि॒वान् वृषा॑ चि॒त्रेषु॑ नान॑द॒न्न सिं॒हः ।
वै॒श्वा॒न॒रः पृ॑थुपाजा॒ अम॑र्त्यो॒ वसु॑ रत्ना॒ दय॑मानो॒ वि दा॒शुषे॑ ॥

By introducing Word - Economy *citreṣu* has been construed with *jaṭharāṣuo* also by Sāyaṇa. He adds *araṇyeṣu* in the second *pāda* with *citreṣu* perhaps following Veṅkaṭamādhava.[206] But even without adding *avanyeṣu* and or construing *citreṣu* with *jaṭhareṣu* we can get the real meaning of the verse *jaṭhara*- represents all types of creatures or their inner body where Agni resides. Agni is called *garbha* (*sa garbha asuraḥ*) 'the embryo', and it displays its powers in various types of manifestations. This gives him various names among which *jaṭharāgni* is very common one. The second *pāda* of the *ṛk* represents Agni as *dāvāgni* which manifests itself in the forests. *Citreṣa* here, refers to the variegated and beautiful forms of the forests where Agni manifests itself roaring like a lion. *Nadanna* is common term for both Agni and the lion.

Citra- bears other significant meanings also as 'excellent, distinguished, beautiful' and so on, as attested by exegetists and lexicographers.[207] But none gives any satisfactory derivation. Sāyaṇa gives only alternatre meanings as *bahuvidha, cayuniya* etc. But he has not analysed it. *Citra* may be derived from *cit* + *ra* as suffix on the analogy of other similar words like *sukra, svitra* and so on. Or, it can be traced with *Vii* 'to select' plus *tru* (*stran* suffix) which seems more plausible with the point of view of the meanings.

Dayamānaḥ - Sāyaṇa explains *dayamānaḥ* as *prayacchan* 'giving' following perhaps, Veṅkaṭamādhava who construes it with *daśuṣe* paraphrasing it as *prayacchota* 'to him who gives'. But *dayamānaḥ* with *vi* prefix primarly means 'distributing and dividing'. Here also the same sense can be imported.

RV. III. 2.12

वैश्वानरः प्रत्नथा नाकमारुंहद्दिवस्पृष्ठं भन्दंमानः सुमन्मंभिः ।
स पूंर्ववज्जनयंञ्जन्तवे धनं समानमज्मं पर्येति जागृंविः ॥

Nothing seems controversial in this *ṛk*. The first pāda presents Agni in the form of the Sun who traverses the sky continually. The phrase *samanam ajmam* in the fourth pāda refers to the same course on which the ever awakened, active and watchful Agni (or the Sun) revolves daily in the heaven.

Sāyaṇa and Veṅkaṭamādhava render *jantave* with *stotre yajamānaya* which declares their prelection for sacrificial sense. Actually this signifies the entire creatures for whom Agni and the Sun produce everything.

RV. III. 2.13

ऋतावानं यज्ञियं विप्रमुक्थ्य १ मा यं दधे मातरिश्वा दिवि क्षयम्।
तं चित्रयामं हरिकेशमीमहे सुदीतिमग्निं सुविताय नव्यसे॥

There is some controversy among the exegetists about ***divi kṣayam*** in the *ṛk*. Some of them regard it as a Bahu. comp. and some take these two words separately. The words recorded in the *saṁhitā* and pāda texts clearly show that they are separate words. This is more obvious through the accent also. Sāyaṇa explains it as *'dyuloke nivasantam'* residing in the heaven, which indicates that he takes it something like a compounded form. He does not construe it as the locative of the verbal form *ādadhe*, Venkaṭamādhava's paraphrasing of the second *pāda* as *antarikṣe dīpte ātmanaḥ āvāsam Vāyu mātarisvā ā dadhe, tam adhikṣitāya vasati itya arthaḥ* indicates that he takes *divi* as the location for the placing of Agni, though his *tam adhisthaya vasati* seems to indicate his doubt also about the exact meaning of the *pāda*.

On the presumption of Bergaingne,[208] Weber,[209] and Oldenberg[210] reads it *divikṣayam* and says that "the blunder has been caused by 10. 63.5 *dadhire dive kṣayam*". But he fails to understand that *dive* can be construed with *kṣayam* as well as with *a dadhe* by the way of 'Word-Economy'. And moreover, the verbal from *dadhe* requires some 'location' for placing 'ṛtāvānam ....' with which *kṣayam* stands as the object of the finite verb. Thus *divi kṣayam* means 'one who dwells in the heaven' as well as "the resident' has ben placed (*ā dadhe*) in the heaven". *Divi* serves these two purposes together, and it should be read as it is. *Kṣayam* is to be construed with *ṛtāvānam yajñiyam vipram ukthyam'* standing all together in acc. sg., it should be construed with *divi* also to arrive at a better sense of the *ṛk*. Thus the view that *'divi kṣayam'* is a Bahuvṛ. Comp. is untenable at the first sight, but by implication[211] it may be accepted for the same of the double meanings.

RV. III. 2.14

शुचिं न यामंन्निषिरं स्वर्दृशं केतुं दिवो रोचनस्थामुंषर्बुधंम् ।
अग्निं मूर्धानं दिवो अप्रंतिष्कुतं तमींमहे नमंसा वाजिनं बृहत् ॥

The accumulation of the attributes in this *ṛk* marks the great power and activity of Agni. He is active like the Sun and wise awake at the dawn. The simile *śucim na yāmann-iṣiram* 'active like the sun on the way' puts Agni near the Sun-god and *svardṛśam* 'obtaining light by (means of) the sun' also equates him with the sun. *Divaḥ ketum* 'the banner of the heaven' again equates him with the sun. His close relationship with the Uṣas is marked by the comp. *uṣarbudham.* Again he is at the top of the heaven identifying himself with the sun moving constantly (*apratiṣkutaṁ*) without facing any resistance. He holds himself the great generative power (*vājinaṁ bṛhat*).

Śucim na yāman can be compared with *citro na yāman* in RV 3.29.6 *Śucim* refers to *sūrya* which can be compared with *sūryaḥ śuciḥ* at RV 1.160.1.

Svardṛśam, acc. sg. which occurs four time in the RV (3.2.14; 5.24.2; 7.32.2; 9.65.11), *sarvapadārthavijñāna-yuktam* 'seeing all and enjoined with the knowledge of every matter', in which the equation of *svar* with *sarv(a)* is clearly based on the hypothesis and may be compared with Yāska's maxim *'akṣaravarṇasāmānyat nirbruyat na tveva na nirbruyat'* (Nir. 2.1) Veṅkaṭamādhava also paraphrases it *'sarvasya draṣṭāram'*. *svardrśa* is a compound in which *svar* and *dṛś*, 'to see' are two words quite clear. It cannot mean 'like the sun' because, then accent should have been on the *upamāna*, i.e. *svar*, but in the present case accent is on the root noun, i.e., *dṛśa* - which is governed by Pan 6.2.139 (*gatikārakopapadātkṛt*).[212] Thus, the comp. will mean "seeing by (means of) the light of heaven (the sun)".[213] Thus Grassmann's[214] meaning "Himmelslicht schauend" is not acceptable. *svardṛśaḥ* can be identified with Avestan *hvarsdaresarjha* or *hvareduresa*.[215] Oldenberg's[216] translation 'sunlike acpect' is nearer to Grassmann's rendering. Geldner[217] renders with "sonnenaugig" which is not upto the mark. Renou's[218] translation "semblable au soleil" (sunlike) is just the same as Oldenberg has done, therefore, needs no further comment. Velankar[219] also follows, the meaning "looking like the sun".

Like *svardṛśam* we can analyse ***uṣarbudham*** also. The same accent-rule can be applied with this comp. also, and it can mean either 'awaken by Uṣas or one who awakes Uṣas'. The first meaning, i.e. "one who is awaken by Uṣas" is more plausible, because Agni is awaken by Uṣas. They come earlier than Agnim in the morning.

Rocanasthām occurs only here. At RV 6.6.2 *rocanasthaḥ* occurs for Agni where Sāyaṇa explicates it *rocante asmin grahanakṣatrādīni iti rocanam antarikṣam, tatra sthitaḥ (agniḥ)'* which appears "better explanation of *rocanastha* than the present one as *'rocanaḥ sūryaḥ tasmin tiṣṭhantam'*; because here Agni has already been equated with the sun and it cannot be repeated again for the same. Moreover, the sun is not a place for standing while the mid-region (*antarikṣa*) is an abode of Agni as stated frequently in the RV. Therefore, *rocanasthām* may be rendered with 'one who dwells in the mid-region'. Otherwise, it should be taken literally to "one who lives in refulgence" or "living in the splendour".

Apratiṣkutaṁ also seems a doubtful word. It occurs first times in the RV (3.2.14; 8.93.12; 97.13; 1.7.6; 8; 84.7; 13; 5.61.13; 7.32.6). There are two interpretations of this word offered by Sāyaṇa. The first is *pratiśabda rahitaḥ* which is based on Yāska's etymological explanation of it as *'apratiṣkuto' pratiṣkṛto' pratiṣkhalito va* (Nir. 6.16). Sāyaṇa gives its derivation from *Ku* (*Kunsabde*) but this derivation seems doubtful. His another interpretations are found in the later Mandalas, i.e. V, VII and VIII, where he explains it as *apratigatos pratiśabdito vā* (5.61.13; 7.32.6). The last one is the explanation of *apratiṣkutaṁ* at 8.93.12 where Sāyaṇa gives its etymology from the *sku* (*sku iti sautro dhātuḥ stambhane vartate*). The same meaning has been repeated at 8.97.13 also. This is entirely different from the previous explanations and appears to be offered by someone else rather than Sāyaṇa. However, this explanations is more suited to the contexts wherever *apratiṣkuta* occurs. The same meaning i.e., "irresistible" may be applied in the present contexts also.

Velankar,[220] construes *apratiṣkutaṁ* with *divaḥ mūrdhnam* which is clear by his rendering "the unrivalled head of the heaven". Perhaps he follows Geldner[221] who translates it with *divaḥ mūrdhānam* as "das unbestrittene Oberhaupt des Himmels". (uncontested; unrivalled - Velankar) is all right, but construing it with *divaḥ* is open to objection. Renou[222] renders it with "inébranlable" (steady, firm) confirms Sāyaṇa's explanation of it as *'apratirodhanīyam* (uncontested). The more relevant and appropriate rendering of *apratiṣkutaṁ* would be irresistible (*apratiha-tagatiḥ*).

Modern exegetists[223] have construed *bṛhat* with *namasā* which is again incongruous, because *namasā īmahe* is a single phraseological unit in the RV and does not need any attributive adjunct to it. At the same time it can be surmized that *bṛhat* is a coordinated adjective to *vāja* and *vājin* which occurs in several contexts of the RV, e.g., 2.2.7; 6.1.11. Therefore, it should be construed with *vājinam* only as Veṅkaṭamādhava and Sāyaṇa have done.

RV. III. 2.15

मन्द्रं होतांरं शुचिमद्वंयाविनं दमूंनसमुक्थ्यं विश्वचंर्षणिम् ।
रथं न चित्रं वपुंषाय दर्शतं मनुंर्हितं सदमिद्राय ईंमहे ॥

The accumulations of epithets in the final *ṛc* of the hymn presents Agni in a beautiful form. His epithetical attribute *mandraṁ*-signifies his pleasant splendour which has been explained by Sāyaṇa as *'stutyam'*, "praiseworthy" and by Venkaṭamādhava as *'mādakam'*, "pleasant, delightful", intoxicating". But actually it indicates the splendid form of Agni as has already been suggested while discussing *mandrasya* as 4a. The same meaning should be applied here also.

Advayāvinaṁ means *dvayahīnam* (only one) *akuṭilaṁ* 'not wicked', according to Sāyaṇa. But Veṅkaṭamādhava explains it as *'satyānṛtābhyamayuktam kevalṁ satyayuktam* 'possessed of only the Truth" which creates doubt about the exact import of the word. The word occurs only thrice in the RV (1.159.3; 3.2.15, 5.75.5). At two places (5.75.5; and *advayāvī*-7.56.18) Sāyaṇa explains it as *māyā rahitaṁ* "without deceit"[224] which places *'dvayāvinaṁ* near *māyāvinam,* and *advayāvinaṁ* near *'māyāvinaṁ* 'not deceitful'; and this can be parenthetically observed that *advayāvin* is grammatically formed like *tapasvin, tejasvin yaśasvin, medhāvin, manasvin* and so on.[225]

As *dvaya* - refers to 'duality' or 'dualism' and *dvayāvin*. 'falsehood, deciet and so on (RV. 1.42.4; 2.23.5; 9.85.1), *advayāvin* - indicates the 'upright and straight forwards' behaviour of the possessor of the quality. While *dvayāvindi* are clipped together with *anhaḥ* 'narrowners', *duritaṁ* 'siḥ', *arātāyaḥ* 'enemies', *aghasansa*- 'sinful' etc. (1.42.4; 2.23.5), *advayāvin* is voked together with *satya* and *dharma* (1.159.3). Therefore, the explanations given by Venkaṭamādhava and Sāyaṇa are justified.

Damūnasam has been explained by Sāyaṇa as '*dānamanasam*', 'one who things of gift-giving' which are based on Yāskas etymology of *damūnas* as *damamanā vā, dāna-manā va, dānta-manā vā* (Nir. 4.4) tracing it to (i) *damat manas*-, or (ii) *dāna + manas*- or (iii) *dantā + manas* -. But actually - *nas* is only a suffix added to *damū* which is identical to Indo-Eurdomus 'house', Latin *domus* 'house'.[226] Thus *damtnas* means 'householder' and it can be equated with *dampati* and *gṛhapati* which are common appelatives for Agni in the RV. Böhtlingk and Roth[227] attest its meaning "zu Hans and Hof gehorig" (belonging to the house and the palace) deriving it from *dam* 'house' with *unas* suffix on the analogy of *Vṛjuhasi* which is a *hapax legomenon* at RV 8.52.2. Geldner[228] gives its meanings "Haus Hüter" (guardian of the house), "Beschützer" (patron, protector) and "Hausgebieter" (lord of house), Renou,[229] prefers the meaning "domestique".

NOTES

1. RV Saṁhitā Vol. V, p. 500 f.
2. Nir. 7.23.
3. *Loc. cit.*
4. J. Gonda, *Epithets in the Ṛgveda*, p. 95 f.
5. Kuiper, E.B.J *Med. Kon. Ned. Akad. v. Wet. Lett.* N.R. 14.5.
6. RV 1.59.1;2.

7. SB. 7.3.1.35. *Vaiśvanaram reto bhutan ...*
8. RV 1.96.3; 3.9.5; 6.8.4. For detailed discussion See H. Oldenberg, Die R*eligion des Veda* (Berlin, 1917), p. 123 f.
9. Cf. RV I.164.46; 3.5.9; 26.2; 29.11 etc.
10. Cf. RV I. 59.2; 5.; 98.3.
11. See Bhave *Soma Hymns.* Vol. III, p. 36.
12. Cf. RV 6.9.7; 3.2.11; 7.5.1.
13. *Worterb.* p. 1350.
14. RV 1.22.10; 3.2.1; 10.35.7.
15. RV 4.36.8.
16. Ṛgartha-dīpikā 3.2.1.
17. Nir. 8.3.1 - *dhisana vag dhiser dadhaty arthe ....*
18. VS 6.26.
19. K.F. Johansson, *Die Albtindische Gottin Dhisana und Verwandtes,* Uppsala - Leipzig, 1917.
20. Jan de Vries, *Altermanische Religion gesichte* II (1957). p. 298 f.
21. A. Hillebrandt, *Vedische Mythologie* I, p. 175.
22. *Vedische Studien II,* p. 82 f.
23. SBE 46, p. 120 f.
24. *Gott. Gel. Anzungen,* 1919, p. 347 ff.
25. Der RV III. p. 41 fn. 2 c.
26. Wackernagel - Debrunner, Altin Gram, II 2, p. 925.
27. L. Renou, *Etudes sur le Vocabulaire du Rigveda* I, p. 52 ff; Et. Ved. et. Pan I, p. 4 f. iv, p. 54, 60; vii, p. 50, cf. also Geldner, o.c. I, p. 372 'Wohl von der gottlischen Inspiration. Sāyaṇa also gives the same meaning in his commentary on the TS 9.1.6;12.3;
28. L. Renou, *loc. cit.*
29. J. Gonda, *The Vision of the Vedic Poets,* p. 116.
30. Nir. 2.25 - *ṛtamityudaka nama*
31. Rg. Dip. 3.2.1.
32. op. cit. p. 329.
33. op. cit., p. 335.
34. H. Lüders, *Varuna* (Gottingen, 1951-59), p. 555 f.
35. H.P. Schmidt. *Vedische Vrata and Avestische urvata.*
36. Nir. 4.19 *'ṛtam satyam yajñam vā'.*
37. J. Gonda, *The Vision* - p. 142.
38. *Loc. cit.*

39. J. Gonda, *Die Religionen Indicens,* I, p. 77 ff.
40. See Valankar *RV. VII Mandala,* p. 226. But this can be translated as 'those who are the increasure of the darkness'. Velankar gets the support of RV. 5.32.6 *asūrye tamasi vāvṛdhānam* (growing in the darkness). But it may be interpreted both ways.
41. This follows Sāyaṇa's explication as *annasya vardhayitāraḥ.* But, can it not be interpreted otherwise as 'those who grow by food or oblation'.
42. Sāyaṇa offers both the meanings, namely, payaso *udakasya vardhayitāraḥ* as well as *pṛṣṇeḥ. payasā vardhamānaḥ.*
43. See Velankar, op. cit., p. 199. This can be compared with his own interpretation of *tamovṛdhāḥ* as 'those that grow powerful in darkness' which is a clear evidence of interpretative contradistinction.
44. For details about the functions of Agni's epithets See J. Gonda, *Epithets in the Ṛgveda* (The Hague, 1959), pp. 79-96.
45. RV 1.3.5; 58.7; 88.6; 120.4; 3.2.1; 37.2; 6.16.13; 7.32.1; 8.78.4; 10.62.7.
46. Nigh. 3.15.24 *'Vāghata iti medhāvinam'.*
47. RV 4.2.13; 8.78.4; 1.7.32.
48. RV 10.62.7.
49. RV 10.62.7.
50. KZ 19, p. 220.
51. W. Neisser, *Bezzen Bergers Beitrage,* Vol. 18, p. 301 f.
52. ZDMG. Vol. 50, p. 423 ff. 52. *Wort.* p. 1248. 53. Der RV. I, p. 335.
53. Études Védiques et Pāṇinéennes, XII, p. 51. See also Ja. 229; 331.
54. For the use of ca see J. Gonda, *Particle ca etc. in the Veda* No. 5, pp. 1-71.
55. *Ṛgartha dīpikā.* 3.2.2.
56. SBE. 46, p. 228.
57. *Die Heiligen Hymnen* I, p. 329.
58. Wörterbuch Zum Ṛigveda, p. 436.
59. *Hymns from the* RV I, p. 318.
60. Der RV I. p. 335.

61. EVP XII, p. 51.
62. *Epithets in the RV*, p. 159.
63. RV Bh 1.3.6.
64. See M. Mayrhofer, Kurz Ety. Wort. I. p. 372.
65. See S.S. *Bhave*, Soma Hymns I, p. 47.
66. Here also Sāyaṇa connects it with *cana*- 'food' and deriwas it from *cay*.
67. See Grassmann *op. cit.*, p. 523; Oldenberg *Loc. cit.*; Geldner *loc cit.*; Renou *Loc. cit.*; Gonda, *op. cit.*, p.114.
68. RV 3.1.5.
69. *Der RV* I, p. 335.
70. EVP. XII, p. 51.
71. *RV Maṅḍala III*, p. 7.
72. RV 1.56.2; 139.2; 2.21.6; 3.2.3; 27.9;10; 62.17; 4.10.2; 5.10.2; 16.2; 18.2; 20.3; 38.4; 66.4; 6.15.3; 23.2; 51.6;7;60.10; 8.25.5; 62.6; 86.1; 9.16.2; 10.5.7; 64.5.
73. RV Bh. 1.2.9; 15.6.
74. Loc, cit.
75. Loc. cit. fn.
76. Loc. cit.
77. Soma Hymns III, p. 68.
78. For details see W.D. Whitney, *Sanskrit Grammar* (Delhi, 1962), p. 155 f, Macdonell, *Vedic Grammar* (tr. in Hindi by Satyavrata Shastri, Delhi 1971), p. 81.
79. *Der RV* 1, p. 170 (fn. 1).
80. *op. cit.*, p. 7 (fn.).
81. Monier Williams, *Sanskrit-English Dictionary* (New Ed., Oxford, 1963), p. 454.
82. SBE. 46. p. 228.
83. *Hymns of the RV.* I, p. 318.
84. *Loc. cit.*
85. *Loc. cit.*
86. Wb. p. 1281.
87. RV Trans II, p. 197.
88. *Der RV, Hymn der Brah.* I, p. 329.
89. *Hymns* RV I, p. 318.
90. SBE. 46, p. 228.
91. *Loc. cit.*

92. *op. cit.*, p. 230 fn.
93. *op. cit.*, p. 335.
94. *Loc. cit.*, EVP.
95. EVP XII, p. 51.
96. *RV. M. III*, p. 7.
97. EVP III, p. 21.
98. Oldenberg ZDMG. 50, p. 443; Berg. Index et Qu. Hym. p. 113, Gonda. *Aspects of Early Visnuism* (Otrecht, 1954), p. 48.
99. Epithets, p. 43; *Aspects of Early Visnuism.* p. 48 ff. *'Gods and Powers in the Veda'*, p. 2 f.
100. Ṛgartha-*dīpikā.* 3.2.1.
101. See his commentary on RV 1.122.13 where he explains *mandāmahe* as *stumo vayan* (we praise), and he explicates this form as pres. first p. pl. of *madi, stutau* (to praise), though here also the form *mandamahe* could be rendered as 'we delight in'.
102. *Sanskrit Worterbuch*, S.V.
103. *Worb.* 1003.
104. *Hymnen* I, p. 329.
105. *Hymns* I, p. 318.
106. SBE 46, p. 228.
107. SBE 32, p. 210.
108. *op. cit.*, p. 499.
109. *Der RV I*, p. 336.
110. *op. cit.* II, p. 135 (RV. 6.39.1).
111. *op. cit.*, III, p. 58.
112. *Et. Ved.* et Pan XII, p. 51.
113. RVM. III, pp. 8.21, 32, 37 etc.
114. S.S. Bhawe, *Soma Hymns*, III pp. 121, 146.
115. *op. cit.*, p. 146.
116. *hapax Legomenon* as 'mathrā in RV. 8.46.23.
117. For details see Wack. Debr. Alt. Gram. II, 2. p. 846 ff.
118. Bhawe also explains it here like root mad by translating *mandayan* as 'exhilerating' and comparing it with *madintama. Soma Hymns* III, p. 119.129.
119. Dhatu Pa. II, 12.
120. Nigh 1.16.
121. J. Gonda, *Epithets in the Ṛgveda*, p. 148.

122. RV 1.26.7; 36.5; 3.1.17; 10.7; 9.67.1; 109.8 etc.
123. RV 4.11.5; 5.25.2.
124. RV 6.4.7; 5.22.1; 9.97.26.
125. RV 9.86.17.
126. SBE 46. p. 228.
127. Hymns. I, p. 318.
128. RV 1.113.13; 5.34.1.
129. RV 4.51.6.
130. Velankar's translation here (7.80.2) as 'unblushing' may be correct for a 'youthful damsel' but with Uṣas, I think 'unperishing' or undecaying' would be more suitable. Here *ahrayama* stands both for the *upameya* and *upamāna*, therefore, both the senses can be applied.
131. S.S. Bhawe, *Soma Hymns.* III, p. 11.
132. *op cit.*, p. 10.
133. Bhawe has left jrayah unexplained and untranslated in his translation.
134. Nigh. II. 14.
135. YV (M) 3.16; (ka) 3,36; MS 1.5.1; Kaths. 6.9; TS. 1.2.14.6 Kauth. 2, 105; Jaim. 3.11.2; TB. 2.4.3. SB. 2.3.4.5.
136. Sāyaṇa explicated *ahrayah* here as 'unashamed'. Griffith has nearly hit the mark here by translating *ahrayah* as 'uninjured' - Hymen. I, p. 99.
137. Sāyaṇa paraphrases *ah* here, *'anavanatah'*, 'unbent before the enemies' which is nearly the same as 'unthreatened'.
138. Here Sāyaṇa, has explicated *ahrayaḥ* as *'Kavayaḥ'*, 'the poets', without giving an explanation for it. *Bhawe* has translated 'priests (or fingers), free from bashfulness', and explained it that "possibly the conception of the deity makes them (poets) feel ashamed when they crush his body, so to say; but if we take *ahrayaḥ* = the not bashful (fingers), the epithet becomes really significant: "even as ladies, the fingers are bold" is the suggestion. Some Hymn III, p. 22. Geldner, considers *ahrayaḥ* for both the priests and fingers. (Der RV. III, p. 39, small fn. 1). But here *ahrayrḥ* seems to suggest the priests who are not affraid of any one, that is, they are not threatened by any one.
139. Sāyaṇa explains *ahrayaḥ* here as *'anavanotavandana* -

nalajjitam 'unbent face or unashamed'. But 'unashamed' does not suit the context as 'unthreatened' does.

140. Various translations have been prosposed for *aśvasūnṛte*- Vom Jubel der Rosse begleited" (Roth in Petr. Dict.); "durch Rosse keritch, an Rossen reich" (Grassmann Wort.); pleased with horses" (Monier-Williams); "literale an chevauxe" (Renou). See J. Gonda, *Epithets* in the RV, p. 98.
141. Here Sāyaṇa explains *ahrayam* as *akṣiṇam* (undecaying) which seems an extension of the meaning 'unthreatened' and is quite suitable. In the following ṛk of the same hymn (5.79.6) he explains *ahrayā* as *akṣīṇāni*, which is again beautiful explanation.
142. For the meaning or *vāja* - as generative power' see J. Gonda, *The Vision of the Vedic Poets,* p. 129 f.
143. *Loc. cit.*
144. *Alt. Gram.* 112, p. 776.
145. AB 5.9.17; Śānkh. B. 25.6; 29.9; Gop. B. 2.6.10.
146. Cf., Wacker-Debru. Alt. Gram 112, p. 816.
147. *Op. cit.* p. 147.
148. *Loc. cit.*
149. A Ludwig, *Der RV.* Hym. Commentor P. I, p. 295.
150. VS 33.73.
151. RV c*ommentaries* III, p. 1289.
152. *RV Trans.* II, p. 197.
153. *Hymns RV* I, p. 318.
154. *RV Ubersetc.* I, p. 57.
155. *Der RV I,* p. 336.
156. *Nigh.* 3.8.16.
157. *Sons. Wort.* S.V.
158. *Wortorb.* p. 1547.
159. Die Hymnen des Rigveda, Maṇḍala I-VI, Wiesbaden, 1955.
160. VS 33.75.
161. For the simile see *atyo na vajam* - RV 3.2.2.
162. RV *Ubersetz* I, p. 59.
163. *Kommentar* iv, p. 295.
164. SBE 46, p. 229.
165. Noten.
166. *Der RV Ukers.* I, p. 336.

167. EVP. XII, p. 51.
168. RV. M. III, p. 8.
169. RV. Commentaries III.
170. RV. *Commentaries* III.
171. SB (m) 1.4.1.24 - *Yajamana vai havyadatiḥ.*
172. *havyadātim* (RV. 3.2.8; 5.55.10; 6.1.9; 47.28; 7.16.9; 10.7.7). *havyadātibhiḥ* 4.8.5; 19.13; 23.15.21; *havyadātaya* - 5.26.4; 51.1; 6.16.10; 48.2; 8.35.9; 101.1.
173. *Der RV* I, p.' 336.
174. *RV.* M. p. 9.
175. *Wortb.* P. 1657.
176. *RV iibersetg.* I, p. 57.
177. SBE 32, w. 334 (RV. 5.55.10).
178. *Der RV Hymmen* I, p. 329.
179. RVB 5.55.10.
180. *Hymns.* RV. I, p. 319.
181. EVP XII, p. 51.
182. RV. 1.45.1; 3.2.8; 4.46.4; 5.9.3; 6.8.15.7.16.1; 8.5.33; 40.11.
183. Rgartha Dip. 3.2.9.
184. See J. Gonda, *Reflections on the numerals 'one and 'two' in the ancient Indo-European languages* (Utrecht, 1955), p. 21 ff.
185. See J. Gonda, *Loka : World and Heaven in the Veda* (Amsterdam, 1966), p. 61 ff.
186. RV. 1.59.2; 3.17.4; 6.6.2; 10.45.1; AU. 13.1.50 etc.
187. RV. Ubarsetg. I, p. 58.
188. RV Trans. II, 198.
189. Hymns. RV. I., p. 319.
190. *Hymn Brih.* I, p. 330.
191. SBE 46., p. 229.
192. Der RV. I, p. 336.
193. *Op. cit.*, p. 231.
194. *Physical Religion,* p. 229.
195. *Religion Vedique,* I, p. 22.
196. *Religion des Veda,* p. 106 f.
197. EVP. XII, p. 51.
198. RV. M. III, p. 9.
199. SBE. 46, p. 34.
200. VM, *op. cit.*, p. 1291.
201. Ludwig, *iibersetz,* I, p. 330, Oldenberg SBE 46, p. 229., Griffith, Hymns I, p. 319;

202. Grassmann iibersetz I, p. 58; Geldner *iibersetz.* I, p. 336.
203. *op. cit.*, p. 9.
204. S.N. Shukla, *Root vis in the RV.*
205. See Gonda Observations, p. 58, and Renou, EVP XII, p. 115.
206. RV with commentaries III, p. 1291.
207. See. H. Oldenberg, Klein.
Roth-Böht. *Sanskrit Worth.* S.V.
Grassmann, Wortb. p. 451.
Walde-Pokor *Vergh. Worth.* II, p. 547; JAOS 67, p. 252.
Pisani, RSO 14, p. 86; *Mayrhofer,* Kurz Ety. Wort. I, p. 387 f.
208. Religion de Vedique I, p. 55.
209. SB. Berlin Akad. 1901, p. 775.
210. RV. Noten I, p. 226; SBE 46, p. 321.
211. See Geldner iibers. I, p. 337 fn., Renou, EVP xii, p. 115.
212. See S.S. Bhawe, Some Hymns I, p. 65.
213. See Gonda, vision, p. 30.
214. Worth. p. 1632.
215. Wackarn-Debr., *Altind* Gramm. II.2, p. 824.
216. SBE 46, p. 230.
217. *Loc. cit.*
218. *Loc. cit.*
219. *Loc. cit.*
220. *Loc. cit.*
221. *Loc. cit.*
222. *Loc. cit.*
223. Geldner, Renou and Velankar.
224. For the sense of *māyā* see J. Gonda, *Four Studies,* pp. 119 ff.
225. See Wackern-Debrun. *Altind. Gramm.* II 2, p. 917 f.
226. For details see Wackern-Debru, Altind. Gramm. IInd, pp. 227; 486; 499; 738; Mayrhofer, Kurz Ety; Wortb. II, p.19 f; S. Varma, Ety. Yāska, p. 97.
227. Sanskrit Worth. S.V.
228. *Loc. cit.*
229. *Loc cit*

The Ṛgveda Maṇḍal III.3

वैश्वानराय पृथुपाजसे विपो रत्ना विधन्त धरुणेषु गातवे ।
अग्निर्हि देवाँ अमृतो दुवस्यत्यथा धर्माणि सनता न दूदुषत् ॥

The general import of the *ṛk* is apparent but the deeper significance of some words in it, namely, *pṛthupājase, vipaḥ, ratnā, dharuṇeṣu* and *duvasyati* create some exegetical problems. These words therefore, need some discussion individually.

The word ***pājasa*** has been explained already at RV 3.2.11; the same meaning can be extended here also.

The form *duvasyati* can be related with *duvasyata* (3.2.8) and *duvasyan* (3.1.2) which have already been explained. The word *ratnā* also occurs at 3.2.11 which has been discussed already and needs no attention here. Now only *vipaḥ* and *dharuṇesu* need to be analysed and discussed here.

Vipaḥ - The initially accented (i.e. accent on the stem) form *vipaḥ* occurs seven times in the RV (3.3.1; 4.48.1; 6.44.6; 49.12; 8.1.4; 19.33; 10.61.3) and *vipaḥ* bearing oxytone, occurs only once (8.63.7). Other compounded forms are *vipaścit-vipaścitaḥ* and *vipahdham* which occur at several places in the RV. Veṅkaṭamādhava[1] and Sāyaṇa invariably render it with *medhāvin, vidvan, vipra* and likewise, all giving the sense of 'wise, full of vision, genius' and so on. The form *vipaḥ* can be either nom. or acc. pl., or abl. or genet. sg. Both, Venkaṭamādhava and Sāyaṇa explicate it here as nom. sg. form giving the meaning '*medhāvinaḥ viprah* (genius or wise) and *medhāvinaḥ stotāraḥ* (wise singers) respectively. Neither of these two scholiasts gives any specific etymological explication to this word. Sāyaṇa tries only once to explain *vipaścit* as *viśeśena ati iti vipa vāk*' (*vipa* - is speech because it protects well) and he forms it with *vipa + cit + kvip* (zero suffix). Being *kṛt* (word formed by primary or *kṛt* suffixes) it bears oxytone. Skandasvāmin[2] the other commentator of the RV, gives its etymological explanation while commenting upon RV 6.44.6 as *vip śabdo'yam vepateḥ kampanārthasya'* (the word *vip* - is derived from the root *vip* in the sense of 'trembling') and he thinks it to be the form of gen sg. of *vip*, which, according to Jog[3] goes against the accentuation rules. But considering all the seven occurrences of *vipaḥ* (accute accent on the initial syllable) it seems rather difficult to accept *Jog's* proposition that in accordance with the Pāṇinian rule *Sāvekacas tṛtīyādirvibhaktiḥ* ("the case affixes of the Instr. and of the cases that follow it have the acute accent, if the stem in loc. is monosyllabic"[4] - Pa. 6.1.168) *vipaḥ* cannot be gen. sg. form of *vip*. *vipaḥ* in RV 4.48.1; 6.44.6; 49.12; 8.19.33 and 10.61.3 seems clearly to be a gen. sg. form. Without going into details it can be indicated that all these occurrences of *vipaḥ* canbe interpreted as a gen. sg. and they give a better sense of the *ṛks* than as nom. or acc. pl. Therefore, Pāṇinian rule on the monosyllabic word-accentuation also needs moderation. In the present context *vipaḥ* can be construed with *ratnā*, taking it as gen. sg; and thus the verbal form *vidhanta* can be interpreted passively as "the precious gifts of the vision (the songs of the poets) have been offered". This makes very little difference in meaning except the change of the syntactical construction.

The exact meaning of *vipaḥ* can be decided on the basis of the root meaning. Several interpreters have given their divergent views on the subject. Oldenberg[5] gives its meaning as "die zitterande Erregung des Diehters" (the trembling achievement of the poet). Rejecting this interpretation Geldner[6] proposes that the root meaning expresses the idea of "die bewegte schwungvoll Rede" (the exciting, animated speech). This has been followed by Renou:[7] "Let mot *vip* se rapporte au macanisme de la pensee védique, ou si l'on prefere aux conditions psychologiques de la jout poetique. Ils' agit proprement du "tremblement" oratoire, de Ils'inspiration "metant en branle" le poeme". Contrary to this, Thieme[8] attributes the sense of "magic conjuration" to the word *vip*-. Preferring Grassmann's[9] explanation of *vip*- as "begeistert" (inspired) Gonda[10] derives it from *vip-vep* "to tremble, shake, quiver" and attributes the sense "vibrant" (speech) to the word. So far as the etymology is concerned there is no question of refuting Gonda's remark that it belongs to the root meaning "trembling" etc., but the exact meaning in the present context would remain only the 'poets or the singers' who are moved by their songs or who tremble or quiver while reciting the mantras. The "Sound vibrations", to which Gonda[11] himself infers in connection with the belief "that mantras exert their power primarily through their "sound vibrations", are connected here directly with the pronouncer himself who is none but the singer. The several similes related with *vip*-clearly indicate its validity as a substantive, therefore it cannot be accepted as an attributive word here. Though its polysemous nature signifies many things, such as "trembling, moving, inspiring, poetry, song, wisdom", yet here the meaning 'exalted or inspired one, i.e. Poet's seems more natural to the context.

Dharuṇeṣu - The word *dharuṇa* occurs thirty five times in the RV as an adj., and sometimes as substantive also. The form *dharuṇeṣu* occurs four times including the present (1.52.2; 3.3.1; 9.73.3; 10.5.6). Sāyaṇa explains it here as *dharmeṣu yajñeṣu* "in religious sacrifices" which seems rather old, because in several other places he prefers its meaning as *dharaka*- "supporter" (1.52.2; 23.13; 73.4; 1.121.2; 9.72.7; 10.5; 1 etc.) and derives it from *dhṛ* "to support" "with the suffix - *una* (*dharayaternilukca* RV 1.52.2). Though he always extends its meaning as 'water, soma juice' etc. yet the original meaning "supporter" is at the same time attached to the extended meaning. Veṅkaṭamādhava also offers the same explanation. Grassmann[12] derives it from *dhṛ* 'to hold fast' and attests its meanings as 'tragent; stutzend' (supporting) 'Trager', 'stutzer' (supporter), 'Grundlage' (bese, foundation) and so on. This can be compared with GK. 'foundation'. Leumann[13] gives the original Indo-Eur. root *dhereu as identical with *dhṛ*. Bergaigne[14] identifies *dharuṇa* with Avestan (*usi*) *dar na*, and derives it from *dhṛ* 'to support, sustain' (tragen, stutzen). Ludwig,[15] Oldenberg,[16] Geldner,[17] Velankar[18] etc. have followed the meaning 'firm foundation', 'ground' etc. as attested by Grassmann. Geldner[19] thinks that *dharuṇeṣu gātave* here stands either for Agni or for the priest himself as a carpet strewn on the ground. He compares it with RV 6.44.6; 67.2 where the prayer itself is strewn like the carpet on the ground. He further remarks that there is some conceptual identity between *dharuṇeṣu* and *dharmaṇi* as already emphasized by Ludwig. The comparative observation of all the occurrences of the word *dharuṇa* - indicates clearly that it is a derivative of *dhṛ* "to sustain, support" etc. This is evident from the internal evidences like *ṛtena dharuṇaṁ dhārayanta* (RV 5.15.2), *dharuṇam rayīṇām* (RV 10.47.2) etc.; and it bears the meanings like "supporter, sustainer, firm ground, foundation" and so on. Ludwig seems to be right in identifying it with *dharmaṇi* which has some coherence with its meanings.

Oldenberg[20] notes on *vipaḥ ratnā* as accusative and instrumental respectively do not seem valid, and his translation[21] of the first hemistitch and especially of *vipo ratnā vidhanta* as "the prayers have worshipped *Vaisvānara* with treasures" seems out of tune here, because here neither *vipaḥ* is acc. nor ratnā instru; rather the first is either nom. or gen. and the second is certainly acc. pl. as is the case with so many other words ending in long *a*.

RV. III. 3.2

अन्तर्दूतो रोदंसी दुस्म ईंयते होता निषंत्तो मनुंषः पुरोहिंतः ।
क्षयं बृहन्तं परिं भूषति द्युभिंर्देवेभिंरग्निरिंषितो धियावंसुः ॥

In this verse the words *dasmaḥ, pari bhūṣati, dyubhiḥ* and *dhiyāvasuḥ* raise some contradictions among the exegetists' views, which can be studies here extensively.

Dasmaḥ - The word *dasma* - appears several times in the RV in various forms. The traditional interpreters have attested its meaning as '*darśanīyaḥ*', beautiful, good looking, etc. But the modern interpreters[22] deriving it from *dama* Indo-Eur.* *dns-mo*, 'exhibit, display, manifest, show', attest its meanings as 'wonderful worker' (wunderkraftig), 'wonderous one' (Wundertrausse) and so on. Grassmann identifies it with GK and proposes its original meaning as 'activities connected with wonderful works". Sāyaṇa gives its etymology from *das* (*upakṣaya*) 'to be exhausted' (Dhat. P. 1.4.) with the suffix *mak* by *isiyudhīndhidasi syādhūsūbhya - mak* (Un. S. 1.150). The exytone can be explained by *ādyudāttaśca* (Pa. 3.1.3). Thus it means *dasyati upakṣayati iti dasmaḥ*, 'one who becomes exhausted is *dasmaḥ*'. Agni is called *dasmaḥ* because he outflows its rays and he appears exhausted. This etymological explanation does not suit those contexts where *dasma* - occurs with other words and deities like *dasmavarcaḥ* (RV 1.173.4 - for *Nāsatyau*), *dasmavarcasām* (RV 8.94.8 - *devanam*' of gods), *dasmatamaḥ* (RV 2.20.6 for Indra) and *purudasmam*[23] (RV 3.54.14 for Viṣṇu). Therefore, a new meaning has to be applied to the word *dasma*.

Now, here it can be proposed that the original root in *dasma* is *das* and not *dans* as proposed by modern scholars like Grassmann and others.[24] Besides, it can also be presumed that the word *dasma* can be put together with *dasyu* and *dasra* which appear to be the derivative of the same root, i.e.

das with the variation of primary suffixes only. While *dasma'* - and *dasra'* - take - *ma* and - *ra* suffixed respectively, *dasyu* - takes - *yu* governed by *Uṇādi* rule *yajimanisundhidasijanibhyo yuc* (Un. S. 3.20) accent calling on the suffix. The meanings of *dasyu* - as 'robber', 'plunderer' 'demon' etc. are well known and here the root meaning can be given as 'to seize, overcome surmount, get possession of master' and so on. Avestan *dahmo, danro* and *dahyu* can be identified very well with all these three Vedic words mentioned above.[25] Thus, the meaning of *dasma* - can be desided on the basis of above root-meanings as 'one who overcomes all, master, possessor of everything' and finally 'most victorious' (*dasmatamaḥ*). The compounds like *dasmavarcaḥ* - will mean 'possessor of lusture' and *purudasma* - 'overcoming all' or 'possessing many things'. These meanings suit in all the contexts of the RV The meaning 'seizing every thing or overcoming all' suits very well in the present context of *dasma* which is again substantiated by the verbal form *pari bhūṣati* occurring in the second hemistitch.

Pari bhūṣati - The form *bhūṣati* with prefix *pari* occurs only here. The traditional interpreters take it in the sense of 'decorating'. But this meaning has been refuted by modern scholars like Gonda[26] who gives the meanings of the *bhūs* 'to make thrive, or prosper, increase, invigorate, strengthen' etc. The compound *pari bhūs* according to him originally means "to strengthen or to bestow favour upon a person or a thing by a circumambulare".

Here with reference to the phrase *kṣayam bṛhantam,* which has been explained rightly by Veṅkaṭamādhava and Sāyaṇa as "sacrificial place" (*nivasam mahāntam uttaravedim,* Veṅkaṭamādhava; *yajñagṛham* - Sāyaṇa), Agni is the agent of *paribhūṣati.* Therefore, the meaning 'to strengthen or bestow favour' does not suit at all. But another explanation proposed by Gonda[27] as "to encompass, surround and to have a propitious influence" seems better which has already been offered by Griffith[28] who renders the third pāda with "the compasseth with rays the lofty dwelling place! Thus, the *pāda* can be rendered fruitfully with "Agni encompasses or surrounds auspiciously the wide dwelling place with the brilliance or rays! Oldenberg's[29] translation of the same as "he takes care of his wide dwelling place day by day" followed by Geldner[30] ("mit jedem neuen Tag nimmt Agni seinem hohen wohnsitz ein") and Velankar[31] (diligently attends at his residence day by day) do not seem upto the mark. Their rendering of *dyubhiḥ* with "day by day" creates doubts. Therefore, a few words on the meanings of *dyubhiḥ*, here, will not be off the point.

Dyubhiḥ - The word *dyubhiḥ* occurs nineteen times in the RV. All the interpreters follow only two meanings of this word, i.e. (1) day and (2) brilliance, rays, light. Yāska,[32] giving its etymological explication, says *dyuriti ahno nāmadheyam, dyotate iti sataḥ, "dyu* - is the name of the day, because it shines ever". This explanation has been followed by almost all the interpreters invariably. Sāyaṇa gives its alternate meaning as *dīptābhiḥ*[33] "by brilliance" *dyotamānaiḥ,*[34] "by shining" and alike. Here his explanation as *dīptībhiḥ* resembles with Veṅkaṭamādhava's paraphrase. Udgītha[35] also gives the same explanation. But Skandasvāmin,[36] Mahīdhara[37] and Uvata follow Yāska's explanation of it as "day". After closer examination of all the contexts it seems more plausible to take *dyubhiḥ* in the sense of "splendour, brilliance, effulgence, radiance" and so on which can be employed suitably in all the contexts of the RV.

Therefore, the interpretation "day by day" given by Oldenberg[38] and others should be discarded. Ludwig[39] hitting the mark has rendered it with mit strahlen (with rays).

Dhiyāvasuḥ - We have already discussed *dhiṣaṇā* and *dhiyā* at 3.2.1 and determined the meaning of these terms as "poetic vision" ("vision-poétique" - Renou) in accordance with the celebrated work of Gonda, namely, *The Vision of the Vedic Poets.* The compound *dhiyāvasuḥ* occurs ten times in the RV (1.3.10; 58.9; 60.5; 61.16; 62.13; 63.9; 64.15; 3.3.2; 8.80.10; 9.93.5). Here and in RV 1.3.10. *dhiyāvasuḥ* occurs separately for Agni but in the rest of the occurrences the phrase *'prātarmakṣū dhiyāvasurjagamyāt'* has been repeated stylistically - for Agni, Indra, Maruts and Soma without carrying for the syntactical relation of gender and number. At RV 1.3.10 Agni, Sarasvati and other gods have been called in one breath *dhiyāvasuḥ.* Thus it appears that originally this adjectival usage was attributed to Agni only, and later on it came into vogue for other deities also through the repetitional style of the poets. Sāyaṇa, explains it here as *prajñayā vyāptaḥ* (possessed with vision) which corresponds to Veṅkaṭamādhava's paraphrase *'prajñāvasuḥ'* enriched with vision! - But elsewhere Sāyaṇa follows Yāska[40] who explicates it as *'karmavasuḥ'*, (enriched with action, action oriented) taking *dhi*- as a synonym of *karma* 'action'! Other exegetists have followed either of the two explanation. Modern interpreters prefer to follow the first explanation, i.e. 'possessed for vision' ("riche en vision poetique" - Renou[41]).

RV. III. 3.3

के॒तुं य॒ज्ञानां॑ वि॒दथ॑स्य॒ साध॑नं॒ विप्रा॑सो अ॒ग्निं म॑हयन्त॒ चित्ति॑भिः ।
अपां॑सि॒ यस्मि॒न्नधि॑ सं॒दधु॒र्गिर॒स्तस्मि॑न्त्सु॒म्नानि॒ यज॑मान॒ आ च॑के ॥

There is not much difference of opinion about the general meaning of the verse. Veṅkaṭamādhava paraphrases *giraḥ* as *'stutiṣca*, 'prayers' while Sāyaṇa explains it as *stotāraḥ,* 'eulogists', 'singers' which seems unusual, because elsewhere he always assigns the same meaning as given by Veṅkaṭamādhava. But here *giraḥ* stands predicatively as the agent noun for the verbal form *saṁdadhuḥ*, "placed well" with the object *apāṁsi* "acts", therefore, though originally *girah* connotes 'eulogies' yet suggestively it indicates the invokers and hence Sāyaṇa is right in his attempt to explain it as *stotārah*, 'singers', *apāṁsi*, 'sacrificial actions' and *girah*, 'prayers'! are to be construed with the verbal form *saṁdadhuh* being its object and subject respectively. The performance of rites (*apāṁsi*) and its cooperation with the poetical compositions (*girah*, elsewhere dhiyaḥ etc.) is too well known in the RV and therefore, here *girah* should be interpreted as prayers or 'poetical compositions, signifying the poets as is explained by Sāyaṇa. The modern exegetists have accepted the general meanings, i.e. "chants" ("le chant" - Renou)[42] "loudations" (Lobesworte - Geldner).[43] "Poems" (Velankar)[44] and so on. But among older generations Wilson,[45] Grassmann[46] and Griffith[47] have followed Sāyaṇa, but Oldenberg[48] prefers "prayers". *cittibhih* - see RV 3.1.3. above —

(ā) *Cake* - The unaccented verbal form *cake* with the prefix *ā* occurs seven times in the RV (RV 1.25.19; 117.23; 3.3.3; 10; 62.5; 8.64.8; 10.40.7), and the accented form (ā) *cake* occurs twice (RV 1.40.2; 8.45.5). According to Sāyaṇa this is a Pl. Ist sg. of the *kai* (*kai gai śabde*- Dhat. p. XXII. 19) 'to sound, make vice! The accent can be explained here by *tiṅnatiṅah* (Pa. 8.1.28) according to which a finite verb is unaccented when a word which is not a finite verb precedes it.[49] So far as its meaning is concerned Sāyaṇa and Veṅkaṭamādhava both paraphrase it as *kāmayate* 'desires' followed by others which betray the original sense in accordance with the formation. If it means 'desires' then it should be a derivative of the *kan* or *kam* 'to wish, desire, crave' etc., with the elision of *n* or *m* in accordance with the *chandās* options as Sāyaṇa has explained it elsewhere (RV 3.62.5). But in all these conditions *cake* should be interpreted in favour of the first person, sg. And thus, the second hemistich has to be rendered with "In whom the poets have placed nicely (their) all activities, I the worshipper, long for the well-being (happiness) in him (form him).

This can be compared with the following *ṛk* number ten where '*vaisvānara tava dhāmani ā coke* refers to the same context, i.e. "O Vaisvanara, I desire (long) for your location of power".[50] The occurrence of *dhāmani* in the verse (10) can be put in parallely with *sumnāni* in the *ṛk* under discussion.

RV. III. 3.4

पिता यज्ञानामसुरो विपश्चितां विमानमग्निर्वयुनं च वाघताम् ।
आ विवेश रोदसी भूरिवर्पसा पुरुप्रियो भन्दते धामभिः कविः॥

In this verse Agni Vaiśvānara is stated to have entered both parts of the universe, i.e. the earth and the sky. He is eulogized on account of his *dhāman*. There is no significant difference of opinion between Veṅkaṭamādhava and Sāyaṇa on the meaning of the entire verse. Veṅkaṭamādhava paraphrases ***dhāmabhiḥ*** with *saīraiḥ svair bahubhiḥ.* "by his many forms", but Sāyaṇa gives its meaning as *tejobhiryuktaḥ* "possessed with brilliance" as usual. He explains *bhandate* as *yaramānena stūyate* is praised by the worshipper', taking it in the passive sense which is a bit different from Veṅkaṭamādhava's explanation of it as stauti, "praises" in active sense. This form of *bhand* 'to praise' occurs only in the RV, therefore, it cannot be compared with other similar contexts. However, Sāyaṇa's rendering seems more suited to the context.

Grassmann renders *dhāmabhiḥ* with "heiliger Bräuche" (holy custom), Geldner with "cigenschaften" (divine attributes) and Renou with "institutions (institutionnelles)". Rejecting all these meanings Gonda[51] puts forth his views to establish its meaning as "display or 'location' (of divine power)".

RV. III. 3.5

चन्द्रमग्निं चन्द्ररथं हरिव्रतं वैश्वानरमप्सुषदं स्वर्विदम् ।
विगाहं तूर्णिं तविषीभिरावृतं भूर्णिं देवास इह सुश्रियं दधुः ॥

The verse refers to Agni in various forms. Many intensive-force-bearing epithets like *candram, candrarathaṁ, harivrataṁ* etc., here signify the favourite terms to convey the idea of brilliancy. These compounds of attributive adjectives here function to intensify the brilliant force of Agni. Veṅkaṭa-mādhava and Sāyaṇa explain *candram* as *kantam*, 'beautiful' and *āhlādakaram*, 'gladenig', respectively. But, actually it indicates the brilliance of Agni and nothing else. Agni is not the only god who is attributed with the epithet *candraratha* - but beside him Uṣas is (RV 3.61.2 and 6.65.2) called *candraratha* - "with a brilliant carriage", which can be compared with RV 1.123.7 *śośucatārathena.*

Harivratam — contains the inherent idea of Agni's "golden colour". His premordial law is to possess the golden colour in all the time and ages. This attributive epithet can be compared with *śucivrata* - at RV 8.43.16; 44.21 and 10.118.1. Moreover, here *vrata* - with *harivrata* - is near the *varṇa*[52] in *sucivarṇam* (the only compounded word at RV 5.2.3). *Harivrata* occurs only here in the RV.

Agni *vaiśvānara* is closely related with natural phenomena like plants, water and so on and therefore, here he has been called *apsuṣadaṁ*, 'dwelling in the water'.

Svarvidam, according to Veṅkaṭamādhava and Sāyaṇa, means *sarvajñam*, "omniscient". Originally it can be related to the light of heaven (*svar* = *sūrya*), and thus it can be interpreted as "knowing" (*vid*, 'to know') or "obtaining" (*vid*, 'to obtain') everything by (means of) the heavenly light (the sun)". The objective accompanies a reference to Indra in RV 1.52.1; 3.51.2; 5.54.1; to Soma in RV 9.8.9; 84.5. also, and it can be placed parallely with *svardṛsam* in 3.2.14

explained earlier as "seing by (means of) the light of heaven (the sun)".[53]

The parallelism of ***tūrṇiṁ*** and ***bhūrṇiṁ*** is remarkable here. The first denotes the attributes of Agni as 'active, prompt, victorious, eager', while the second one, i.e. *bhūrṇiṁ*, refers to his qualities connected with sustenance and support for all. Sāyaṇa's alternate interpretation of it as *śatrūṇāṁ hiṁsitāram*, "killer of the enemies" is not as reliable as the first one, i.e. "quick mover". Grassmann's[54] renderings of *bhurṇiṁ* as 'mighty' (excited, wild) followed by others,[55] offers another angle of meaning related with Agni's virtues. This explanation comes from the *bhur* which contains several shades of meanings.

Taviṣībhiḥ *āvṛtam* refers to Agni's 'might' and 'vigour' with which he is always associated; and this is a suggestive expression of Agni's 'flames' and 'brilliance'. Thus in its 'entirety' this verse represents a series of attributes for laudatory purposes.[56]

RV. III. 3.6

अ॒ग्निर्दे॒वेभि॒र्मनु॑षश्च ज॒न्तुभि॑स्तन्वा॒नो य॒ज्ञं पु॑रु॒पेश॑सं धि॒या ।
र॒थीर॒न्तरी॑यते॒ साध॑दिष्टिभिर्जी॒रो दमू॑ना अभिशस्ति॒चात॑नः ॥

The intimate relation between sacrifice and *dhīḥ*, 'the vision' has been emphasized by this *ṛk*. Agni, performing the intricate sacrifice by his vision moves between men and gods.[57] There is not any significant difference of opinion among the exegetists. But Sāyaṇa's explanation of *dhiyā* as *Karmaṇa*, 'by action', is certainly different from that of Veṅkaṭamādhava's rendering of it as *prajñāya*, 'by vision', which certainly seems up to the mark. Grassmann's[58] translation of it as "mit Verstand" (with understanding, intellect) and Ludwig's[59] rendering as "durch seine Erfindung" (through his device) also lack authenticity.

Geldner's translation "durch die Dichtung" (by the poem) is also doubtful. Here "die Dichtung' (the poetry) cannot fit, and therefore, this translation is open to objection. Renou's rendering of it as "grace a la vision (qu'el accords as poete) seems more plausible and is certainly based on the findings of Gonda.

The compound ***abhiśasticātanaḥ*** occurs only here in the RV. All the interpreters have interpreted it in the sense of 'remover of the evils or enemies'. Though the usages of the word *śasti* alone (RV 4.3.3; 15; 20.10; 1.186.3) create some doubt about the exact meaning as they are the derivative of *sams,* "to praise", yet the occurrences of *abhiśasti* - (RV 3.30.1; 5.3.7; 12; 7.94.3; 1.71.10) remove this doubt of meaning. Therefore, we can render *abhiśasticātanaḥ* as the "reppelling far away the baneful speaker" with Renou's rendering as "repoussant au lion les paroles funestes",[60] or Geldner's translation of it is "der üble Nachrede entfernt".[61] It means that we can equate *abhiṣasti* with *mṛdhravācaḥ* (RV 1.174.2; 5.29.10; 7.6.3 etc.), whom Agni presses down and who are supposed to be the antagonists of the Vedic religion.

The shift of accent on the second member of the comp. can be explained by Pa. 6.2.139 *gatikārakopa-padātkṛt.*

Oldenberg[62] followed by Geldner and Velankar[63] has raised some doubts about the comp. *sādhadiṣṭibhiḥ.* Sāyaṇa has construed it with *devebhiḥ* and explained it as *sādhitayajñaiḥ* taking it as a *tatpuruṣa* comp. Veṅkaṭamādhava construes it with *manuṣyebhyaḥ,* paraphrasing it as *sādhad yajñebhyaḥ.* According to Whitney[64] and Oldenberg it should be a Bahuv. comp. as the accent shows; and thus it means "one who causes the sacrifice to be successful".

RV. III. 3.7

अग्ने जरस्व स्वपत्य आयुन्यूर्जा पिन्वस्व समिषो दिदीहि नः ।
वयांसि जिन्व बृहतश्च जागृव उशिग्देवानामसि सुक्रतुर्विपाम् ॥

Syntactically the first two *pādās* have three distinct clauses, namely, (i) *agne jarasva*, (ii) *svapatya āyunyurjā pinvasva* and (iii) *samiṣo didīhi naḥ*. This leads us to say that Sāyaṇa's paraphrasing and construing *jarasva* with *āyuni* is open to objection. Besides, Veṅkaṭamādhava's interpretation of the second clause as *haviṣa asmākam kāmān pinvasva* is also doubtful. The meanings of *jarasva* given by Sāyaṇa as *devān stuhi* 'praise the gods', is also not satisfactory. Veṅkaṭamādhava leaves it as it is.

Jarasva : The accented form *jarasva* occurs only here. Unaccented *jarasva* occurs thrice in the RV (1.123.5; 7.9.6; 76.6) among which 1.123.5 and 7.76.6 are the repetitions of the same *pāda*. Sāyaṇa. explains this everywhere as *'stuta bhava or stuhi* which is based on the explanation of Yāska.[65] But Yāska's etymological explication cannot be accepted[66] because all the contexts where *Jarasva* occurs indicate some activity of 'motion'. Modern researches have shows that *jar* means 'to move, come near, to wake up, awake'[67] etc. which can be utilized fruitfully here. The meaning of *jarasva* as 'be awakened wake up' is quite congenial to all the contexts cited above. Thus here *agne jarasva* can be rendered with 'O Agni, be awake (be enkindled)'.

The second clause ***āyuni ūrjā pinvasva*** had been explained by Veṅkaṭamādhava as *haviṣa asmākam kāmān pinvasva*, leading *āyuni* with the first clause. Ṣāyaṇa explicates it as *rasenānnena vā devān prīṇaya*. He also construes *āyuni* with the preceding clause. Oldenberg, Griffith, Geldner etc. have followed Sāyaṇa. As mentioned above *svapatya āyuni ūrjā pinvasva* is a complete syntactical unit and should be rendered accordingly. *Āyuni* occurs thrice in the RV (3.3.7; 9.100.1; 10.5.7) and everywhere it has a locative adjunct. In two other places it has the preceding adjective *pūrve* which suggests that the loc. *svapatya* in the present context should be construed with *āyuni*, and thus this clause can be rendered with "well (fill, heighten)[68] energy in the life of (our) good progeny".

The third clause, i.e. ***samiṣo didīhi naḥ*** has been explained by Veṅkaṭamādhava as *annāni ca asmān prayaccha,* "bestow food upon us". Sāyaṇa has given a slightly different explanation. He explicates it as *asmākam sasyārthaṁ vṛṣṭīḥ saṁdīpaya* "shine forth the rains for the sake of our food". The word *vṛṣṭiḥ, 'rains'* here appears to be from his own imagination, because *iṣaḥ* has nothing to do with the rains, and moreover, it does not suit the verbal form *didīhi.* As the word *iṣaḥ* has several meanings such as 'food, desire, strength' and so on, it can be interpreted here in any of these senses. But in confirmity with *ūrja* preceding *iṣaḥ,* it should be taken here to mean 'vigour, strength, freshness', and therefore, the clause can be rendered with "make shining or brighten or illuminate our vigour or strength".

In the third pāda ***vājan*** is to be supplied after *bṛhataḥ* (cf. 2.27; 6.1.11); and thus *jinva vājan* at RV 3.15.6 can be compared with the present context. Veṅkaṭamādhava supplied *aśvān* here, perhaps, implying the sense of *vājan.* But vāja-refers to the 'generative power' rather than 'horse'. Agni is *uśij*[69] of the gods because he is sought for as the oblation-bearer. He is the great power of the poets, through whom they receive visionary powers. But as the following verse suggests (*yantāram dhīnam uśijam ca vāghatam*), *uśij* here has to be construed with *devānam* and *vipām* both.[70]

Jinva has been rendered by Sāyaṇa with *dehi.* But originally it means 'inspire', 'increase', 'make active', 'quicken', 'impell' and so on. Thus with *vayāmsi* and *bṛhataḥ vajan* the meaning 'increase or quicken' will be suitable.

RV. III. 3.8

विश्पतिं यह्वमतिथिं नरः सदा यन्तारं धीनामुशिजं च वाघताम् ।
अध्वराणां चेतनं जातवेदसं प्र शंसन्ति नमसा जूतिभिर्वृधे ॥

Sāyaṇa construes *jūtibhiḥ* with *jātavedasam* in commentary, but in view of 3.12.3 *yajñasya jūtyā*, "by means of the impetus of the sacrifice", *jūtibhiḥ* refers here to the impulsions of the sacrifice by which the worshippers praise and appease Agni for their own prosperity (vṛdhe). The accumulation of epithets and attributes in this verse refers to the divergent functions and qualities of Agni, and thus intensifies the effect of the *mantra* upon the listener.

RV. III. 3.9

वि॒भावा॑ दे॒वः सु॒रणः॒ परि॑ क्षि॒तीर॒ग्निर्ब॑भूव॒ शव॑सा सु॒मद्र॑थः ।
तस्य॑ व्र॒तानि॑ भूरिपो॒षिणो॑ व॒यमुप॑ भूषे॒म दम॒ आ सु॑वृ॒क्तिभिः॑ ॥

Upa bhūṣema and ***suvṛktibhiḥ*** create some doubts here Sāyaṇa explains *upa bhūṣema* as *prakāśayāmaḥ*, 'we illuminate', which does not see suitable in confirmity with *vratāni*. Veṅkaṭamādhava paraphrases it with *alaṅkurmāḥ*, 'we decorate', which is again doubtful. His explanation of *pari babhūva* as *paryābhavat*, 'surpassed, overcame', is certainly better than Sāyaṇa's explication as *pari* to *gṛhṇāti*, 'overtakes'. With *śavasā sumadrathaḥ* (having a good chariot, Agni by his power encompassed the people) the meaning 'overcame, surpassed or encompassed 'will be more suitable'.

In connection with *vrata* - the meaning of the compounded verb ***upa bhūṣema*** to show or to express one's confirmation consolidation (in the literal sense) of power". Here poets confirm their sollidarty with the powers of Agni through their good prayers (*suvṛktibhiḥ*).

Suvṛktibhiḥ originally means the "thing properly measured or strewn" (Cf. *vṛktabarhiṣaḥ* - 1.333; 14.5; 3.2.5), and it can be derived from *vṛj*, '*to cut*, divide'. Thus *suvṛktibhiḥ* refers to the mantras which are well-divided and measured.[71]

RV. III. 3.10

वैश्वानर तव धामान्या चके येभिः स्वर्विदभवो विचक्षण ।
जात आपृणो भुवनानि रोदसी अग्ने ता विश्वा परिभूरसि त्मना ॥

This verse has many common traits of the earlier verse four in which *dhāmabhiḥ* refers to the "location (of divine power)". Due to these divine powers Agni became the knower of the heavenly light, or became omniscient by the means of the light of the heaven (the sun). Sāyaṇa explains it as *tejaḥ;* Grassmann[72] "heiliger Brauch", Geldner[73] "Eigenschaften" and Renou[74] "institutions". Finally Gonda[75] determines its meaning, "display or 'location' (of divine power)".

Vicakṣaṇa has been rendered by Renou[76] with "Ó (dieu) qui regardes au loin" making Agni "a distant looker". But actually this indicates towards his 'visionary powers' through which he can see everywhere and everything.

The verbal form (*ā cake* has been discussed already at RV 3.3.3 in the sense of 'desiring, longing'. Therefore, Sāyaṇa's explication *abhiṣṭaumi"*, I praise vigourously" is to be rejected, and "I long or crave (for your powers)" should be prefered.

The third *pāda, jāta āpṛṇo bhuvanāni rodasī* can be compared with RV 3.3.4 c. In both the places, the inherent idea is the same, viz. "Agni pervades the entire universe with its light'. The same notion is also seen in where Agni is stated to encompass the three worlds. Sāyaṇa's explication of *paribhūrasi* as *parigrahītāsi*, "thou art the protector' should be replaced with "thou are the encompasser' in accordance with the explanation of *paribhus* - gives earlier at RV 3.3.2.

RV. III. 3.11

वैश्वानरस्य दंसनाभ्यो बृहदरिणादेकः स्वपस्यया कविः ।
उभा पितरा महयन्नजायताग्निर्द्यावापृथिवी भूरिरेतसा ॥

So far as the word-meaning is concerned both Veṅkaṭamādhava and Sāyaṇa agree with each other. But the general import of the first two *pādas* differs as is clear from their respective interpretations. Veṅkaṭamādhava renders ab with *vaiśvānarasya karmabhyaḥ mahatvam the ekaḥ prāpnoti sobhana karmecchayā kaviḥ,* "due to his desire for good deeds the genius one (Agni) obtains eminence through the deeds of Vaiśvānara: Sāyaṇa paraphrases it as *vaiśvānarasya agneḥ daṁsanābhyaḥ toṣakārībhyaḥ kriyābhyaḥ bṛhat mahaddhanaṁ bhavatīti yat tadavitatham. yataḥ kāraṇāt ekaḥ mukhyaḥ kaviḥ agniḥ svapasyayā śobhanayajñā-dikarmecchayā yajamānādibhyo dhanam ariṇāt dadāti,* "there comes the immense wealth through the beneficial activities of Vaiśvānara Agni; and due to this the eminent poet Agni bestows riches upon the worshippers for the desired performance of good sacrificial deeds".

This comparison here indicates a clear difference over the use of the verbal form *ariṇāt* which has been taken by Veṅkaṭamādhava in a passive sense while Sāyaṇa interprets it in transitive sense. This makes much difference in the general meaning to the verse. Actually this difference arises out of the interpretation of the word *bṛhat.* Veṅkaṭamādhava interprets it as *'mahatvamiha'*, importance and 'construes it with *ekaḥ kaviḥ*', the only poet, i.e. Agni, while Sāyaṇa explains it as *'bṛhat mahaddhanaṁ* - 'the great wealth' and directly construes it with the radical form *'ariṇāt',*' bestows, makes to flow' as its object. If it really means 'wealth' it cannot be interpreted for Agni, as Veṅkaṭamādhava has done, rather it has to go for the 'worshipper' as done by Sāyaṇa. Oldenberg[77] and Geldner[78] have followed Sāyaṇa.

We can supply *vājam* after *bṛhat* as suggested earlier with *jinva bṛhataḥ* at RV 3.3.7. Thus it will give a clear sense of "bestowing or flowing or releasing 'the great generative power' from the inherent powers (*daṁsanābhyaḥ*) of

Vaiśvānara". As Vaiśvānara "originally meant to possess the total amount of vital strength.[79] The wish is expressed here to receive *vāja* - (generative power) through Agni's help. This explanation is in confirmity with the word *bhūriretasā* (possessing ample seminal fluid) used at the end of the verse.

The word ***daṁsana*** refers to Vaiśvānara's 'marvellous power' and can be related with *daṁsaḥ, daṁsana -, dasma -,* dasra - etc. Sāyaṇa's explanation of *daṁsanābhyaḥ* as *'toṣakārībhyaḥ kriyābhyaḥ,* "satisfying action" is not upto the make. This word can be identified with Avest. *Danhah* - "dexterity".[80]

NOTES

1. *Ṛgarth-dīpikā* 3.3.1.
2. RV Bh. 6.44.6.
3. K.P. Jog, *"On Veṅkaṭamādhava's Interpretation of the similes* beginning with *vipo na* in RV. 4.48.1; 6.44.6 and 8.19.33" JOI Baroda. Vol. XVIII, No. 3, March 1969, pp. 187-197.
4. S.C. Basu, *Siddh. kau.* Vol. III, p. 127.
5. ZDMG. 63, p. 299; 54. p. 171.
6. Geldner and Pischel, *Ved. Ṣtu.* III, p. 97 ff.
7. Renou, EVP 1,
8. P. Thieme, "*Der Fremdling in Ṛgveda*", *Abh. Zu Kunde des Morgenlandes* 23(1938), p. 43 n.
9. Grassmann, *Wort.* p. 1282 f.
10. J. Gonda, *The Vision,* p. 37-4; 172;195.
11. *Ibid* p. 38.
12. *Ibid* p. 685.
13. KZ. 32, p. 306.
14. *Indoir. Quellen u-Forsch.* 6.39.
15. Ludwig, *A Kommentar* zur RV. p. 296.
16. SBE. 46, p. 232.
17. *Der RV.* I, p. 337.
18. H.D. Velankar, *RV M.* III., p. 11.

19. *Loc. cit.* fn.
20. *op. cit.*, p. 234.
21. *Loc. cit.*
22. See Böhtlingk and Roth, *Sank. Wort.* S.V.; Grassmann *Wo.* pp. 569; 534; Wackern. 112, p. 450; 749 f.; Mayrhofer II, p. 28; Gonda, *Epithets,* pp. 62; 110. Ludwig, *Loc. cit;* Oldenberg, *Loc. cit.* Geldher, *Loc. cit.*, Renou, *Loc. cit.*
23. Sāyaṇa explains *puru* here as *bahukarmaṇām* "performing various deeds" which is nearer to the modern interpretations.
24. See Pischel, *Ved. St.* II/1, p. 104 ff.
25. See Mayrhofer, *op. cit.*, p. 28 f.
26. J. Gonda, *Four Studies in the Language of the Veda* (Mouton & Co.'s - Grawenhage, 1959), pp. 71-93.
27. *op. cit.*, p. 78.
28. *Hymns RV I.* p. 320.
29. *Loc. cit.*
30. *Loc.cit.*
31. *Loc. cit.*
32. Nir. 6.1.
33. *RV Bhāṣya* 9.112.2; 10.3.3.
34. *Ibid.* 5.53.3.
35. RV Bhāṣya of Udgīthācārya on RV. 10.7.4.
36. Nir. Bh. 6.1.
37. VS Bhāṣya. 11.27.
38. *Loc. cit.*
39. *Der RV. Uber.* 1, p. 331.
40. Nir. 11.26.
41. XII, p. 52.
42. Renou L, EVP, Vol., XII p.22
43. See also Geldner, *Der RVI*
44. See Valankar, *RV Maṅḍala III*
45. *RV translation II,*
46. Grassmann, *Worterbuch*
47. *Hymns of the RV I*
48. Oldenberg, *Noten I*
49. S.C. Basu, *Sidhānta-Kaumudī* Vol. III, p. 203.
50. For the explanation of *dhāmani* see Gonda, *The Meaning of the Sanskrit term dhāman*, p. 24.

51. For details see J. Gonda. *Loc. cit.*
A. Bergaigne, *Religion Vedique* III, p. 227.
52. H.P. Schmidt, *Vedisch Vrata Und Avestisch Urvāta*, p. 99.
Renou, EVP XII, p. 115.
53. See J. Gonda. *Vision*, p. 30.
54. Grassmann, *Wortb.* p. 954.
55. Wackern. *Altind. Gramm.* II. 2, p. 740.
Waild Pokorny, *Ety. Dict.*, II, p. 157.
Mayrhofer, *Kurz. Ety. Wortb.* II, p. 515.
56. Cf. J. Gonda, *Epithets*, p. 190.
57. For details see Gonda, *The Vision*, p. 142.
58. *RV Ubers.*, I, p. 59.
59. *Op. cit.*, p. 555 f.
60. Renou EVP. XII, p. 53.
61. Geldner, *op. cit.*, p. 338.
62. *RV Noten* I, p. 226.
63. *RV M. III.* p. 12.
64. *Sanskrit Grammar*, 1299 b, 1309 b.
65. *Jarā stutir jarateḥ stuti karmaṇaḥ* - Nir, 10.8.
66. Yāska's etymology and root meaning of jṛ, 'to praise', is acceptable to S. Varma on philological grounds. However, they do not suit the Ṛgvedic contexts. See S. Varma, *Ety. of Yāska*, p. 44.
67. See Bailey, TPS 1953, p. 33 ff; Walde-Pokorny, *Vergl. Wortb. der indger.* I, p. 599 f. SBE 46, p. 233; Neisser, Bezzenberger's *Beitrage* XIII, p. 297. Geldner, *op. cit.*, p. 338, Velankar, *Loc. cit.*
68. For the meaning of *pinva* see Brugmann, *comp. Grammar*, IX, pp. 136 with Indo-Eur. **pi-nu* 'swell' Avestan *frapinao-iti* is equal to Skt. *prapinvati* (swells, spreads).
69. For detailed discussions and meanings of *uśij* as 'zealous' (*vas-; us',-* "to wish, desire") an ancient type of priest (cf. also the Avest. usig-Ya 4420: a supporter of the old religion to which Zarathuṣtra was opposed)
70. See A. Bergaigne, *La Religion Vedique*, I, p. 57 ff: Wackern-Debru. *Altind. Gramm* 112, p. 160, 321; T. Burrow, *Annals of Orien. Res.* M. Uni. 1, p. 7. ff. Who makes an attempt to identify the term with Hittite Verbal root *"huek-huk"*, "to set free from witchcraft, charm, care", J. Gonda p. 119; see Velankar, loc. cit. fn.

71. For controversies and discussions on *suvṛkti* - see Yāska, Nir. II.24 Roth-Boḥt, *Sans. Wortb.* s.v.; Max Müllar, SBE 32, p. 109; Oldenberg SBE 46, p. 202; Grassmann Wortb., p. 1553.
72. *Wortb.* p. 677.
73. *Loc. cit.*
74. *EVP XII.* 53
75. *Dhāman,* p. 24.
76. *Loc. cit.*
77. *Loc. cit.*
78. *Loc. cit.*
79. J. Gonda, *Epithets,* p. 95.
80. For details see Mayrhofer, *op. cit.* II, p. 9.

***

The Ṛgveda Maṇḍal III.4

समित्संमित् सुमनां बोध्यस्मे शुचाशुंचा सुमतिं रांसि वस्वंः ।
आ देंव देवान् यजथांय वक्षि सखा सखींन् त्सुमनां यक्ष्यग्ने ॥

Nothing is much controversial in this *ṛk.* Veṅkaṭamādhava[1] explains **vakṣi** as *vaha,* 'conduct' taking it in the sense of imperative or optative while Sāyaṇa interprets it in the present sense as *āvahasi,* 'you conduct'. Even this difference is set aside when we compare other similar contexts, because both of these scholiasts possess this style of interpretation.

The phrase *samitasamit* refers either to 'the extreme effulgence' or 'to the every log' which is burnt in order to produce Agni. Sāyaṇa's interpretation of it as *atyartham samiddhastvam,* 'extremely shing you', confirms the first possibility. But Veṅkaṭamādhava's explanation of it as *samidham samidham,* 'with every *samidh*' (log) confirms the second meaning which appears more plausible and stands parallel to *śucāśucā,* 'with every flame'. This compound comes in the category of other similar comp. like *divedive,* 'day by day or every day', and can be placed with *prakalvin* at RV 7.18.15 which stands as the means for measurement and thus is adverbial instrumental. Velankar[2] thinks it to be 'adverbial nominative', but even being in nominative case it acts for instr. which is confirmed by *śucāśucā* also.

Vasvaḥ (gen. sg. of *vasu*) seems to stand here for Agni himself who is invoked to grant his bountiful or gracious or brilliant 'wisdom', Veṅkaṭamādhava's as well as Sāyāṇa's interpretation of it as 'the wisdom connected with riches *vasuno dhanasya tadvisayām (buddhim)* is too literal. Here it can be compared with *sumatim vasvaḥ* at 7.39.1a. Geldner's[3] interpretation followed by Velankar, as 'divine favour' (die Gnade des Gottes) is more plausible than Griffith's[4] 'boon of riches'. Oldenberg[5] has also rendered it with '(thy) *Vasus* 'favour' where *vasu* stands for Agni.

RV. III. 4.2

यं देवासस्त्रिरहंन्नायजंन्ते दिवेदिंवे वरुंणो मित्रो अग्निः ।
सेमं यज्ञं मधुंमन्तं कृधी नस्तनूंनपाद् घृतयोंनिं विधन्तंम् ॥

In this verse ***tanūnapāt*** stands for Agni himself whom all the gods, especially Varuṇa and Mitra (as well as Agni himself) worship. The terms *triḥ ahan* refer to the 'three *savanas* of the day'.

Tanūnapāt- this appears somewhat strange here that Agni worships himself, i.e. his own form *tanūnapāt*. Agni has been assigned this name seven times in the 'RV', and all the related verses appear to be nearer each other so far as their contents are concerned and can be assigned later date as Wilson has proposed. The hymn under discussion is an āpri-hymn and is later than the other hymns. The relation with the other hymns can be established on the basis of common terminology used in the verses connected with *tanūnapāt*. The tautological expressions, artificial phraseology and wilful mystification are the main traits of these Āprī hymns. For example, *madhumantam* (1.13.2), *ghṛtavantam* (1.142.2.), *madhvāsamajyate* (1.188.2), *madhvā samañjan* (10.110.2), and *imama- ñjaspām* are the common phrases scattered in these hymns which can be equated with the expressions like *yajñam madhumantam, ghṛtayonim vidhantam* in the under discussion. Potdar[7] has studied all the Apri-hymns together and determined the chronological order of these hymns which according to him also belong to a later period.

According to RV itself *tanūnapāt* is a form of Agni when he remains unmanifested, i.e. when he remains in the embryo. RV says:

tanūnapāducyate garbha āsuro
narāsaṅso bhavati yad vijāyate
mātariśvā yadamimīta mātari
vātasya sargo abhavat sarīmaṇi / RV. 3.29.11

"Being the Germ celestial he is called Tanūnapāt, and when he manifests in varied forms he becomes Narāśaṁsa. He is Mātariśvan, because he is formed in his Mother. During his fast course he has become the rapid flight of wind".

Sāyaṇa's explication of it as *tanūnāṁ sarīrāṇāṁ na pātayitaḥ,* 'because he is not the injurer of the bodies' is open to doubts, *tanūnapāt* can be equated with *apāmnapāt* and *aponapāt,* and thus *tanū* stands as the synonym of *apām* here. This is confirmed by Yāska's explication of its etymology as *āpos'tra tanvā ucyante tatā antarikṣe* etc. (Nir. viii. 5) - "*tanū* means 'water', so called because it is spread (*tan*) over the atmosphere".[8] Linguistically this explanation stands partly true because *napāt* literally means 'grandson' which is identical with Indo-Eur. nepot 'grandson or nephew', Avestan *napam,* Lat. neptis, GK and so on.[9] The word naptṛ denotes kinship and can be put together with *pitṛ, mātṛ, bhrātṛ, duhitṛ* etc. in which the radical part *pi, ma, bhra-, duhi* - are quite distinct; and on the basis of this anology we can assume that in *napāt* there exists a distinct part nap which has not been attested anywhere. Now this *nap* is either na + p (a part of the *pat* 'to fall') or a root itself. In both the cases the radical meaning is doubtful. However, on the basis of *apatya, naptṛ* and *napāt* it can be surmised that a and *na* are negative particles, giving the meaning 'net', and thus these words mean 'who do not fall' or who cause the 'continuity of the generation'. Thus we can form *naptṛ* from *nap* with *tṛ* (*trn*) suffix, and being nit it initially accented (see RV 1.22.6; 37.11 etc.). *tanūnapāt* being RV comp. takes the acute accent on the first member. Thus, *tanūnapāt* literally means 'one who is a 'descendant, i.e. son or grandson'. Agni's mythology clearly exemplifies this statement.

RV. III. 4.3

प्र दीधिंतिर्विश्ववांरा जिगाति होतांरमिळः प्रंथमं यजंध्यै ।
अच्छा नमोंभिर्वृषभं वन्दध्यै स देवान् यंक्षदिषितो यजींयान् ॥

Dīdhitiḥ - The explanation of *dīdhitiḥ* offered by Sāyaṇa as *stutirdiptirvā* 'eulogy or brilliance' corresponds with Veṅkaṭamādhava's paraphrase *'dīpthiḥ'* 'light', and both stand a good chance of refutation. The translation 'Andacht', "prayer" Grassmann,[10] Geldner[11] and Wackern-Debru[12] also does not offer anything new. " The noun *dīdhiti-* belongs to the word family[13] of *dhi* which has the same function as the *dhiḥ* or the *dhitiḥ* indicating the sense of "visionary insight or wisdom." Velankar's[14] translation "pious thoughts" stands a good chance of hitting the mark.

The noun **dīdhiti** - occurs 9 times in the RV in different forms as *dīdhitiḥ* (1.186.11; 3.4.3; 5.18.4), *dīdhitibhiḥ* (7.1.1.), *dīdhitiṁ* (3.31.1; 4.2.16; 9.102.1; 8) and *dīdhiti* (5.42.1). The formation can be explained from the reduplicated *dhi*-with the suffix *ktin* (*striyāṁ ktin* - Pa. 3.3.94). Being *nit* it will have the acute accent on the initial syllable by Pa. 6.1.197.

Sāyaṇa construes ***idaḥ.***, acc. pl. of id (*is*), with the third pāda which seems deceptive because it has the direct connection with the verb *pra jigāti* in the first *pāda* and syntactically it has nothing to do with the third *pāda.* Similarly Velankar's translation of *idaḥ* as 'of our sacrificial food', taking *idaḥ* as gen. sg. form rather than acc. pl., is also open to objection. He construes *prathamaṁ* with *yajadhyai* as his translation 'to worship him first' indicates. But *prathamaṁ* stands here as an attributive qualification for *hotāram* which can be substantiated by the expressions like *hvayāmyagniṁ prathamaṁ svastaye* 1.35.1; *taṁ medheṣu prathamaṁ devayantiḥ* 1.77.3; *yo jāta eva prathamo manasvān* 2.12.1 and so on. Here and likewise in other places the attribute *prathama-* refers to the supremacy of the deity over other gods.

RV. III. 4.4

ऊर्ध्वो वां गातुरध्वरे अकार्यूर्ध्वा शोचींषि प्रस्थिता रजांसि ।
दिवो वा नाभा न्यसादि होता स्तृणीमहि देवव्यचा वि बर्हिः ॥

Vāṁ - There is some controversy over *vāṁ* among the exegetists. According to Veṅkaṭamādhava it stands for Agni and Soma as is clear by his paraphrase *agnisomau.* Sāyaṇa explicates it as *agniśca barhiścobhau vāmityucyete,* "Agni and barhi 'sacrificial grass' are called vāṁ", but this interpretation has no ground because vāṁ occurs frequently for Agni-Indra, Indra-Viṣṇu, Agni-Viṣṇu, Aśvins and so on. Therefore we cannot rely on Sāyaṇa's interpretation here. Max Müller[15] proposes the change of vāṁ into *vā,* and explains it in favour of either the road going upward or heaven's navel where Agni makes himself seated. But this explanation seems just hypothetical. Ludwig[16] thinks *vāṁ* to be used for heaven and earth; but this explanation also seems deceptive. Oldenberg[17] says that "the structure of the phrase gives the impression - though this impression is by no means certain - that vāṁ, which belongs to *gātu* is to be supplied to socinisi also". Further he remarks hypothetically that vāṁ represents the two important fires, i.e. *Āhavanīya* and *Gārhyapatya,* or it might be for two *adri* - (press-stones). But his supposition has no ground here, therefore, it needs no attention, Geldner[18] gives the opinion of Sāyaṇa only. Velankar[19] follows Oldenberg's interpretation as "two stones" which is not to the point.

Vāṁ (daivyāhotārāṁ) - As *vāṁ* is closely connected here with *hotṛs* who has been mentioned as seated at either of two places, i.e. heaven or mid-region. In the third *pāda*, this gives ample evidence to relate vāṁ again with two *daivyā hotārā* mentioned in the seventh *ṛk* of the same hymn. But who are these two heavenly priests? *daivyā hotārā* occurs together 11 times in the RV[20] and in all those hymns there are some common traits and sequences which give a remarkable uniformity of thought expressed in those hymns. In all those hymns Narāśaṁsa and Tanūnapāt are two forms of Agni mentioned together or separately in the same hymn, and they represent Agni's manifestation in the heaven and on the earth or mid-region. After these two forms of Agni forms a sequence of three verses comes in almost all hymns in which *Naktoṣas (Rātri* and *Uṣas*), *Daivyāhotārā* and *Bhāratī Sarasvatī* come one after another. This phenomenon is common in all these eleven hymns which are scattered in I, II, III, V, IX and X Maṇḍalas of the RV. They constitute a common ideological framework and appears to be the creation of one particular group of the poets. Most of these hymns are Apri hymns as is the case with the hymn under consideration. Thus, through a close examination of these occurrences of *daivyā hotārā* it becomes clear that these two are none but the two unmanifested and manifested - forms of Agni who are called *Tanūnapāt* and *Narāśansa* (*tanūnapāducyate garbha asuro narāśaṁso bhavati yad vijayate*). And this again leads to another conclusion that vāṁ here in the present *ṛk* refers to none other but these two forms of Agni, i.e. *Tanūnapāt* and *Narāśansa.*

Devavyacaḥ - This comp. occurs only here in the RV *devavyacaḥ tamaḥ* (5.33.2; 26.8) and *devavyacastamam* (1.142.5) also occur. Other compounds with *vyaca* - are *uruvyaca* - (1.160.2; 6.36.3; 7.31.11 etc.) and *samudravyaca* (1.11.1).

Vyaca - can be derived from *vyac* 'to become wide, extend, contain' with the suffix *asun*. Being *nit* it should have the initial acute accent but due to Bahv. Comp. the accent has been shifted to the first member (*bahuvrihau prakrtyā purvapadam* - Pa. 6.2.1). Thus it will mean 'which is extended by the gods', i.e. *barhiṣ*. Sāyaṇa and Veṅkaṭamādhava explain it as *'devairvyāptam*, "pervaded by the gods", which is also plausible.

RV. III. 4.5

स॒प्त हो॒त्राणि॒ मन॑सा वृणा॒ना इन्व॑न्तो॒ विश्वं॒ प्रति॑ यन्नृ॒तेन॑ ।
नृ॒पेश॑सो वि॒दथे॑षु प्र जा॒ता अ॒भी॒३॒॑मं य॒ज्ञं वि च॑रन्त पू॒र्वीः ॥

From the commentaries of Veṅkaṭamādhava and Sāyaṇa as well as from the translations by Occidental and Oriental scholars it appears that they have missed the mark.

The word ***pūrvīḥ***[21] in the present *ṛk* seems to refer to the Uṣas, which is clear from the following *ṛk* i.e. *ā bhandamāne uṣasā upāke* as well as from the 'eleven hymns' referred to earlier in connection with *daivyā hotārā*, where the Night and the Dawn play a prominent role. With the help of the premordial law (Truth) or fundamental order, i.e. *Ṛta*, *Uṣas* plays the role of inspiring, invigorating and activising the entire world which has been expressed here by *invantaḥ visvam - ṛtena* inspiring all through *Ṛta*". They go about this by choosing seven *hotṛs* through their mind.

Sapta hotrāṇi - which occurs only here means according to commentators 'seven sacrificial activities of priests'.[22] Or, this may be related with the myth of the seven founders of sacrifice (*yajño nā sapta dhātrbhih* - RV 9.10.3)[23] Besides, the number 'seven' is often used in the Veda to denote 'completion and perfection of the modalities' of sacrificial worship.[24]

Now, the view that *ab* refers to the gods and *cd* to the deified doors,[25] seems untenable. The whole verse refers to the varied forms of *uṣas, vicarantī (uṣasanakta)* at RV 6.49.3 and *sūryamāsā vicarantā* at RV 10.92.12 also substantiate this point well. *Prajātāḥ* can be compared with *ṛtajātasatyāḥ* at 4.51.7 assigned to Uṣas.

RV. III. 4.6

आ भन्द॑माने उ॒षसा॒ उपा॑के उ॒त स्म॒येते त॒न्वा॒३॒ विरू॑पे ।
यथा॑ नो मि॒त्रो वरु॑णो॒ जुजो॑ष॒दिन्द्रो॑ म॒रुत्वाँ॑ उ॒त वा॒ महो॑भिः ॥

Nothing seems very controversial here. Sāyaṇa's interpretation of *smayete* and *mahobhiḥ* needs a closer look. He explains *smayete* as *prakāśete* 'both *Uṣas* and *Rātri* - 'shine together', *mahobhiḥ* has been rendered by him as *tejobhiryukte ime dyāvāpṛthivyau kurutām,* 'make the sky and the earth full of light", and thus he supplies a verb in the second hemistich which seems unnecessary. This trend has been followed by modern exegetists also. But we can get the clear meaning even without that.

Smayete tanvā virūpe refers to *Uṣasanakta* in their visible, beautiful womanly form. This is a stylistic expression of sublime eroticism giving an aesthetic brilliance to the Vedic poetry. They have been entreated to come to the sacrificial platform in their beautiful form (*bhandamāne*) smiling (making themselves attractive) their variegate (*virūpe*) form (*tanvā*) a order to please or make satisfied (*jujoṣat*) the gods Mitra, Varuṇa, Indra and their hosts, *mahobhiḥ*- refers to the accompanying powers of Indra and other gods, and not their brilliance as Sāyaṇa thinks.

Bhandamāne, though originally connected with *band* or *bhand*, 'to praise', signifies here the aesthetic beauty of *uṣasanakta* whose celebrity and sublime form has often been exalted in the RV. Here they have been prayed to come before the gods, therefore, the meaning *stuyamāne* given by Veṅkaṭamādhava and Sāyaṇa does not suit the contexts. Therefore, the meanings 'beautiful, exalted, splendid, lovely' etc. have to be accepted.

RV. III. 4.7

दैव्या होतारा प्रथमा न्यृञ्जे सप्त पृक्षासः स्वधया मदन्ति ।
ऋतं शंसन्त ऋतमित् त आहुरनु व्रतं व्रतपा दीध्यानाः ॥

Daivyā hotārā has been explained earlier in the form of Agni's two names, i.e. *Tanūnapāt* and *Narāsaṁsa.* Here *sapta pṛkṣāsaḥ* creates some problem. According to Sāyaṇa as well as Veṅkaṭamādhava it refers to the seven priests (*hotāraḥ* or *ṛtvijaḥ*) who prepare the sacrificial food. But as *pṛkṣa* stands for the Bull and the horses, it cannot be taken in the sense of either 'food' or 'priests'. The close examination of all the occurrences of *pṛkṣa* clearly indicates that it means 'vigorous', 'strong', 'powerful' and so on. *Pṛkṣa* can be identified here with Indo-Eur. *pṛkṣo.*[26] Thus, *sapta pṛkṣasaḥ* refers here to the 'seven priestly forms, referred to earlier with *saptahotrāṇi*- at RV 3.4.5 and named at RV 2.1.22, who rejoice with the celestial food (*svadhaya madanti*). Thus Sāyaṇa's explication of *mādanti* as *mādayanti* has no bearing here. To take *sapta pṛkṣāsaḥ* for *ṛtivijaḥ* 'priests' is entirely unacceptable. The phrase *svadhayā madanti* occurs thrice with the gods. Therefore, here also it should be taken for god Agni and not for *ṛtvijās.*

The second part of the verse also has no connection with the worldly sacrificial priests, rather it is connected with Agni's forms who follow the path of *Ṛts,* and therefore, they themselves are called *Ṛta.* Pursuing the religious order they protect the religious ordinances while receiving visions.

The form ***dīdhyānāḥ*** has been explained by Sāyaṇa as *dīpyamānāḥ,* 'shining' or *dīpayantaḥ* 'illuminating', (Agni) which seems faulty. The form occurs nine times in the RV

(3.4.7; 7.8; 4.33.9; 50.1; 7.90.4; 5; 91.4; 10.67.2; 181.3) and mostly it is related with *manasa* which indicates the thinking or imagining process rather than the 'shining'. Therefore, it should be taken in the sense of "visionary illumination with their thought".[27]

RV. III. 4.8

आ भार॑ती॒ भार॑तीभिः स॒जोषा॒ इळा॑ दे॒वैर्म॑नु॒ष्ये॑भिर॒ग्निः ।
सर॑स्वती सारस्व॒तेभि॑र॒र्वाक् ति॒स्रो दे॒वीर्ब॒र्हिरेदं स॑दन्तु ॥

In this verse the three goddesses Bhāratī, Idā and Sarasvatī have been invoked. They represent here some order of preference at the sacrifice. Bhāratī's and Sarasvatī's are the imaginary female, and male followers of Bhāratī and Sarasvatī among the celestials. Idā is followed by Devās (in general) and Agni by the deifined ancesters like Aṅgirasas".[28] Nothing is controversial in the *ṛk*.

RV. III. 4.9

तन्न॑स्तु॒रीप॒मध॑ पोषयि॒त्नु देव॑ त्वष्ट॒र्वि र॑रा॒णः स्य॑स्व ।
यतो॑ वी॒रः क॑र्म॒ण्यः॑ सु॒दक्षो॑ यु॒क्तग्रा॑वा॒ जाय॑ते दे॒वका॑मः ॥९॥

वन॑स्प॒तेऽव॑ सृ॒जोप॑ दे॒वान॒ग्निर्ह॒विः श॑मि॒ता सू॑दयाति ।
सेदु॒ होता॑ स॒त्यत॑रो यजा॒ति यथा॑ दे॒वानां॒ जनि॑मानि॒ वेद॑ ॥१०॥

आ या॑ह्यग्ने समिधा॒नो अ॒र्वाङिन्द्रे॑ण दे॒वैः स॒रथं॑ तु॒रेभिः॑ ।
ब॒र्हिर्न॒ आस्ता॒मदि॑तिः सुपु॒त्रा स्वाहा॑ दे॒वा अ॒मृता॑ मादयन्ताम् ॥११॥

Veṅkaṭamādhava and Sāyaṇa supply *retaḥ* after *tat* in their commentaries, which seems perhaps a drawn conclusion on the basis of the verb *jāyate* in the second hemistich. *Yataḥ* also has been explained by Veṅkaṭamādhava. as *retasoh*, 'from the semen'. But *tat* refers to *turīpam* and *poṣayitnu* here. Both of these words occur thrice in the RV, each time in a repetition of the same phrase. The present verse has been repeaed at RV 7.2.9, and *tannastu-rīpamadbhutam* at RV 1.142.10 can be equated with *tannasturīpamadha poṣayitnu* in the present ṛk. *Poṣayitnu* occurs separately at RV 4.57.1 which can be compared with (*tvaṣṭa*) *poṣāya viṣyatu* at RV 1.142.10. Thus the inherent idea is the same everywhere.

Turīpam has been explained by Veṅkaṭamādhava as *tarakam* which has been followed by Sāyaṇa also. Grassmann gives its meaning as 'Samenflussigkeit' (seminal fluid) which is based on Sāyaṇa's interpretation. This has been followed by subsequent interpreters, But this betrays the root meaning completely. The *tur* is apparently comprehensible in *turīpam*, and the same can be seen in *turaḥ* (RV 1.18.2), *turaṇyan* (RV 1.121.1), *turaṇe* (RV 1.121.5), *turaspeye* (RV 10.96.8), *turagātu* (RV 1.164.30) etc. Thus *turīpam* can be derived from *tur* + *i* + *pa* (*tur* and *i* as two roots and *pa* as a suffix) which will gives the sense of 'making quick, inspiring, stimulating quickening, enlivening' and so on. Thus it becomes an attributive adjective of Soma, which can be substantiated here by the use of *yuktagrāvā* in the fourth *pāda*. All the qualifying words used in this *ṛk*; namely, *turīpam, poṣayitnu, rarāṇaḥ, vīraḥ, karmaṇyaḥ, sudakṣaḥ* and *yuktagrāvā*, indicate only towards this possibility. In the remaining two ṛks nothing seems controversial.

NOTES

1. Ṛgveda Saṁhita with the commetaries of Skandaṣvāmin, Udgītha, Venkaṭamādhava and Mudgal, Part (iii), edited by Vishva Bandhu, Hoshiarpur, 1963 p. 1296
2. See H.D. Velankar *RVM.* III, p.14
3. Uberstzt I, p.339
4. *op. cit.*, p. 321.
5. *SBE* 46, p. 236.
6. RV 1.113.2; 142.2; 1.188.2; 3.4.2; 3.29.11; 9.5.2; 10.110.2;

7. K.R. Potdar, *Āpri Hymns in the Ṛgveda (A Study and a Theory)*, JUB, Vol. XIV (Sept. 1945) pp. 26.43 and vol. XV (Sept. 1946) pp. 29-57.
8. See S. Varma. Ety. of Yāska, p. 59.
9. For identification see KZ. Benfew, 9. 111 ff; Brugmann, *A comp. Gramm.* II, p. 383, 390; III, p. 281; Wackern, *Alt. Gramm.* 112, p. 269, 417, 694 f.
10. Grassmann, Wortb. S.V.
11. *Der RV.* I, p. 339.
12. Wackern. Debrunner, op. cit. p. 629.
13. J. Gonda. *Vision*, p. 226
14. *Loc. cit.*
15. SBE. 46, p. 238; *RV. Noten*, p. 227 (quoted by Oldenberg).
16. *Loc. cit* (quoted by Oldenberg).
17. *Loc. cit.*
18. *Loc. cit.*
19. *Loc. cit.*
20. RV. 1.13.8; 142.8; 188.7; 3.4.7; 7.8; 5.5.7; 9.5.7; 10.65.10; 66.13; 110.7.
21. cf. *ṛtasya pūrvīḥ* - RV. 3.5.2.
22. cf. H. Oldenberg *Religion des Veda*, p. 383 f. RV 2.1.2. also mentions the names of Hotṛ, Potṛ, Nestṛ, Āgnīdhra, Prasastṛ, Adhvaryu and Brahmā - the seven priests.
23. Bergaigne, op. cit. III, p. 232.
24. Ludwig, KZ 28, p. 243; KR. Potdar. Sacrifice in the Rgveda, Bombay 1953, p. 123 ff; J. Gonda. *Dhaman*, p. 52.
25. See H.D. Velankar. *RV M. III*, p. 15 fn. (He follows apparently Geldner who annotates as "*pūrvih*, die *Tore* wie *bahvih* 1, 188.5: vgl. 7.2 5c". see *Ubersetzt* I, p. 339, fn.
26. For details see H.W. Bailey. TPS. 1953, p. 29 ff; Ilya Gershevitch, *The Avestan Hymn to Mithra* (Cambridge 1959), p. 224.
27. For details see J. Gonda. *Vision*, p. 295 ff.
28. See Velankar, *RV M. VII*, p. 13 fn. 8.
H. Grassmann, *Wörterbuch* Zum Ṛigveda, p. 542.
See Wackern, *Alt. Gramm*, 112, p. 744.
Mayrhofer, *Kurz. Ety. Wortb.*, I, p. 515

The Ṛgveda Maṇḍal III.5

प्रत्य॒ग्निरु॒षस॒श्चेकि॑ता॒नोऽबो॑धि॒ विप्र॑ः पद॒वीः क॑वी॒नाम् ।
पृ॒थु॒पाजा॑ देव॒यद्भि॒ः समि॒द्धोऽप॒ द्वारा॒ तम॑सो॒ वह्नि॑रावः ॥

In this *ṛk* Agni appears to play the role of *Uṣas* who is generally called to rouse the sun and to smash the darkness. The verse can be compared with similar statements elsewhere (RV 4.51.2; 7.80.2).

There is not much difference of opinion among the exegetists about the general meaning of this verse.

Padavīḥ - Sāyaṇa and Veṅkaṭamādhava[1] differ with each other only on *padavīḥ*. According to Sāyaṇa it means *mārgam gacchan*, 'traversing on the way', Veṅkaṭamādhava paraphrases it as *padāni dhātā*, 'pace giver'. The comp. occurs six times in the RV and appears to be formed from *pada* + *vī*- 'to go' etc. As the *vī*- has several meanings we can interpret this comp. variously, but the phrase '*padavīḥ kavīnām* occurs thrice[2] which indicates that Agni (here) and Soma (RV 9.96.6; 18) are the 'path-shower or guide'. This meaning suits all the contexts.

As - *vī* - is formed by *vī* + *kvip* it should be unaccented according to *anudāttau-suppitau* (Pans. 3.1.4), but here *padavīḥ* has its accent on the last syllable which can be explained by Pans. 6.1.223. *samāsasya*-.

There is some difference in meanings of *pṛthupājāḥ* which can be seen here also in the same light as it has been explained earlier (RV 3.2.11).

(prati) Abodhi - This is an aorist form of *budh* 'to awaken' or 'to awake' third sg. which has been taken here in the present sense by Sāyaṇa to indicate universality for Agni. Veṅkaṭamādhava explains it in the past tense. The *ṛk* can be rendered as follows:

"Inspiring the Uṣas (to rise), Agni, the excited (inspired and elequent) guide of the sages, is awakened. The oblation-bearer, enkindled by the god-devoted men and possessed of ample lusture has flung open the doors of darkness".

RV. III. 5.2

प्रेद्ध॒ग्निर्वा॑वृधे॒ स्तोमे॑भिर्गी॒र्भिः स्तो॒तॄणां॑ न॑म॒स्य॑ उ॒क्थैः ।
पू॒र्वीर्ऋ॒तस्य॑ सं॒दृश॑श्चका॒नः सं दू॒तो अ॑द्यौदु॒षसो॑ वि॒रोके ॥

In this verse *cakānaḥ* and *viroke* are controversial words explained differently by Veṅkaṭamādhava and Sāyaṇa.

Cakānaḥ - According to Sāyaṇa it means 'desiring' (*kāmayamānaḥ*) but Veṅkaṭamādhava[3] explains it as 'shining' (*dīpyamānaḥ*). The form occurs eight times in the RV (3.5.2; 5.3.10; 27.3; 6.36.5; 7.27.1; 10.64.16; 123.8; 148.3). Other two forms *cakānāḥ* (2.31.7; 4.16.15; 6.29.2; 10.7.8) and *cakānā* (RV 6.68.3) also occur. Sāyaṇa explains and derives it differently at different places, which creates doubts whether really the same Sāyaṇa has explained these forms everywhere. At RV 2.31.7 he derives it from *kan* (*dīptikāntigatiṣu*) with *lit* and kānac, and explains it as *'kāma-yamānaḥ'*, 'desiring' which seems correct in the context of *śravasyavoḥ vājam cakānaḥ* 'the fameseeker, desiring the generative power'. This meaning can be applied suitably at RV 5.3.10; 27.3; 6.29.1; 10.148.3. At 6.29.1 Sāyaṇa explains it as *'kāmayamānaḥ'* but derives it from *kām* and *kai* (*cakāna iti kāmayateḥ chandasaṁ rūpam, athavā cakānaḥ sabdavantaḥ; kai gai śabde ityasṁat titaḥ kānaci rūpam*), which is evidently different from his previous derivation. At RV 6.68.3 he derives *cakāna* from *kay* (*kayathiḥ śabdakarma*) which seems to be the explanation offered by some other exegetist rather than by Sāyaṇa.

Cakānaḥ should be derived from *kan* 'to shine, desire, go', only and should be interpreted according to the contexts. As at RV 10.123.8 *bhānuḥ śukreṇa śociṣā cakānaḥ* (the sun shining with his brilliant rays) *cakānaḥ* should be taken to mean 'shining'. Sāyaṇa[4] has also explained it as *'dīpyamānaḥ'*. This meaning can be applied at RV 4.16.15; 10.77.8; 6.36.5; 68.3 where Sāyaṇa fails to hit the mark. Veṅkaṭamādhava's explanation of *cakānaḥ* as *'dīpyamānaḥ'* in the present context[4] seems more plausible with Agni than Sāyaṇa's as *'kāmayamānaḥ'*. Geldner's rendering of the third pāda as 'der die vielen Anblicke des rechten Brauchs gern hat' seems uncalled for, because 'the many appearances of the righteous custom (sacrifice)' has nothing to do with the present context. Velankar[5] seems to follow Geldner without going into pros and cons while translating it as - "Being fond of the many lovely faces of *Ṛta* (i.e. sacrifice)", and annotating it as '- *pūrvīḥ ṛtasya saṁdṛśaḥ'* are the many aspects of ṛta which is here symbolised by the sacrifice as at RV 6.51.1c. Agni himself is called the *anīka* (the face) of the sacrifice at RV 10.2.6a, since Agni plays the most important part in the sacrificial ritual". Renou's[6] rendering of this as 'ayant toujours aimé' les nombreux champs-de-vision de l'Ordre-sacre' is not different from above two explanations.

Purvīḥ ṛtasya saṁdṛśaḥ here refers to *uṣasaḥ* in the fourth *pāda*. This statement can be substantiated by the comparison of those passages where either *'ṛtasya pūrvīḥ* comes as a joint phrase, or *pūrvīḥ* occurs alone in the contexts of Agni and Uṣas. Some of those passages are quoted here to justify the statement: - RV. 3.1.11: *āpaḥ pūrvīḥ - ṛtasya ....*

3.6.7 a: *divaścidā te rucayanta rokā*
b: *uṣo vibhātīranu bhāsi pūrvīḥ*
3.7.9 b: *pūrvīḥ .... raśmayaḥ suyāmāḥ*
6.28.1d: *indrāya pūrvīruṣaso duhānāḥ*

In all the above passages *Uṣas* is called *pūrvīḥ*. At RV 3.6.7 the word *rokā* can be compared with viroke in the context under discussion. These evidences confirm that *ṛtasya pūrvīḥ* are none but *Uṣasaḥ* who are supposed to be originated from the *ṛta*. This statement may stand in contradistinction with the descriptions about the origin of Uṣas from Indra, Agni etc. (*yaḥ sūryam yaḥ uṣasam jajāna* RV 2.12.7), but that can be solved by the comparison of those passages where *Uṣas* is called *purāṇī* (RV 3.61.1; 4.51.6), 'ancient' or unceasing. At one place they (*uṣas*) are called to be 'originated from *Ṛta*, the Truth *or Ṛta* '*ṛtajātasatyāḥ*'[7] (RV 4.51.7) which can be again compared with *ṛtasya pūrvīḥ*. Thus the fourth pāda can be rendered as "(Agni) shining forth (*cakānaḥ*), resembling with (*saṁdṛśaḥ* - looking alike) Uṣas, the foremost (creation) of Ṛta".

'Viroke' - This form occurs only here. *Virokiṇaḥ* occurs twice (RV 5.55.3; 10.78.3). Similarly *rokaḥ* (RV 6.66.6) and *rokaḥ* (RV 3.6.7) also occur. Sāyaṇa explains *viroke* as '*virocane prātaḥkāle*' in the brilliance, i.e. morning. Veṅkaṭamādhava renders it with '*prādurbhave*' in the appearance of the Uṣas in the morning' is the meaning of the fourth pāda. Here *viroke* is in the *bhave* sense and subsequently it takes locative.

General meaning of the verse is clear.

RV. III. 5.3

अधांय्यग्निर्मानुंषीषु विक्ष्व१ंपां गर्भों मित्र ऋतेन साधंन् ।
आ हंर्यतो यंजतः सान्वंस्थादभूंदु विप्रो हव्यों मतीनाम् ॥

In this verse Agni's supremacy over all visionary powers and human beings has been described.

Adhāyi - The verbal form *adhāyi*, 3rd sg. passive of *dhā*, indicates here Agni's placement in the houses clans of human beings. Here the phrase *adhāyyagnir- mānuṣīṣu vikṣva* can be compared with other phraseologies 'expressing specific similar thoughts'[8] as at RV I. 60.4ab: *uśik pāvako vasurmānuṣeṣu vareṇyo hotādhāyi vikṣu.*

> (the yearning purifier, good one, the choice-worthy, the *Hotṛ*
> (Agni has been placed in the human dwellings).
> RV 7.7.4 c: *viśāmadhāyi viśpatirduroṇe agnir* .../
> (the lord of the clans, Agni has been placed in the house of the clans).

Agni has been placed among men, but by whom? None of the interpreters has indicated towards this fact except Sāyaṇa. Sāyaṇa explains *adhāyi* as *'devaiḥ āhitaḥ* - placed by the gods'. To satisfy this urge we can look into the RV itself where Agni's three forms have been described, among which one has been placed on the earth.[9] The same form has been indicated here.

Adhāyi will be formed with *dhā* in aor. with *at* as an acutely accented augment by Pa. 6.4.71 and insertion of *yuk* by Pa 7.3.33 (*āto yukciṇkṛtoḥ*). On the place of *cli* it will take *cin* due to passive construction by Pan. Su. 3.1.66 (*ciṇbhāvakarmaṇoḥ*). While interpreting the aorist will be taken in the sense of present tense governed by Pan. Su. 3.4.6 (*chandasi luṅlaṅlitaḥ*).

The phrase *ṛtena sādhan* refers to Agni's placement which has been made effective by Ṛta. This can be compared with RV 7.34.8. In other contexts[10] *Sādhan* occurs with Agni where he himself is making the things effective. The gods place Agni making him effective in every ways. This idea has been communicated very well by RV 1.96.1 where *āpaḥ* and *Dhiṣaṇā,* 'the Visionary Power', make agni effective.

Haryataḥ - In the third pāda Agni has been described as ascending to the highest peak. His attribute here as *haryateo*- has some special connotation. Sāyaṇa explains it here as *spṛhaṇīyaḥ* 'loving one, attractive' as has been done by Veṅkaṭamādhava and other subsequent exegetists.

Haryata - is a derivative of *harya* 'to go quickly or to shine' (*haryagatikāntyoḥ*) with *ata*-suffix (governed by Una. S. 3.110 *'bhṛmṛdṛsiyajiparvipacyamitaminamiharyebhyo' taca*) by which other similar words as *'bharata'*, *'marata'*, *'darsata'*, *'yajata'*, *'pac-ata'* etc. are formed. Being *cit* it has acute accent on the final syllable governed by Pa. 6.1.16 *'citaḥ'*. The suffix *ata* - is similar to Indo-Ger. *e-to*[11] and Iranian - *ata* - found with the Avestan words like *barata yazata, n mata, r mata* etc.[12]

Grassmann[13] thinks that *hary* - is a denominative from *hari* but Whitney[14] takes it as derivative from *hṛ*. In the first case the meaning may be 'to become golden', then extended to be desirable', 'loving' etc., though not certain. But in the latter case we have to change the meaning as 'being angry' which is not suitable either with Agni or with Soma with whom this epithet occurs frequently. *Hṛ* is supposed to come from *ghṛ* (with the loss of the plossive element), and is identical with Avestic *zar* to grieve, do anger etc. Thus if we accept Whitney's proposition the meaning of *haryata* will be changed.

In the present context the root meaning *'kānti'*, 'shining', 'beautiful' is more agreeable, therefore *haryata'* may be rendered as 'shining, brilliant, attractive', but with Soma it may mean 'going hurriedly, tumultuous, impetuous',[15] taking the root meaning *'gati'*.[16] We can render the present *ṛk* as follows:

"Agni, the embryo of waters, friend (of all) is placed among human settlements (clans) being affective by Ultimate order (Truth). The shining and holy Agni mounted upon the highest peak (of heaven);[17] and the inspired one has become worthy of being invoked by the visionary powers (prayers)".

RV. III. 5.4

मित्रो अग्निर्भवति यत् समिद्धो मित्रो होता वरुणो जातवेदाः ।
मित्रो अध्वर्युरिषिरो दमूना मित्रः सिन्धूनामुत पर्वतानाम् ॥

In this verse the previous statement about Agni as a friend *'mitraḥ'* has been elaborated. Agni, in 'any capacity and in any form' manifests himself to do friendly things for both, gods and men. The association of *Jātavedas* with Mitra-Varuna's duality is an indication of the same idea.

The word *iṣiraḥ*, which comes here for the first time in the third maṇḍala, is indicative of Agni's active role with the households who are suggested by the use of *damūnāḥ* 'the house-lord'. Because of his intimate association with the dwellings of men[18] Agni is *damūnāḥ.*[19]

RV. III. 5.5

पाति प्रियं रिपो अग्रं पदं वेः पाति यह्वश्चरणं सूर्यस्य ।
पाति नाभा सप्तशीर्षाणमग्निः पाति देवानामुपमादमृष्वः ॥

In this verse Agni has been extolled as protecting the entire world in which heavenly as well as earthly beings are bound together. The words like *ripaḥ, veḥ, agram padam, yahvaḥ, saptaśīrṣāṇam, upamādam, ṛṣvaḥ* connote some suggestive meanings here on which some of the interpreters do not have complete agreement.

Ripaḥ - This finally accented form occurs here and once at RV 10.79.3 The oxytone bearing form *ripaḥ* occurs four times in the RV (2.32.2; 7.32.12; 60.9; 104.18). In both the places *ripaḥ* has been explained by Sāyaṇa as *'pṛthivyaḥ'* of the Earth'. But *ripaḥ* has been explained by Sāyaṇa as *'hiṁsā'*, 'injury, hate' etc. This creates doubts whether both the forms belong to the same stem, or, are altogether different. Sāyaṇa has not offered any derivational explanation for it. Veṅkaṭamādhava's[20] explanation of *ripaḥ* varies from Sāyaṇa's interpretation. He renders it *'śabdayataḥ'* (*pakṣiṇaḥ*) 'of the tattering birds' which is not clear. But his explanation of oxytonic *ripaḥ* is almost the same as Sāyaṇa has offered. He explains it as *'hiṁsakaḥ'*[21] 'injurers'.

Veṅkaṭamādhava and Sāyaṇa explaining *ripaḥ* at RV 3.5.5 and 10.79.3 have followed Nighaṇṭu[22] where *ripaḥ* is attested as a synonym of 'earth'. But this meaning does not suit the contexts, therefore should be forthrightly rejected.

Böhtlingk and Roth[23] following Sāyaṇa, attest the meanings of *rip*-fam. (from *rip*) as 'Betrug' (deceit); Kniff (trick), 'Betruger' (deceiver) and 'Erde' (earth). Grassmann[24] and Wackern[25] have followed these meanings. According to them the root-meanings are 'schmieren'. (grease, to smear), 'Kerben' (adhere, stick), 'betrügen' (deceive). Wackern compares it with GK (fatty, greasy).[26]

So far as the meanings of oxytonic *ripaḥ* as 'deceit, injury' etc. are concerned, which can be exemplified by the contexts like RV. 4.5.5 *patiripo na janayo* (like the women deceiving their husbands) and RV 7.32.12 *ya indro harivān na dabhanti tam ripo.* (Indra, who is possessed of horses, is not deceived by his enemies), there is no doubt about the derivation and other such problems. *Ripaḥ* can be derived from the root *rip* - (*hiṁsavancanalepanadisu* 'to injure, deceive, besmear'), but *ripaḥ* is problematic.

Here it may be proposed that *ripaḥ* is actually *rupaḥ.*[27] This assertion is based on the comparison of similar contexts. Some of them are being quoted here:

RV 3.5.5 (present context): *pāti priyam ripo agram padam veḥ*

RV 4.5.8 *pāti priyam rupo agram padam veḥ*

RV 4.5.7 *sasasya carmannadhi cāru pṛśneragre rupa ārupitam jabāru*

RV 3.7.7 *adhvaryubhiḥ pañcabhiḥ sapta viprāḥ*
priyam rakṣante nihitam padam veḥ.

Among these passages RV 3.5.5 and 4.5.8 are almost the same except the word *ripaḥ* and *rupaḥ* which can be altered easily. rupaḥ at 4.5.7 can be put parallely with *rupo agram* (4.5.8) and *ripaḥ agram* (3.5.5). *agram padam veḥ* at RV 3.5.5 is parallel to *agram padam veḥ* at 4.5.8 and *ghrtavat padam veḥ* at 3.5.8 as well as (*priyam rakṣante*) *nihitam padam veḥ* at 3.7.7.

Through these parallelism this point emerges clearly that *ripaḥ* and *rupaḥ* are the same. Now which one could be the possible reading is the main problem. As the occurrences of *rupaḥ* are more in number and at the same time it goes well with the contexts, it seems plausible to accept *rupaḥ* at 3.5.5. and 10.79.3. The *ripaḥ* in the sense of injury etc. does not fit well at these places, and other meanings, like 'earth' are also not applicable.

But what is the meaning and etymology of *rupaḥ*? Wackernagel[28] and others have reconstructed *rupaḥ* from *rup* identical with *rupyati* in *Taittirīya-brāhmaṇa*[29] and *ruppati* in Pali which means 'to fear, pull, suffer' etc., and which was later on changed into '*rup*'. They have identified it with Latin *rumpo.* But this view seems untenable, because if we have to trace back *rup,* why not with the *rup* which is found in *ropaṇa, āropaṇa* - etc., and which consequently means 'to put, plant, establish' and so on. Thus here *rupa* will be formed with *rup* + *ac* = *rupa,* being *cit* it gets tone; and means 'emplanted, established'. Here Sāyaṇa and others have taken *rupaḥ* as the form of Gen. sg., but is actually agent noun here and is in nom. sg. Thus *pati priyam rupaḥ agram padam veḥ* 'the emplanted Agni protects the dear and lofty place (heaven, here Vedi) of the bird (sun). The same meaning and nom. sg. form can be applied in all the contexts,[30] namely, RV 4.5.7; 8; 10.79.3. This assertion is more strengthened by the fact that in the contexts cited above, namely, 3.5.6; 7 *agniḥ* stands as the subject which can be equated with *rupaḥ.*

Veḥ - The literal meaning of *veḥ* (gen. sg. of *vi* - bird) is 'of the bird' which might be intended here by the poet, because Agni protects the birds in the sky, but the suggestive meaning appears to relate it with *sūryasya* in b, which can be compared with the similar conext RV. 3.54.6. Sāyaṇa's explication *'gantyāḥ sarvabyāptāyāḥ'* 'gong or pervading all round' (the earth) is literally all right, but his construing it with *ripaḥ* (according to him 'each') is not plausible, because 'the foremost foot' (of the earth) does not creat a poetical propriety here, rather with the sun it beautifies more and more the poetic sensibilities of the Vedic poets. Veṅkaṭamādhava's rendering *'śabdayataḥ pakṣiṇaḥ* is not clear.

Max Müller's[31] doubt about the phrase *agram padam veḥ* as 'a description of sunrise' actually accentuates this point more that *priyam agram padam veḥ* is a picture of the first beautiful rays of the sun whom Agni protects rising himself in the morning. Bergaigne's[32] as well as Oldenberg's[33] interpretation of this pāda is not plausible. Geldner's[34] explanation of *padam veḥ* as 'the lofty place of Varuṇa' on the basis of RV 1.25.7 (who *Varuṇa* knows the place of the birds flying through the sky) is not upto the mark. How *Varuṇa* can be 'bird' here on that basis is not clear. Renou's[35] explanation of *veḥ* as 'de l'oiseau (solaire)' - (solar bird) is far better that others. Velankar's[36] annotation of *padam veḥ* as *'antarikṣa'* or the 'heaven where the sun moves' is nearer to the point explained above. Thus it is clear that *veḥ*[37] refers to the 'sun' and *'priyam agraṁ padam'* his 'course' or 'sky'.

Saptaśīrṣāṇam - This comp. occurs only twice in the RV (13.5.5; 8.51.4). Sāyaṇa explains it as *'marudgaṇam'* 'host of the Maruts'. Veṅkaṭamādhava[38] renders it with *'saptadhiṣṇva śīraskam yajñaṁ'* the sacrifice having its seven heads in the form of *dhiṣṇva*'. Naturally his interpretation is accentuated by the predilection for sacrificial connection with the verses, otherwise with *'sūryasya caraṇam'* 'food of the sun' there is no need of attaching any sacrificial meaning with the verse. If we add suggestive meaning with *'sapta'* why not with all other words? Therefore, Veṅkaṭamādhava's interpretation does not seem tenable. So far as Sāyaṇa's explication *marud* is concerned that is also doubtful. At RV. 8.51.4 (*Khila Sūkta*) Sūrya has been assigned with this epithet, and Indra's attribute as *'saptaraśmi'* (RV 2.12.12; 18.1) also indicates that *saptaśīrṣāṇaṁ* here stands either for Sūrya or for Indra. Indra is the God of mid-region, and this goes well with *nābhā* (in the mid region) on the present verse. Therefore, the explanation *marud* offered by Sāyaṇa is not suitable. Max Müller's[39] explanation of *saptās* as 'the *vraja* of Paṇi, opened by Agni', is entirely wrong, because here *saptās* is directly connected with *nābhā* which refers to sky, and moreover, Agni does not open it, rather he 'protects it' (*pāti*), the fact which cannot be ignored here. Bergaigne[40] explication of this as 'a group of seven priests (celuiqui a sept tetes est sans doubt un personnage equivalent a lui seul au groupe des sept pretres) is ingenious. Not only this but even Oldenberg's[40] interpretation of it as connected with litergy is also not plausible. Geldner[41] follows Oldenberg, and Renou has nothing to offer new. His rendering of *nābhā* as im Nabel (at the navel) is correct, but its implied meaning 'navel of the earth' is doubtful. Velankar[42] follows Renou in translating it, but his annotation is marked by the same remarks as given by Oldenberg and Geldner. All of them seem to be obsessed with the litergical predilection in interpreting this *ṛk*.

Upamādam - This occurs only here in the RV According to Sāyaṇa it means *upamādakam yajñam* 'exhilerating sacrifice' which is in complete confirmity of Veṅkaṭamādhava's rendering *'upamādayitāram yajñam'*, Geldner and others have followed this interpretation, but their annotation about *upam* being Soma seems plausible. Renou[43] compares it with *sādhamāda.*

Rayaḥ-Sāyaṇa, following Veṅkaṭamādhava has explained it as *darśaṇīyaḥ* 'beautiful', 'graceful', but he has construed it with *agniḥ* which is syntactically incorrect. As *agniḥ* is the subject in the third pāda, *ṛṣvaḥ* (though standing for Agni) is the subject of *pāti* in the fourth pāda; and thus it should be construed only with *pāti,* and not with *agnih.* In all the four pādās there are four verbal forms, i.e. *pāti* (four times repeated), and with all these forms there are four agents, i.e. *ripaḥ (rūpaḥ), yahavaḥ, agniḥ* and *ṛṣvaḥ.* Their separate usage has some special connotation. The first *rūpaḥ* 'settled' or 'emplanted' goes well with *padam* 'place' (of establishment or settlement), while *yahavaḥ* 'the grate' is compatible with the lofty sun (*sūryasya*). *Agniḥ* in the third pāda is connected with *saptaśīrṣāṇam,* because he himself is *saptajihva-* (3.6.2) and *saptaraśmiḥ* (2.5.2; 3.1.4; 6.35c); and *ṛṣvaḥ* has complete identity with Soma (*upamādam*) because both of them are possessed with beautiful form, ie. *ṛṣvaḥ* (5.5.7; 10; 9.89.4). Thus the sublime effect of the usages cannot be denied by construing these words with each other. They should remain intact.

Etymologically ***ṛṣva***- comes from *ṛṣ. arṣ*- to flow or move quickly, to pierce, penetrate deeply and so on, which is identical with *gav.* 'to go up' from which comes 'standing high' - Originally this root is *i* or *ṛ*- 'to go' as found in *inoti* and Avestan *isaiti* 'sends forth', and thus it may be extended to go upward.[44] From this point of view *ṛṣva* may be interpreted in many ways as 'lofty, great, going upward, penetrating, piercing' and so on.

The verse may be rendered as follows:

"The implanted one (Agni) protects the dear and foremost foot of the bird (the sun or Viṣṇu), the great one protects the pace of the Sun; Agni guards the seven headed (Indra) in the midregion, and the graceful one protects the exhileration of the gods, i.e. Soma".

RV. III. 5.6

ऋभुश्चंक्र ईड्यं चारु नाम विश्वांनि देवो वयुनांनि विद्वान् ।
ससस्य चर्म घृतवंत् पदं वेस्तदिदग्नी रंक्षत्यप्रंयुच्छन् ॥

Sāyaṇa differs with Veṅkaṭamādhava on the meaning of *ṛbhuḥ, cāru, sasasya,* and *ghṛtavat.* Others have either followed Sāyaṇa or expressed doubts on some points or other.

Ṛbhuḥ - The word *ṛbhu* - occurs frequently in the RV (1.20.4.51.2; 110.7; 2.1.10; 3.5.6; 36.2; 54.12; 60.2; 4; 4.33.5; 6.3.9.7.48.2; 9.21; 6 etc.) either as an epithet to Agni (2.1.10; 3.5.6; 6.3.6), Indra (10.23.2), Soma (9.21.6), or as a name of a group of minor deities who are called *ṛbhavaḥ* and have been referred to in eleven hymns of the RV. Later on they have been mentioned as the three sons of the poet Sudhanvan Aṅgiras.[45] Here the word stands as an attributive qualificator of Agni. Veṅkaṭamādhava[46] explains it as *'dīptaḥ'*, 'shining', but Sāyaṇa gives its meaning *'mahān'*, 'great', though at other places he also renders it with *'bhasamānaḥ medhāvī vā'*, 'shining or genius'. The explanation is certainly based on the etymological exegesis of Yāska[47] which in itself seems faulty.[48]

Etymologically as *ṛṣva* is from *ṛṣ* so *ṛbhu* is from *ṛbh.* The word *ṛṣva* can be put parallely with *ṛbhva,* and *ṛsu* (RV 1.127.10) with *ṛbhu.* Again it can be equated with *vibhu* and *prabhu* (RV 1.9.5). Now there are two possibilities of deriving *ṛbhu*-one is from a supposed *ṛbh* with *u* suffix (Pa. 3.2.180) and other is from-ṛ + *bhu* as *vi* + *bhu* in *vibhu* and *pra* + *bhu* in *prabhu;* but the first possibility is more plausible on the anology of *ṛsi, ṛsabha, ṛsva* etc. Moreover, in *vibhu* - and *prabhu* the first members are the known prefixes which are called *gati,* while in *ṛbhu ṛ* cannot be prefix, and there is no justification for deriving this word from two roots together which may fall in the line of Yāskan etymology giving no proper derivational validity. Therefore, it is presumed that a *ṛbh* existed in Vedic language which lost its existant role due to some unknown factors. Some scholars have derived *rbha* from *ṛabh.* 'to be skilful' which seems absurd, because the derivation from *rabh* - is unsound due to change of *rabh* to *ribh* rather from *ṛbh* - it may be sound; and *ṛbh* - may be changed into *arbh* as some other possible changes are known to the Vedic language, for example changes from *ṛs* to *arṣ; ṛc* to *arc; gṛbh* to *garbh; kṛt* to *kart; gṛt* to *gart* and so on. Thus on the basis of these anologies, it can be surmized that *ṛbh* is very much possible which can be seen in the word *arbha* and *arbhaka* -. Though some scholars have derived *arbha* - from *ṛ* with primary suffix - *bha* - which has been determined by Uṇādi-sūtra 3.152 *artigṛbhyam bhan,* but in this derivation the possible meaning is not certain; because *ṛ* means 'to go', and the meaning of *gṛbhaka* and *arbha* seems to be 'small' in comparison with *mahat* with which it occurs always in the RV. Moreover, it can be identified with Lat. Orbus (deprive of, divest of and Arm. *Ord* (orphan) which confirms the meaning of *'arbha* and *arbhaka'* as 'small' (klein). Here one may question the validity of accentuation, because *ṛbhu* is always finally accented while *arbha* and *arbhaka* are initially accented which is confirmed by suffix *bhan* having *n* as an *it* and due to it, it should take accute accent on the first syllable by Pāṇinian rule *ñnityādir nityam* (6.1.197), but this can be answered that all such formations which are governed by the rule *uraṇraparaḥ* (Pans. 1.1.51) have the tendency of taking accute accent on the first syllable, which can be exemplified by *karta, garta, karma, garbha, marta* and so forth. On this anology *arbha* - and *arbhaka* can be initially accented.

Cāru - The word cāru has been explained by Sāyaṇa as *'manojñam'* "pleasant". Veṅkaṭamādhava gives its meaning *'kalyāṇam',* 'favourable'. Both of them construe it with *nāma* which is explained by them as *udakam* "water" on the basis of Yāska. But *cārunāma* is a common phrase in the RV used for the Gods and can be placed parallely with *priyam nāma* (7.56.10: Maruts; 9.75.1: Soma; 10.85.5: Manyu; 10.123.7: Gandharva) which connotes the idea of 'beloved, dear' and so on. But as *cāru* occurs as an adjective to *atithiḥ* (2.2.8-Agni himself), *adhvara* (1.19.1; 9.44.4) and gods it may mean "beloved, precious, esteemed, valued, dear" and so on, and it can be identified with Latin *carus* which bears the same meaning. Lüders[49] connects it with the cosmic *ṛta* and remarks "das Beiwort caru - ist charaktaristisch fur das kosmisch *ṛta.* (Es) spricht fur die Baziehung auf ile kosmische Wahrheit". But this view is doubtful. Geldner[50] gives its meanings gern geschehen, teueren, liebling" etc. Renou[51] renders it with "précieux" (precious), and Thieme[52] with "lieh" (dear). Thus in all meanings "dear, gracious, beautiful, precious, esteemed, beloved, engagings the affections, inspiring sympathy" and so on can be assigned to *cāru* in various contexts.[53]

So far as its derivation is concerned it is quite doubtful. Sāyaṇa, derives it from *car* with *ñuṇ* suffix (*dṛsanijani-caricaṭibhyo ñuṇ* - Un. S. 1.3) in which *ñ* and *u* are indicatory, and due to indicatory *ñ* it will take acute accent on the initial syllable. In this way *cāru* means 'one who walks' which is unacceptable. Grammatically *cāru* is nearer to *kāru,* and as *kṛ kar* inter alia means 'to praise, sing'. The *car* also may mean 'to love, praise, esteem, honour' and so on. Besides, as *kāyamānaḥ* and *cāyamānaḥ* connote the similar idea *kāru* - and *cāru* may also be taken nearer to each other due to their inherent meaning and grammatical formations. The suffix *uṇ* in *kāru* is similar to *ñuṇ* in *cāru* making the difference of only which stands indicate the initial acute accent. Thus *kāru-karu:* as a substantive means 'who praises' and *cāru* 'praiseworthy'. The same meaning has been extended in various connotations in different contexts.

Vayunāni - *vayunāni* has been explained by Veṅkaṭamādhava as *'praiṇānani'* and by Sāyaṇa *'jñtavyāni padārthāni'* matters worthy of knowing' which indicates the difference of views. The meaning given by Sāyaṇa precludes "other matters, i.e. which are not worthy of knowing". This creates another notion that Agni does not know many things. But this is not true with Agni, because he is all-knowing god, which is obviously clear with *viśvāni* as an adjective to *vayunāni* in the present context. Actually *vayunani* refers to the 'ritual ways' which are completely known to Agni.[54]

Sasasys which occurs four times in the RV (3.5.6; 4.5.7; 4.7.7; 5.21.4) has been explained here as *svapataḥ śantajvālasyāpyagneḥ* "even of sleeping and pacified Agni" by Sāyaṇa. Veṅkaṭamādhava explicates it as *'svapataḥ sthavarasya'*, "sleeping and unmoving (creatures)" in which *sthavarasya* gives quite different notion. Thus both of them appear at a loss in clarifying the exact meaning of the pāda.

Sasasya carman produces some mystic element about Agni. Compared to other contexts like *sasasya carmannadhi cāru preśneḥ* 4.5.7; *sasaya yad viyutā sasminnūndhan nṛtasya dhāman raṇayanta devāḥ* 4.7.7; *sasasya yonimasadaḥ* - 5.21.4 etc. *sasasya* is parallel to *ṛtasya;* and thus it indicates some location. As *ṛtasya* is related with *dhāman* "location of power" so *sasasāy* is related with *padam* and *yonim.* Thus it connotes two things together, namely, the location of water, i.e. mid-region, and location of fires, i.e. sacrificial place. *Sasaysa carman* in the present context can be compared with *sasasya ūdhan* in 4.7.7; and both of these contexts indicate the "rain-water" connected with the mid-region. *Veḥ* in the present context also means 'clouds' or 'water' which goes and pervades the sky. Thus *sasasya carman* mystically means 'rain-clouds which are helpful in the growth of 'grass', 'the literal meaning of *sasa.* In the context of sacrificial setting *'sasasya carman'* connotes the idea of *barhiṣ* which are strewn on the ground sprinkled with water. Agni protects them.

Further, *veḥ* may refer here to the sun whose 'course' (*padam*) which is full of 'rain' or 'brilliance' (*ghṛtavad*) is protected by Agni. However, even in this context *padam veḥ* together seems to suggest the mid-region (*antarikṣa*) where water originates and helps in the growth of the 'grass' (sasa). All these meanings can be assigned to the *pāda.*

Sasasya yonim and *ṛtasya yonim* in 5.21.4 also refer to the location of the water suggestively though they are meant for the sacrificial place also. But everything is enjoined with mystic way of expression in such contexts, and the exact meaning is not possible without elaboration of the inherent theme.

RV. III. 5.7

आ योनिंमग्निर्घृतवंन्तमस्थात् पृथुप्रंगाणमुशन्तंमुशानः ।
दीद्यांनः शुचिंर्ऋष्वः पांवकः पुनःपुनर्मातरा नव्यंसी कः ॥

Yonim ghṛtavantam should be interpreted in the context of *sasasya carma ghṛtavad padam* as explained above. Sāyaṇa explains it here as *'dīptimantam sthānamāyatanam'* of the shining place' which is similar to Veṅkaṭamādhava's interpretation of it as *'udakavantam sthānam'*. The first two pādas refer to the first-place on the altar literally, but mystically they refer to the place of water, i.e. sky; because the forth pāda refers to the two worlds or parents of Agni whom he makes ever new. In other words it can be surmized that Agni causes rains by which the green grass making the earth new; and the sky becomes new by the clouds.

Uśantam uśānaḥ has been explained by Sāyaṇa and Veṅkaṭamādhava as *"kāmayamānaḥ*', 'desiring the desirous' which seems deceptive, because 'to shine' which is more probable here in the context of Agni than the meaning 'to desire'. Thus the renderings 'den verlangenden' (eagerly longing for the eagerly desirous - Geldner, followed by Velankar) and "desirant (Agni qui lui-meme le) desire" (Renou) can be accepted.

Pṛthupragāṇam, which appears only here, has been explained by Sāyaṇa as *'pṛthugītim'* having wide praise'. Veṅkaṭamādhava explicates it as *'pṛthupragāmānam vistīrṇāvakāśam'* amply spacious place' which is more probable in the context of *yonim* 'resting place, altar'. Geldner's rendering 'mit breitem Zugang' (with vide access) also accepts the same notion of 'wide space' which has been followed by Renou[55] (large ' acce's) and Velankar[56] (amply spacious).

RV. III. 5.8

सद्यो जात ओषंधीभिर्ववक्षे यदी वर्धन्ति प्रस्वों घृतेनं ।
आपं इव प्रवता शुम्भंमाना उरुष्यदग्निः पित्रोरुपस्थें ॥

The use of passive ***'oṣadhībhir vavakṣa'*** is significant here. This refers to the 'wild-fire' which grows in the forest through the plants and creeps. At the same time they also grow by the rain. The second pāda has been construed and explained by Sāyaṇa with the third and the fourth pādās but there is no necessity to construe it with cd, because it is in itself a separate syntactical unit and should be interpreted solely. *Prasvaḥ* refers to the grown plants which grow more by the rain (*ghṛtena*) which comes through Agni. In the summer Agni burns all the wild plants and just after that they grow profusely when rain comes. The same idea has been expressed here in the second *pāda.* The third *pāda* refers to the lightening-course of Agni who shines and grows in the lap of the parents (sky and earth)[57] like the rains or streams shining in the way. "Waters rushing over a slope display a bright glow on their surface'[58] as is clear from *apām na urmavo rusantaḥ* at RV 6.64.2.

Uruṣyat - *uruṣyat* has been explained by Sāyaṇa as *'asmān rakṣatu'*, 'protect us' which is similar to Veṅkaṭamādhava's explanation *'rakṣati'*, 'protects'. But, here it seems to indicate the extending activity of Agni and could be taken near to *uru* 'wide'. Though traditionally *urṣayati* has been taken to mean 'to protect' (*urusyati rakṣakarmā*) Nir. 5.23, yet it seems to originate from *uru* 'wide', then extended to mean 'widening '. As *urṣyat* here stands for Agni himself. The meaning 'protection' is not suitable, hence, the sense 'has extended himself' prevails.

RV. III. 5.9

उदुं ष्टुतःसुमिधां युह्वो अंद्यौद् वर्ष्मंन् दिवो अधि नाभां पृथिव्याः।
मित्रो अग्निरीड्यों मातरिश्वा ऽऽदूतो वंक्षद् यजथांय देवान् ॥

The second pāda of the verse refers to Agni in the form of the Sun.[59] On the naval of the earth (*adhi nābhā pṛthivyāḥ*) Agni is displayed as the sacrificial fire, but *divaḥ varṣman adyaut* 'cose on the body of the heaven' clearly dipicts the Sun. Mitrah and Mātariśvan are also the forms of celestial Agni (*mātariśvā yadamimīta mātari*[60] *samidhā* may refer here to the 'flaring up' as Velankar thinks, but it serves the purpose of sacrificial *samidhā* also by which Agni shines, Sāyaṇa explains it as *'samindhanena'* by *'samidh'*.[61]

RV. III. 5.10

उदंस्तम्भीत् सुमिधा नाकंमृष्वो३ ऽग्निर्भवंन्नुत्तमो रोंचनानांम् ।
यदी भृगुंभ्यः परिं मातरिश्वा गुहा सन्तं हव्यवाहं समीधे ॥१०॥

इळांमग्ने पुरुदंसं सनिं गोः शंश्वत्तमं हवंमानाय साध ।
स्यान्नंः सूनुस्तनंयो विजावा ऽग्ने सा तें सुमतिर्भूत्वस्मे ॥ ११ ॥

Rocanānām refers to the luminaries, i.e. all the gods in the heaven among whom Agni is the best and the greatest (*uttāmaḥ*). This form *rocanānām* occurs only here in the RV. *Rocaneṣu* occurs at 6.44.23 (*divi rocaneṣu triteṣu*) where again it refers to gods. The explanation of Sāyaṇa there as *'rocamāneṣu tritīye sthāne tateṣu deveṣu* is more plausible and can be extended in the present context also.

Mātariśvā in the third pāda refers to the Wind by which Agni is enkinled in the altar which has been referred here as *guhā*. Sāyaṇa construes *uttamaḥ rocanānām* with *mātariśvā* which seems deceptive, because the third pāda has no syntactical relation with the second. Moreover, *uttamaḥ* has direct relation with *agniḥ*.

Bhṛgubhyaḥ is in dative for whom *Mātariśvān* brought Agni (see RV 1.60. 1d).[62]

NOTES

1. *RV Commentaries* III, p. 1299.
2. RV 3.5.1; 9.96.6; 18.
3. *Loc. cit.*
4. Sāyaṇa-bhāṣya on RV 3.5.2
5. *RV M.* III, p. 16.
6. *EVP*, Vol. III, p. 54.
7. Sāyaṇa explicates this compound as *'ṛtārtham Yajñārtham jātasca tāḥ satyāṇ satyaphalāsca tādṛsyaḥ'*. The comp. comes only here, and as I think it means the *Ṛta*, and true because of their 'origin from truth and omnipresence'.
8. For details on the repetitions of similar phraseologies to express similar thoughts see J. Gonda, *Stylistic Repetition in the Veda* (Amsterdam 1959), p. 128 ff.
9. RV 10.88.10; *stomena hi divi devāso agnim ajījanat*
   RV 3.2.9; *tāsāmekāmadadhurmartye* -
   RV 1.96.1 cd; *āpaśca mitraṁ dhiṣaṇā ca sādhan devā agnim dhārayan draviṇodām*
10. RV 3.1.17; 18; 4.1.9; 16.3; 6.66.7; 1.96.
11. See Karl Brugmann, *A Comparative Grammar* II, p. 226.
12. See Wacker. Debr. *Alt. Gramm.* II, 2.0.168.
13. *Worterbuch Zum Ṛigveda*, p. 1652.
14. *The Roots*, p. 203.

15. See S.S. Bhave, *Soma Hymns*, II, p. 41.
16. For *viprah* and *matinam* see J. Gonda, *The Vision*, pp. 13; 36f.
17. *sānu* may be here the summit of the *Ṛta* which is universal and fundamental order, harmony and structural unity, the ultimate "truth" on which the world and ritual is founded'. For *ṛta* see J. Gonda, *Die Religionen Indiens*, I. P. 77 ff.
18. For an elaborate explication of this idea see J. Gonda, *Epithets in* the *Ṛgveda*, p. 94 f.
19. Sāyaṇa and Veṅkaṭamādhava explain damūnās as '*dānamanā dāntamanā vā* and *dāmamanā* respectively, which are not acceptable to modern scholars for details see discussion of 3.1.11.
20. *Loc. cit.*
21. *op. cit.* (on RV 2.32.2).
22. Nigh. 1.1
23. Sanskrit Wörterbuch
24. *Wort* p. 1165.
25. Wackernagel-Debrunner, *Alt. Gramm* I, p. 210.
26. *Ibid.* 112 p. 471; 853 f.
27. See Geldner, *Der RV. III*, p. 341, see this possible supposition of replacing *ripo* by *rūpo.*
28. Wackernagel-Debrunner, *Altind. Gramm.* 1, pp. 63; 98, 219; Karl Brugmann, *Comp. Gramm.*, I, p. 208.
29. TB. 2.1.1.2.
30. Sāyaṇa explains everywhere *ripaḥ* and *rūpaḥ* as *pṛthivyāḥ* 'of earth' and nowhere he cares about the subject of the verbal forms like *pāti* and *avidyat rūpaḥ* is the subject everywhere.
31. SBE, 46, p. 242.
32. *Religion Vedique,* II, p. 77 ff.
33. *SBE,* 46, p. 240.
34. *RV. Ubersetz,* I, p. 341.
35. *EVP XII,* p. 54.
36. *RV M.* III, p. 117.
37. cf. RV 1.25.7.
38. See commentary of Vaṅkatamādhava on RV 3.5.5
39. SBE, 46, p. 145.
40. *op. cit.*, p. 242. Oldenberg thinks that *saptas* at RV 8.51.4 is an epithet of words which signify 'hymn' (prayer), but the word *arkam* there evidently stands for the sun and not for 'hymn'.

41. *Loc. cit.*
42. *Loc. cit.*, p. 17 f.
43. Renou, *EVP XII*, p. 115. Renou equates *upamadam* with *sādhmādam* doubtfully, which gives the clue that *upamadam* has a close connection with the intoxication. *Sādhmāda*, a substantive, may refer to the place of sacrifice where the poets share soma-beverage with the gods as at RV 3.35.4; 43.3, or to the sharer of this pleasures as at RV 1.121.15; 5.20.4, or sharing of soma as at RV 4.23.2, or to Soma itself as at RV. 8.2.28; 1.187.11. Similarly *upamādam* may be interpreted for place, person and Soma. But as in the *ṛk sūrya*, and other gods have been referred clearly here. Soma will be more suitable.
44. See Grassmann, *Worterbuch*, p. 294; Karl Brugmann, *Comparative Grammar* II, 216; 345; IV. 193; Wackernagel, *Altind. Gramm.* I, 56; II 870; S. Varma, *Ety. of Yaska*, p. 55.
45. Macdonell, *Vedic Mythology*.
46. *op. cit.*, p. 1301.
47. Yāska, *Nir.* 11.151.
48. S. Varma, *op. cit.*, p. 106.
49. H. Lüders, *Varuna*, p. 602 and n. 1.
50. *RV. Obersetz* I, p. 341; 279.
51. *EVP XII*, p. 54.
52. P. Thieme, *Der Fremdling in Rgveda*, Leipzig 1939, pp.19.
53. For details see J. Gonda, *Notes on names* and the *Name of God in Ancient India*, Amsterdam, London - 1970, pn.40 ff.
54. *Loc. cit.*
55. *Loc. cit.*
56. *Loc. cit.*
57. Cf. H.P. Schmidt, *Brhaspati and Indra*, p. 69 f.
58. Geldner's supposition 'the *arani*'.
59. See Velankar, *Loc. cit.* fn.
60. See also Nir., 7.26 - '*mātaryantarikṣe śvasiti, mātaryāśvanitīti vā*'.
61. Velankar's statement that Sāyaṇa construes *samidh* as an ablative' is strange, because *samindhanena* is not ablative but instrumental.
62. See Velankar, *Loc. cit.* fn.

***

The Ṛgveda Maṇḍal III.6

Traditionally this hymn belongs to a particular sacrificial formula and is employed with a *prātara anuvāka* (hymns to be recited in the morning litanies) in *Patnivrata* ritual. This has led to the almost all exegetists to interpret it with reference to sacrificial settings as is evident through the commentaries of Sāyaṇa and Veṅkaṭamādhava. Modern scholars have also followed the same pattern. But a close observation and analysis of the entire hymn reveals the fact that some of the verses depict the vivid picture of morning light in which the most charming Dawn rolls down to propitiate Agni. This fact could not attract the attention of any one of the exegetists which would have facilitated to understand the inherent meanings of the hymn as a whole. These indivation that the Uṣas plays a beautiful role here is revealed through the usages of many words as well as phrases in this hymn, which are particularly associated with Uṣas mythology, or belong to the epithetical group of those words which have been employed with Uṣas in the RV. This statement can be corroborated by the textual evidences of the present hymn compared with similar concepts or words like *vājinī* (*ṛk.* 1); *āskre sapatī - urugāyasya dhenū* (ṛk. 4); *divas cidā rokā uṣaso* (*ṛk.* 7); and *ṛtāvarī ṛtajātsya* (*ṛk.* 10). These can be compared with the other concept, words and phrases employed with Uṣas in the RV. Thus a fresh interpretation can be attempted through the study of the individual words and the phrases.

RV. III. 6.1

प्र का॑रवो मन॒ना व॒च्यमा॑ना देव॒द्रीचीं॑ नयत देव॒यन्तः॑ ।
द॒क्षि॒णा॒वाड् वा॒जिनी॒ प्राच्ये॑ति ह॒विर्भर॑न्त्य॒ग्नये॑ घृ॒ताची॑ ॥

In this verse the words *kāravaḥ, devadrīcīm, dakṣiṇavād-vājinī* and *ghṛtācī* are significant, for a new look to them would enable us to comprehend the meaning of the verse in a better way.

Kāravaḥ - The voc. sg. of *kāru* - occurs only here in the RV. Nom. pl. *kāravāḥ* occurs at several places. The etymology of *kāru*- seems ambigous. Sāyaṇa has tried to explain it from the *kṛ* with the Un. suffix - *uṇ (kṛvāpājimisvadi sādhyasūbhya uṇ*- Un. S. 1.1). There are three words of the same category, namely, *kāra*-, kārin and kāru, all of them bearing the acute accent on the final syllable. Sāyaṇa traces all of them to the *kṛ* with some variations of the sufixes only. So far as the frequency of their occurrences is concerned *kāru* - occurs fifty three times, *kāra* -nine times and kārin - seven times in the RV. By the time of the AV the usages are not very common. In the most of the later Vedic literature we find only the repetitions of the Ṛgvedic verses only. Therefore, a correct etymology cannot be ascertained only on the basis of the frequency of usages. All the usages in the RV are closely connected with some kind of singing activity, hence it seems natural to derive this word from a root which bears the meanings, "to sing, praise, eulogize" and so on. The *kṛ*. "to make, do, perform" can be applied on only one ground that there are references in the RV in which poets mention the poetic creation or making of new eulogies. They themselves are called *brahmakārā* (RV 6.29.4), "the creators of the words" and *brahmakṛtaḥ* "the poets" (RV 7.32.2; 10.50.7; 54.6; 66.5). Thus the *kṛ* can be extended into the *kir-kar* (for kārin).

Though due to the suffix *uṇ* (elision of *ṇ*) the *vṛddhi* is possible by Pan. S. 7.2.115 (*aco ñṇiti*) if we accept the elongated *kṛ* in the sense of "singing, praising" it would facilitate in solving the etymological intricacies of these words. From the *kṛ* we can form *kār* easily. The meaning "artisan" or "fashiner" must have been developed on the thesis that *kāru* - etymologically belonged to the *kṛ*, but this notion carries originally no weightage as seen in the contexts of the RV. Therefore, it is more plausible to derive *kāru* from the *kṛ*, "to praise, sing". Some one may argue here that even from the *kṛ* - *kar* the word *kāru* can be derived by the Pāṇinian rule *ata upadhāyāḥ* (Pā. S. 7.2.116) with the suffix *uṇ* as stated above. But in that case the meaning will remain only "artisan" which does not suit for all the contexts of the RV. Hence this will be more sound and solid to derive it from *kṛ* "to praise, sing" and confirm its meanings "singer, poet, eulogist" and so on.

Devadrīcim - This occurs only here, but a similar comp. *devadrīcā* occurs twice in the RV (1.93.8; 163.12). The words *rīci* and *rīcā* occur no where separately. The comp. *devardrīca* has been employed once with nom. dual. form *agnisoma* (Agni and soma) at RV 1.93.8, and at 1.163.12. It stands for the sg. form *arvā vāji*. Thus its formation and declensions are doubtful. But at RV 1.163.12 it has been employed in the way of stylistic repetition of the phrase *devadrīcā manasā* occurring at RV 1.93.8 without carrying the case-relationship. It indicates that the stems should be *devadrīc* - (m) and *devadrīcī* - (femn.); and thus *devadrīcā* must be the nom.-dual of the mas stem.

The comp. *devadrīcī* can be equated with *kadrīcī* (RV 1.164.17) and the formation can be explained with other similar words like *visvācī* (RV 7.43.3, 1.139.2), *purūcī* (RV 3.58.8; 10.18.8) *ghṛtācī* (RV 1.167.3) and Avest. *zairici* (form *zairi* "golden").

The derivation of *devadrīcā* creates problem, however we can make some attempt on the analogy of some similar words. There are some formations in *dry-anc, dryak, dric* and *drik* in the RV; like *madryañca* - (RV 7.24.13), *madryak* (RV 3.41.1; 6.38.2), *madrik.* (RV 1.177.1), *sadhrīcī* (RV 1.164.31) etc., and all the endings, viz. *dryañc* etc., originally of the same root. According to Pan. S. 6.3.92 *devadrīcī* can be analysed as *deva + dri + ac* or *añc + i.*

According to Pan. S. 6.3.95 *sahasya sadhriḥ* the word *saha* is changed into *sadhra,* but it appears linguistically illogical, because in that case the formations of *madryañca, madrik* etc. cannot be explained. According to Wackernagel-Debrunner these formations have *dry, dryak, dric,* and only from these adverbial bases we get such formations with the help of the root *ac* or *añc.* But if we observe closely all the formations *like sādhryañca sadhri, madryañca, madri, tadryañca* (JB 2, 4-26), *vadryañca* (MS), *devadryañca, asmadryañca* and so on. It can be analysed obviously that before the *ac- añc* there is prefix - *ri* - and not *dri.* For example we can analyse *sādhryañca* as *sādh + rik + añc, madryañc* as *mad + ri + anc; asmadryañc* as *asmad + ri + añc; yadryañc* as *yad + ri + añc, kadryañc* as *kad + ri + añc: devadryañc* as *devad + ri + añc,* and so on. Therefore, on the place of *dri, drik, dry,* as given by Wackarnagel-Debrunner are interchangeable to each other in accordance with the *sandhi* rules and vowel formations, *sadhry, madry* and *devadry* etc. are the changed forms of *sadhri; madri* and *devadri* = respectively due to the sandhi of *i + a* (*a* of *ac añc*). The *añc* or *ac* takes the suffix *a* (*kha* or *i nip*) accordingly to form *sadhrīcī* and so on. The *i* of *ri* - is lengthened, perhaps, to facilitate the pronunciation.

After a closer examination of these forms, it appears that the medial suffix *ri* - indicates the direction of the activity. Thus, *devadrīcī* would mean, "going or traversing towards the gods" which seems suitable in the present context also. Here *devadrīcīm* refers to Uṣas who traverses towards the gods in the east. In the context of the sacrifice it indicates the on going activity of the ladle which approaches the gods in the east.

Dakṣiṇāvāḍ- This refers to the ladle which brings *dakṣiṇā*, "gift" to the priest. However, its inherent meaning seems to be *dakṣiṇātaḥ ūhyamāna*, "called upon or brought to the southern part or from the right side of the *āhvanīya* fire". Veṅkaṭamādhava also paraphases it in the same manner *yuyam apareṇa āhavanīyam dakṣiṇohyana ṇa sruk adhvaryubhiḥ hriyamāṇa*. But both these explications seem lacking the essence of the real meaning of the compound. On the analogy of *havirvaṭ* (RV 1.72.7), *havyavaḍ* (RV 1.12.6; 67.1; 3.2.2; 11.2; 27.5; 5.4.3 etc) and *madhyamavāt* (RV. 2.29.4) other it should mean "carrying *dakṣiṇā*", or "carrying towards south or brought from or to the right side", but the previous meaning seems more plausible. *Dakṣiṇāvāt* stands here as an adj. to *ghṛtācī*, "shining like *ghṛta* or bringing *ghṛta*". It may be interpreted in favour of Uṣas who is shining and brilliant.

The morning litany expressly brings the Uṣas in the context. Though the sacrificial settings refer to the particular objects yet poetically the objects are connected with the natural phenomenon which seems to be Uṣas here and none else.

RV. III. 6.2

आ रोद॑सी अपृणा॒ जाय॑मान उ॒त प्र रि॑क्था॒ अध॒ नु प्र॑यज्यो ।
दि॒वश्चि॑दग्ने महि॒ना पृ॑थि॒व्या व॒च्यन्तां॑ ते॒ वह्न॑यः स॒प्तजि॑ह्वाः ॥

The first pāda of this *ṛk* has been repeated at RV 7.13.2b and RV 10.75.6b. It indicates that Agni pervades the entire universe as seen as he is born. He is larger than the universe and cannot be contained in it. We can compare here the *Puruṣa* who pervades the earth and goes beyond it - *sa bhūmiṁ viśvato vṛtvātyatiṣṭhaddaśāṅgulam* "pervading the entire earth from all directions he (*Puruṣa*) stood up ten *aṅgulās*".

Thus here also the cosmic activity of Agni has been exemplified. The verbal form (*pra* -) *rikthāḥ* (pf. of *ric* "to excel") gives the sense of "surprising". The second pāda is to be constructed with the third pāda due to the use of *mahinā* by greatness "which is instrumental in surpassing others."

Vahnayaḥ - refers to the varied forms of Agni who manifests in many things as well as with many names like *Tanūnapāt, Vaisvānar* and so on. *Saptajihvaḥ* signifies the seven colours of Agni's flames. There is nothing controversial in this *ṛk*.

RV. III. 6.3

द्यौश्चं त्वा पृथिवी यज्ञियांसो नि होतांरं सादयन्ते दमांय ।
यदी विशो मानुंषीर्देवयन्तीः प्रयंस्वतीरीळंते शुक्रमर्चिः ॥

Yajñiyāsaḥ refers here to the gods as explained by Sāyaṇa. We can compare it with RV 10.53.2: *yajāmahai yajñiyan hanta devāṅ* and RV 10.88.13: *vaisvānaraṁ kavayo yajñiyāso'gnim devā ajanayannajuryam* here refers to the sacrificial place where Agni is placed ceremoniously. The use of dative here seems to refer to Agni's own residence which he may take gladly. *Śukramarciḥ* refers to Agni's brilliant rays which can be compared with RV 8.44.4

ut te bṛhanto arcayaḥ samidhānasya dīdivaḥ
agne sukrāsa īrate /

"O luminous Agni, vast and bright thy rays upwards ascend as thou art enkindled high".

RV. III. 6.4

महान् त्सधस्थे ध्रुव आ निषत्तो ऽन्तर्द्यावा माहिने हर्यमाणः ।
आस्क्रे सपत्नीं अजरे अमृंक्ते सबर्दुघे उरुगायस्यं धेनू ॥

The multitudinous facets of Agni's personality are revealed in this ṛk through the words like ***dhruvaḥ*** and ***haryamāṇaḥ***. Sāyaṇa explains *haryamāṇḥ* as *Kāmayamānaḥ*, "desiring". The root *hary* - implies two meanings, namely, "to desire" and "to move or go" (*haryakāntigatyoh*); and thus Sāyaṇa's explanation can be accepted on one ground and rejected on another. But as Agni is always mobile in between the Heaven and the Earth the second meaning, i.e. "moving on" is more plausible. On the basis of his word economy theory.

Velankar[1] thinks that *dhruvaḥ* stands also for the loc. *dhruva*[2] but there is no need to construe it twice. Similarly *haryamāṇaḥ* is only a participle and should not be taken as a finite verb or supplied with *īyate*,[3] because *ānisattaḥ* serves the purpose of the finite verb. And thus, the first two *pādā*-s may be rendered as, "moving between the heaven and the earth the mighty and firm (Agni) is well - seated in (his) residence".

The third and the fourth *pādā*-s refer to the Heaven and the earth as stated by Geldner. This can be substantiated by RV 1.95.1; 96.5; 3.1.10 where Agni is mentioned as the calf of these two celestial cows.

The meaning of ***āskre*** is doubtful. According to Sāyaṇa it means *ākramaṇaśīle* "attacking or overpowering nature" but Veṅkaṭamādhava renders it as *āskrandanasil*, "pouring, sprinkling". Modern scholars identify it with Avestan *āskreiti* "connection" and assign it the meanings "united, joined". But the etymology remains still ambiguous.[4]

Sabar in *sabardughe*, has been traditionally accepted as the synonym of *payaḥ* "milk".

RV. III. 6.5

व्रता ते अग्ने महतो महानि तव क्रत्वा रोदसी आ ततन्थ ।
त्वं दूतो अभवो जायमानस्त्वं नेता वृषभ चर्षणीनाम् ॥

The premordial orders of Agni have been eulogized through out the RV. A glance at this *ṛk* also reveals the same concept. Here the phrase *kratvā rodasī ā tatantha* can be compared with *dyaus pṛthivi agna tatantha, vratā, kratvā* in the present *ṛk* can be put parallely with *ṛtena* in 5.1.7. Thus *kratvā* refers to Agni's power and divine order, and not *prakāśena* as Sāyaṇa has explained. Only by suggestion we can imply the meaning *prakāśa*, 'light'.

The phrase *tvam netā vṛṣabha carṣaṇīnām* can be compared with RV 3.62.6 *vṛṣabhaṁ carṣaṇīnām* .... *bṛhaspatim.* where *vṛs cara* reveals the close relationship with Indra also[5] who has often been associated with this kind of epithet. Sāyaṇa explains *carṣaṇīnām* as *yajamānānām,* "of the worshippers", but this meaning is altogether unacceptable, because *carṣaṇī* refers to the tribes or the people in general as Veṅkaṭamādhava's paraphrase *manuṣyāṇām,* 'of the human beings' clarifies.

RV. III. 6.6

ऋतस्यं वा केशिनां योग्याभिर्घृतस्नुवा रोहिता धुरि धिंष्व ।
अथा वंह देवान् देंव विश्वांन् त्स्वध्वरा कृंणुहि जातवेदः ॥

Sāyaṇa construes ***yogyābhiḥ*** with *keśinā ghṛtasnuvā rohitā-* and *tasya* with *dhuri.* But *tasya* can be construed with *yogyābhiḥ* as well as with *dhuri;* and thus *ṛtasya* means the 'fundamental order's as well as 'sacrifice, denoting the fundamantal order' symbolically. *Ṛtasya dhuri* can be compared with *ṛtasya dhūrṣadamagnim* in RV 1.143.7 and *ko adya yuṅkte dhuri gā ṛtasya* in RV 1.84.16.

Here ***keśinā,*** "two horses having long manes" presents difficult. None has tried to explain who are these two horses. The form *keśinā* occurs seven times in the RV 1.10.3; 82.6; 3.6.6; 41.9; 8.14.12; 17.2; 10.105.2) and *keśavantā* once (RV 10.105.5). Everywhere it is related with Indra. In most of the contexts *keṣinā* is attributive adjective of *hari* "the two horses (of Indra)" *hari* or the noun 'horse'. "Their name *hari* obviously is of a secondary character; as it literally means "brown, tawny, by it is one of those colour names which by way of ellipsis or otherwise (taboo) were applied to animals".[6] Thus here, *keśinā* actually occurs by way of stylistic repetition with Agni as an overlapping statement. Originally this trait belongs to Indra. No doubt Agni's horses are called *hari*, but the attribute *keśinā* is certainly not a common word for Agni's horses as stated above.

RV. III. 6.7

दिवश्चिदा ते रुचयन्त रोका उषो विभातीरनु भासि पूर्वीः ।
अपो यदग्न उशधग्वनेषु होतुर्मन्द्रस्य पनयन्त देवाः ॥

Veṅkaṭamādhava explains *divaḥ* as *'dīptasya* (tava) construing it with te. Thus his difference with Sāyaṇa's explanation of it as *'sūryādapi'*, 'even from the Sun' is evident. As *divaḥ* occurs frequently for the 'sky' there is no question of construing it with *te* and thus it should be taken to mean 'from the sky'. Agni's brilliance shines brilliantly even from the sky and he follows the shining Dawns, which identifies him with the sun.

In the third *pāda* ***apaḥ*** and ***uśadhak*** creat difficulty. Sāyaṇa explains both together as *apaḥ kāmayamānaḥ dahaṁśce vardhase.* But, as *apaḥ* occurs frequently in the sense of 'work, activity' and so on, it cannot be taken here as a verbal form *uśadhak* in here an adjective to *apaḥ* and both together mean 'burning activity' (in the forests) of the brilliant *hotṛ* which is praised by the gods. The third and the fourth pādā-s should be construed together like this; *'agne yat vaneṣu hotuḥ mandrasya uṣadhak apaḥ devaḥ panayanta'*, "O Agni, when the gods praised the burning activity of the brilliant priest in the woods". Thus it renders a complete syntactical unit of an adverbial clause, and it should precede the first two *pādās.* Sāyaṇa's construction of the third pāda with the first, and second with the fourth is not very sound. He supplies *rokan* after *hotuḥ* .which is unnecessary.

RV. III. 6.8

उ॒रौ वा॒ ये अ॒न्तरि॑क्षे॒ मद॑न्ति दि॒वो वा॒ ये रो॑च॒ने सन्ति॑ दे॒वाः ।
ऊमा॑ वा॒ ये सु॒हवा॑सो॒ यज॑त्रा आयेमि॒रे र॒थ्यो॑ अ॒ग्रे अश्वाः॑ ॥ ८ ॥

ऐभि॑रग्ने स॒रथं॑ याह्य॒र्वाङ् नाना॑र॒थं वा॑ वि॒भवो॒ ह्यश्वाः॑ ।
पत्नी॑वतस्त्रिं॒शतं॒ त्रींश्च॑ दे॒वान॑नुष्व॒धमा व॑ह मा॒दय॑स्व ॥ ९ ॥

स होता॒ यस्य॒ रोद॑सी चिदु॒र्वी य॒ज्ञंय॑ज्ञम॒भि वृ॒धे गृ॑णी॒तः ।
प्राची अध्व॒रेव॑ तस्थतुः सु॒मेके॑ ऋ॒तावरी ऋ॒तजा॑तस्य स॒त्ये ॥ १० ॥

इळा॑मग्ने पु॒रुदंसं॑ स॒निं गोः श॑श्व॒त्तमं॒ हव॑मा॒नाय साध ।
स्यान्नः॑ सू॒नुस्तन॑यो वि॒जावाऽग्ने॒ सा ते॑ सुम॒तिर्भू॑त्व॒स्मे ॥ ११ ॥

In these verses the word **ūmāḥ** has been explicated by Veṅkaṭamādhava as *rakṣakaḥ,* 'protectors' Sāyaṇa explains it as '*ūma saṁjñakaḥ pitaraḥ santi.*' The word occurs thirteen times in the RV (ūmāḥ - 3.6.8; 4.19.1; 5.52.12; 7.39.4; 10.6.7; 31.3; 77.8; 120.3; *ūmāsaḥ* 1.166.3; *ūmebhiḥ* 5.51.1; *ūmebhyaḥ* 10.32.5; *ūmāsoḥ,* 1.169.7). Elsewhere Sāyaṇa also gives its meanings *aviaraḥ,* "helpers' (RV 1.166.3) and *rakṣakaḥ,* 'protector'. Therefore, here also it can be taken to mean protectors, helpers' and so on. It can be derived from the *sv,* 'to protect'.

This verse is to be construed with the following verses. All the following verses do not need any discussion because of their simplicity.

NOTES

1. RV M. III, p. 20 fn.
2. See Pischel, *Vedst.* II, 220; Geldner, *Komment,* p. 44; Oldenberg, *Notes* I, 228; Velankar, *Loc. cit.*
3. Geldner, *Komment;* p. 44.
4. Wackernagel-Debrunner Altind. *Grammatik* II. 2,73,637; 851, 853. Mayrhofer *op. cit.*, I, 85; Viśva Bandhu. VP vol. 6, sect. I pt. II, p. 735.
5. See Schmidt, *Bṛhaspati und Indra,* p. 131.
6. Gonda *J., Epithets,* p. 147; see also (*Darling, A Dict.* of *Selected Synonyms in the Principal I-E. languages,* p. 136 (quoted by Gonda).

* * *

The Ṛgveda Maṇḍal III.7

प्र य आ॒रुः शिंतिपृ॒ष्ठस्यं धा॒सेरा मा॒तरां विविशुः स॒प्त वाणींः ।
प॒रि॒क्षितां पि॒तरा॒ सं चंरेते॒ प्र संस्त्रांते दी॒र्घमायुंः प्र॒यक्षे ॥

The present *ṛk* raises some difficult questions with words *āruḥ, śitipṛṣṭha -, dhasaḥ, mātarā, sāptavāṇīḥ, parikṣitā, pitarā* and *prayakṣe.* With whom all these epithets and phrases are to be construed, is a doubtful question which will need some comparison of other related contexts for an explication.

Śitipṛṣṭhasya - The comp. *śitipṛṣṭha* - occurs only twice in the RV, i.e. here and at RV 2.1.25 as *śitipṛṣṭha* for the 'horses' of Indra. Another similar comp. is *śitipādaḥ* RV 1.35.5 which may be compared with *śitipṛṣṭha* above. Here Sāyaṇa's paraphrase of *śitipṛṣṭhasya* as *nīlapṛṣṭhasya* 'of blue backed' may be compared with his own explications of *śitipṛṣṭha* as *śvetapṛṣṭhau evam bhūtaśvau,* 'two horses having white back', and of *śitipādaḥ* as *śvetaiḥ pādairupetaḥ.* 'possessed with white legs'. In other two places he explains *śiti* as 'white', and here as 'blue'. Which of these two meanings will be valid has to be decided. Here Sāyaṇa seems to follow Veṅkaṭamādhava who renders it with *nīlapṛṣṭhasya udakasya* 'of the blue backed water', which appears some how obscure because of *udakasya* which here has no relation whatsoever with Agni. The modern exegetists like Roth, Grassmann, Oldenberg, Griffith, Geldner and Velankar follow the meaning 'white backed'. Thus a controversy seems to prevail over these two explications, i.e. 'white' and 'black'.

The occurrences of *'śiti'* - in latter Vedic literature indicates the greater possibility of its usages in the sense of 'white' rather than 'black'. Moreover, *śiti* seems identical with *śveta* which has the confirmed meaning 'white'.

Āruḥ - It is perfect, 3rd plu. form of the root *ṛ 'gatau'*. The accented form occurs only here in the RV and unaccented form occurs at RV 3.1.4 which has already been explained. The accent here can be explained by Pan. S. 8.1.66 (*yad vṛttannityam*) according to which if the verbal form is preceded by the word *yad* (here *ye*), it retains it accent; and thus the accent falls on the suffix by Pan. S. 3.1.1. (*pratyayaḥ*) and 3.1.3 (*ādyudāttaśca*).

Ye - There is some controversy over this form among the scholars. With reference to this pronominal form Ludwig remarks 'Wahrrcheinlisher ist, dass wirthier eine archaistische anwendung der form auf *ye* fur fem. vor uns haben', (it is probable that here we have an archaic use of the form *ye* for fem.). Griffith takes it apparently for fem. Oldenberg disagrees with these two statements and proposes to alter the reading of *ye (ya)* as (*yaḥ*) construing it with *sapta vāṇīḥ* and thus according to him *saptavāṇīḥ* would stand as the subject. Geldner and Renou apparently follow Sāyaṇa who explains it as *'raśmayaḥ'* (rays) which has been explicated by Geldner as 'the rays of the sun' and by Velankar as *'arcayaḥ'* on the basis of the RV 4.6.10 (*ye arcayaḥ caranti*) and 5.9.5 (*adha sma yasyāarcayaḥ*). Velankar's remark that these 'flames' or 'rays' are alluded to sometimes as in the masculine (5. 1.5; 7) and sometimes in fem. gender (5.5. 2,3,8a) appears noteworthy.

Dhāseḥ - The word *dhāsi*- occurs in different forms in the RV. The form *dhasiḥ* occurs once (RV 9.85.3), *dhāsina* twice (4.3.9; 6.67.6), *dhāsim* eight times (1.62.3; 4.55.7; 5.12.4; 41.17; 7.6.2; 8.43.47; 29; 10.30.1), *dhāsimiva* once (RV 1.140.1) and *dhāseḥ* five times (RV 1.122.13.3.7.1; 3; 57.1; 10.89.11). Sāyaṇa has invariably explained it as a synonym of 'food' on the basis of Nigh. 2.7.11 where it has been attested with other words of the same meaning. He derives it from *dhet* 'to drink' (*dhīyate pīyate iti* - Dhat. Pa. 1.951) with Uṇādi suffix *si.* But he also gives another optional derivation, from *dha* 'to sustain' (Dhat. Pa. 3.10). Veṅkaṭamādhava explains it from *dhe* giving its meaning as *patur (agneḥ).* Grassmann and Roth attest both of the derivations and meanings given by Sāyaṇa. Ludwig, Griffith, Oldenberg follow the first meaning i.e. 'food'. Geldner renders it with 'Sitze', 'seat', which has been followed by Velankar.

The meaning has been controversial even after these renderings. According to Wackernagel-Debrunner *dhāsi* mean milkdrink (Milchanute), refreshment, (Labung), in the masculine, it stand for abode place, and homeland, (Heimate). This conclusion is based upon the analogy with the Avestan word *dajhi-dahi-* 'country, homeland'. In the first case he derives *dhāsi* -m. form *dhā* - 'to suckle, suck, nurse' (perhaps following Sāyaṇa) and in the second from *dhā* 'to place, sit, lie'. Janert traces the origin of *dhāsi* from Indo-Eur. *dhn-si-idg. dhn (in dhānayati)* and rejects the meaning 'drink' (Trank) suggested by B. Schlerath. However, he obviates the difficulties of his own interpretation of *dhāsi* as 'water course' (Rinnsol, Rinnung), 'fluid ray' (flu Bigkeitsstrahl) through the meanings and the etymologies given by Schlerath. But even this interpretation and analogical explication do not sound correct. Indo. Germanic root **dhen* (in *dhānayati*) cannot be placed with *dhā*; because the *dhān*- actually connotes the sense of setting something in motion, while *dhā* indicates just the opposite idea; i.e. setting something in stationary stake, viz 'placing something properly'. Here *dhāsi* appears to be derived from *dhā* 'to place' in ordinary sense. The *dhā* often conveys the idea of "to establish, to institute, to create, lay down, dispose"[1] ("Boser quelque chase qui subsistera desormais, qui est destine' a 'durer; etablir dans l 'existence, creer")[2], ("to put anything which exists, henceforth which is destined to remain; to establish in the existence, to create"). Thus we can derive *dhāsi* from *dhā* and attest its meanings as 'establishment, creation, institution, foundation, disposition, existence', and so on. The occurrences of *dhāsi*-in the RV signify only such meanings and not 'food' or 'drink' as supposed by Sāyaṇa and others. These meanings can be assigned suitably to all the occurrences of *dhāsim*-at various places in the RV To exemplify these meanings, we can quote here the following contexts:

RV 1.62.3b. *vidat saramā tanayāya dhāsim*

'Sarmā found a place (Position) for her offspring.[3]

1.122.13ab: *mandāmahe daśatayasya dhāsar -*
dviryat pañca bibhrato yantyannā.

We extoll the existence of the tenfold whom the food go on sustaining for ten (all) times.[4]

1.140.1: *vedipade priyadhāmāya sudyute*
dhāsimiva pra bharā yonimagnaye

'To splendid Agni seated by the altar, loving well his abode,[5] bring the food to his place as (one brings to his) residence.[6]

These examples clarify the position that *dhāsi* - cannot mean 'food', 'drink' or 'nourishment', rather it should be translated as 'place', 'abode', 'residence', 'existence' and so on; and it should not be derived from the *dhet* 'to drink', but should be connected with the *dhā* 'to place', 'dispose', 'create' and so on. Here *dhāseḥ* can be translated as 'from the abode', taking it as an abl. Sg.[7]

Mātarā- Here *mātarā* (loc. du. of *mātṛ*) stands for the two worlds, i.e. the earth and the sky. For details see RV 3.1.7. above.

Sapta vāṇīḥ- This phrase occurs only five times in the RV (3.1.6; 7.1; 8.59.3; 9.103.3; 1.64.24). Veṅkaṭamādhava explicates here as *sapta ca, gamana svabhāvā nadīḥ,* (RV 3.1.6).

Sāyaṇa follows this maxim of 'seven rivers' here also. Besides these two scholiasts many subsequent oriental as well as occidental exegetists also follow this line.[8]

Parikṣitā - The comp. *parikṣit* occurs thrice in the RV (1.123.7 - *parikṣitoḥ*: 3.7.1; 10.65.8 - *parikṣitā*). Other similar formations in the RV are *adhikṣitaḥ* (RV 8.40.3; 41.9) and *upakṣitaḥ* (8.10.33). The word *parikṣit* can be formed with *kai* 'to dwell' (Avestan *sit* - 'to reside') with the zero suffix *kvip* (Pan. S. 3.2.76) and by insertionof *tuk* (Pan. S. 6.1.71) with the prefix *pari* (*pari* + *kṣi* + *t* + *kvip* = *parikṣit*). The accent will fall on the second member of the comp. which can be explained by Pan. S. 6.2.139. The lengthening of the final vowel can be explained by Pan. S. 7.1.39.

The phrase '*parikṣitā pitarā*', "the surrounding parents" stands for "heaven and earth".

Pitarā - there is no controversy over this term. All the exegetists agree on its interpretation as 'the sky and the earth'. This can be compared fruitfully with the RV. 10.65.8 the phrase *parikṣitā*

Āyuḥ - Veṅkaṭamādhava renders it with *annam* which has been followed by Sāyaṇa optionally. Sāyaṇa's optional meaning '*jīvanam*' appears to be more suitable and this has been followed by subsequent interpreters.

Prayakṣe - This form of *yaj* with the prefix *pra* occurs only twice in the RV (3.7.1; 31.3). *Prayakṣan* occurs at RV 2.5.1. As the *yakṣ* or *yaj* conveys various meanings like 'to honour, worship, give' etc. *Pryakṣe* can be interpreted variously, but here, with *āyuḥ* its meaning as 'to offer', 'to bestow' would be more suitable. Veṅkaṭamādhava and Sāyaṇa have explained it in the sense of worship while most of the modern exegetists have taken it to mean 'conferring, bestwing, offering' etc., which appear convincing. Perhaps here the idea of 'bestowing long life' conveys the sense of the beginning of the day of the year as Max Müllar has shown (See SBE 46, p. 250).

RV. III. 7.2

दिवक्षंसो धेनवो वृष्णो अश्वां देवीरा तंस्थौ मधुंमद् वहन्तीः ।
ऋतस्यं त्वा सदंसि क्षेमयन्तं पर्येकां चरति वर्तनिं गौः ॥

The verse stands here as a riddle arousing many doubtful connotations. The words *divakṣasaḥ. dhenavaḥ, ekā gauḥ,* though simple in appearance, on the peripheral meanings, are impregnated with suggestive senses. A full treatment of these words and their implicative meanings would solve the difficult problem of interpretation of this verse.

Divakṣasaḥ - This form occurs only twice in the RV (3.7.2; 10.65.7). Once the form *divakṣaḥ* also occurs at RV 3.30.21 where it is an epithet of Indra, which is suggestive of Indra's presence in the present context also. If we compare the hymn 10.65 with the present hymn, i.e. 3.7, it will be more clear. In 10.65 Indra and Agni have been invoked together where many appellatives and epithets as well as attributive phrases and oppositional descriptions are the same as in the present hymn. Therefore, if here the epithet *divakṣasaḥ* is interpreted as Indra it would not be inappropriate. Thus *divakṣasaḥ, dhenavaḥ* and *vṛsaṇaḥ* will be construed as a whole to convey the idea of 'waters' or 'lights' of heaven dwelling mightly and which have been mentioned explicatively in the second pāda as *'aśvā devīrā tasthau - madhumadvahantīḥ'*, 'the pervading goddesses carrying the sweet juice (Soma)'.[9] The terms *dhenavaḥ* is parallel and complimentary to *aṣvaḥ devīḥ* in the following pāda. Veṅkaṭamādhava and Sāyaṇa have construed *aṣvaḥ* with *dhenavaḥ,* which has been followed by other. For example, Velankar[10] has put *dhenavaḥ* and *aṣvaḥ* together as predicate, but if *aṣvaḥ* is also construed with *devīḥ*[11] which is confirmed by *vahantīḥ,* it would be fitting to the context. Or *dhenavaḥ* and *aṣvaḥ* stand together as an accumulation of adjectives qualifying *devīḥ,* where *devīḥ*- is more repetition of the same phenomenon. Thus we can render the first two pādās with "the cows of the heaven dwelling with powerful (Indra) are all pervading, and he (Indra) has mounted upon the pervading goddesses carrying the sweet drink".

The symbolism of 'cow' is to be explicated here. 'Cow' signifies six phenomena in the RV, namely, (i) rays (as at RV 1.10.8; 92.2; 5.74.4), (ii) Waters or streams (as at RV 1.33.3; 10; 2.34.1; 5.29.3), (iii) cows in general (as at RV 1.83.4; 5.91.22; 103.5; 126.5; 6.54.5 etc.), (iv) Uṣas or light (as at RV 1.62.3; 5.14.4), (v) praise or eulogy according to Sāyaṇa (as at RV 2.21.5) and speech 'vāk' as explained by Yāska in terms of *mādhyamika vāk.*

Out of above six meanings interpreters have accepted three, i.e., rays, waters or streams and *mādhyamika vāk.* But it seems a fetched to attach the last one, i.e. *mādhyamika vāk* here, as there is no ground for it. Rather it would be in the fitness of the context to accept either 'rays' or 'streams', as we have sufficient grounding for this assertion on the basis of the comparison of such other similar contexts. At RV 2.35.9 the 'celestial waters" *(yahvīḥ)* are said to be the carier of Apam Napat's (Agni's another form) greatness.

> *tasya jyeṣṭhaṁ mahimānaṁ vahantīr -*
> *hiraṇyavarṇāḥ pari yanti yahvīḥ*

'The gold-coloured maidens, carrying his highest greatness, surround him.'[12]

The word ***madhumad*** in the present context can be compared with RV. 2.35.11 where *āpaḥ* carry the *ghṛta* and *anna* (clarified butter and good) of Agni. Thus the usage of participial form *vahantīḥ* signifies the role of the great *āpaḥ devīḥ* in all these contexts, and on this ground it can be surmised that *dhenavaḥ, aśvaḥ,* and *devīḥ* are none else but 'celestial waters' which pervade the entire region. Agni mounts upon them in the form of lightening which can be compared with RV. 2.35.9 ab:

apaṁ napādā hyasthādupasthaṁ
jihmānāmurdhvo vidyutaṁ vasānaḥ.

'Apām Napāt has mounted upon the bosom of the crooked ones, standing erect and wearing brilliance (*vidyutam*).[13]

But, notwithstanding this, the phrase *ekā gauḥ* in the fourth pāda refers to something else than the 'celestial water'. It refers, perhaps, to the 'rays' with special reference to *ṛtasya sadasi* 'in the seat of *Ṛta*' which might be here the 'sacrificial setting' where Agni arrives from the heavenly region escorted and surrounded by 'one' i.e. 'Agni's flame'. This can be compared with RV 3.2.9 where one of the three *samidhās* have been mentioned to be put in the world.

The phrase *vartanim pari carati* may be compared with *vartiḥ (pari yatihah)* at RV 6.53.2 and *pariyāti vartiḥ* at RV 7.69.5. In all these contexts *varti*- refers to the 'course'. The prefix *pari* in all these contexts suggests the span of the course through which the object accompanies the subject. Here, in the context under discussion, *ekā gauḥ* accompanies Agni all along his way from heaven to earth, and this accompaniment can be of none but of 'rays' or 'brilliance' or 'light' that proceeded from heaven with Agni.

RV. III. 7.3

आ सीमरोहत् सुयमा भवंन्तीः पतिंश्चिकित्वान् रंयिविद् रंयीणाम् ।
प्र नीलंपृष्ठो अतसस्यं धासेस्ता अंवासयत् पुरुधप्रंतीकः ॥

This verse relates how Apām Napāt became transformed into sacrificial fire from celestial form. The phrase *suyamāḥ bhavantīḥ* refers to the *dhenavaḥ ,aśvaḥ* and *devīḥ* of Agni, i.e. his 'rays' or 'flames' referred to earlier in above verse. Sāyaṇa explains *suyamāḥ* as *'sukhena niyantum sakyāḥ'*, 'early controllable', construing it with *bhavantīḥ* who are the mares (*vaḍavāḥ*) of Agni. He does not explicate these *vaḍavāḥ*. Veṅkaṭamādhava[14] leaves this point entirely. The meaning 'easily controllable' has been followed by Griffith[15], Grassmann[16], Geldner[17], Renou[18] and Velankar.[19] Oldenberg[20] renders it with 'well-manageable'.

Suyamāḥ, perhaps, means 'well controlled' here, because Agni has a good control over his rays and when he desires to manifest them, he makes them to come forth from his form or seat which has been indicated here in the second hemistich.

Nīlapṛṣṭho atasasya dhāsaḥ - This phrase can be compared with '*sitipṛṣṭhasya dhāseḥ at* RV 3.7.1 *atasasya* has been explained by Sāyaṇa as *satata gamanasya* 'of constant moving', deriving it form *ata 'sātatyagamen*'. But on the basis of comparison with other contexts *atasa* means 'tree' or 'bush' which is confirmed by Sāyaṇa's explications elsewhere.[21]

None of the exegetists has tried to give the etymology of *atasa*. Sāyaṇa's derivation of *atasa* from *ata* 'to move constantly' is open to objection, because 'tree' or 'bush' has nothing to do with 'constant moving' therefore, this derivation should be rejected outrightly. Grassmann[22] says that 'der Ursprung ist unbekannt' (the origin is obscure) but doubtfully proposes its derivation from *tanis* with *a*. This derivation, though hypothetical, leads to get another clue of etymology. On the basis of the meanings, which are clear from the point of view of the various contexts, it is evident that *atasa* refers to the phenomenon which is not moving, rather is static like 'tree'. Therefore, if we derive *atasa* from *tas* with a privative *a*, which is used often in Vedic language to signify objective ideas with a negative concept,[23] it would not be out of focus. This derivation takes in its perview not only *atasa* but another obscure etymological problem of the word *taskara* - 'thief' which occurs five times in the RV

(1.191.5; 6.28.3; 8.29.6; 10.4.6) and goes without etymological explications. Yāska has given the views of the etymologists as *'tatkaro bhavati yat pāpakam iti'* (he does what is sin), and of the grammarians as *'tanotervā syat santata-karmā bhavati ahorātra-karma vā'*[24] (it may be derived from *tan*, or he is a constant doer or is doing sections in the night and the day). Lindner[25] proposes its etymology from *tanis*[26] 'to shake, agitate' etc. But this etymology is unstable because of its root meaning. Equally unsafe is the equation of *atasa* with GK *diu-d ic* 'thorn, hedge' proposed by Charpentier[27] and Sutterlin[28] as well as Uhlenbeck. The word *taskara* - in opposition to *atasa* signifies the 'movement', and therefore, if we derive it from the root *tas* -, hypothesizing its meaning as 'move constantly or here and there' the problem will be solved. *Taskara* - moves here and there, and *atasa*, the tree, stands constanly. This meaning of *taskara* - is implied in the explication proposed by Yāska in the phrase *ahorātrakarma*. With this hypothesis we can add another hapax legomenon tasara - (RV 10.130.2) which has been derived by Wackernagel from *tanis* 'to move here and there', with the - *are* - suffix on the anology of *trasara* -, *drarara* - etc.[29] But he could have derived it from *tas* as he derives *trasara* from *tras* - "Zittern"[30] (tremble, shiver). On this very anology we can be sure to derive *tasara* -, *taskara* - and *atasa* - from root *tas* 'to move constantly'. One can raise some doubt about the accentual differentation among the words *tasarā, taskara* and *atasa*, because while the first two bear the acute on the initial, the third, i.e. *atasa* has its accent on the final syllable. The accentual problem of *atasa* has its accent on the final syllable. The accentual problem of *atasa* can be explained very well by Pan.S. 6.2.157 *'ackāvaśaktau'* (a word formed with the *krit* affix *ac* and *ka* preceded by the particle *nan* (*a*, has acute on the final when the meaning is 'not capable'). By this aphorism the meaning of *atasa* as 'not capable of moving constantly' is also exemplified. The accent here could have been explained by Pan. S. 6.2.172 *'nañ subhyām'* also but the part meaning 'not capable' would have been left unexplained. Thus the formation of *atasa* can be explained as *nañ + tas + ac = a + tas + a = atasa,* a *bahuvṛ* comp. meaning 'one who is not capable of moving constantly, i.e. 'tree'. The other meanings proposed by Sāyaṇa and followed by subsequent scholars as *tṛnsgulmādi,* 'bush', etc. do not come in the perview of this word in any context.

The word ***tasara***, referred to above may be derived from *tas* 'move constantly'. As *tasara* has the context of 'moving back and forth, being the weaving shuttle[31] it exemplifies clearly the meaning of the root *tas* 'to move'. The word *tasara* may be formed with *tas + ac + rak* (Uṇādi S. 2.13) = *tasara.* The original accent remains on the root itself. In the same way *taskara* will be formed by *tas + kṛ + ta* (Pa. 3.2.20 *'krño hetutācchīlyānulomyeṣu*) = *tas + kar + a = taskara.* Here this word appears to be *bahavr.* comp., and thus means 'one who does moving world constantly' i.e. 'thief'. The accent will be governed by *'bahuvr'*, Pan.S. 6.2.1.

Thus, these three words, i.e. *atasa, tasara* and *taskara* come in one lexical group which has its origination from the *tas.*

Here *atasasya dhāseḥ* signifies the 'seat of Agni, the wood' where he resides, and when produced he becomes 'blue backed' due to smoke, and makes his flames, referred to here in the verse by *tah,* 'to come forth'.

Pra' atasayata - This form indicates the Agni's action of 'making to come forth his flames which reside (*vas*) in his own body'. Though the flames come out from his 'seat' (*dhāseḥ*). Yet they appear to remain in Agni's entire body forefully, which has been indicated here by the use of prefix *Pra.* Sāyaṇa explicates it as *'prakarṣeṇa vāsayati sma. nivāsena srame'panite satatagamanaṁ posayitum sakyamityarthaḥ.*

NOTES

1. J. Gonda, *The Vision of the Vedic Poets* (The Hague, 1963), p. 174.
2. E. Benveniste, *"Problems semantiques de la reconstruction"* in word 10 (New York, 1954), p. 252.
3. Here Sāyaṇa explains *dhāsim* as *'annam'* (*Sarama svaputrāya annam avindat* which has been followed by several exegetists including Geldner who renders it with 'Nahrung' (nourishment). Why he deviates from the meaning 'Sitze', as given in the present context, is unthinkable.
4. Here again Sāyaṇa explains *dhāseḥ* as *'annasya* (*dasa-vayavasya*) which seems improbable because of *anna* (*ni*) in the same context. Here *dhāseḥ* is to be construed with *mandāmahe* as well as with *yat.* Geldner again follows Sāyaṇa. Here he renders *dhāseḥ* with 'Speisung' (food) again follows Sāyaṇa. *dasatayasya* and *dvi-panca* are parallel. This can be compared with post Indo-Eur. / *dekm* (t) / 'ten' as a compound containing PIE (de) 'two' plus the zero grade of the root/kemo, from which the noun (komt-) 'hand' is derived with the agent suffix - . See Oswald Szemerengi, *Studies in the Indo-European System of Numerals* (Heidalberg, Carl Winter, 1960), p. 69. The word *pañca* has been used to express "totality" and as Albert Goetze has shown that it can be applied to the whole body of nobility in the socio-political context of the early Kingdom. See Albert Goetze, *Kleinasien* (= *Kultur geschichte des Altan Orients* III: 1.3.3.1), (Munich, C Beck, 1957, 2nd edition), pp. 86-88. *pañca* can be compared with Hittite *panku* 'all'. For details see E. Polome' *The Indo-European Numerals for Five and Hittite Panku* - 'all' in *Pratidanam* (Fest. to Prof. F.B.J. Kuiper), (Mouton, The Hague, 1968), pp. 98 ff.

   The translation of *dhāma* see J. Gonda, *The Meaning of the Dhāman,* (Amsterdam, 1967, p. 23 ff.) His criticism of Geldner's rendering as "Geburtsstatte' and Renou's as 'institutions'.

6. Sāyaṇa explains *dhāsim iva* here as *'havirūpam annamiva'* like the offering', but here it can be placed with *yonim* 'place' which has been used as a parallel to *dhāsim.* Geldner seems doubtful about this. Griffith has nearly hit the mark while translating 'his place of birth' but missed doubtly because he translates *yonim* as 'food' and *prabhara* as 'I bring', bhara being 2nd p. sing. of *bhr.*
7. See Oldenberg, *RV Notes*, p. 229; SBE. 46, p. 251.
8. For details see above 3.1.6.
9. "The Sweet drop" *madhuman drapsaḥ* is another name for the soma beverage; RV 9.69.2 *madhuman drapsaḥ pari vāramarṣati.* See J. Gonda, *Epithets* -, p. 214.
10. *Ṛgveda Mandala* III, p. 23 (fn.).
11. 'Word Economy' theory should be applied.
12. Velankar's rendering (RV M. II, p. 99) adopted here.
13. *vidyuta*-signifies both lightning and brilliance. See Velankar.
14. *Loc. cit.*
15. *Loc. cit.*
16. *op. cit.*, p. 1548.
17. *Loc. cit.*
18. *Loc. cit.*
19. *Loc. cit.*
20. *Loc. cit.*
21. RV Bh. 1.58.2; 4; 4.4.4; 4.7.10.
22. *op. cit.*, p. 27.
23. L. Renou In the BSOAS (London) 10, p. 15; J. Gonda, *'Ahiṁsā and Similar concepts'* in *'Four Studies in the language of the Veda* (Mouton & Co. 1959), p. 95 ff.
24. Nir. 3.14.
25. B. Linder, *Altindische Nominallildung* (Jena, 1978), p. 69, quoted by Wackernagel in Alt. Gramm. II, 2, p. 541.
26. Vaj. Priti, 3.5.1; gaṇapāṭha.
27. Jarl Charpentier, *Beitrage aur kunde der Indogermanischen Sprachen* (Gotingen) 30, p. 157.
28. Vhlenbeck *C.C.* and Sutterlin in IF4, p. 104.
29. Wackern. Debr. *Alt. Gram.* II, 2. p. 215.
30. *Loc. cit.*

31. RV 10.130.2:
ime mayūkhā upa sedurū sadaḥ
sāmāni cakrustasarāṇyotave
"These pags are fastened to the seat of worship; they made the Soma-hymns their wearing shuttles". Sāyaṇa explicates *tasarani* as *'tiryaksarani tirascinasutrani'* which is apparently wrong with the point of view of etymology. *Tiryak* has nothing to do with *tasara.* According to Uvata - Mahidhara *tasara* is an instrument of weaving *'tasaram vayanasadhanan* V. S. 19.83.

***

BIBLIOGRAPHY

TEXTS

Atharvaveda Saṁhitā, S.D. Satavalekar, Edited, Svādhyaya Maṇḍala, Pardi, Śaka 1965

Atharvaveda Saṁhitā with Commentary of Sāyaṇa, Vishva Bandhu, Edited, Vishveshvaranand Vaidik Research Institute, Hoshiarpur, 1961

ṚK - Prātiśākhya, Śaunaka, Edited by Mangla Deo Shastri, Allahabad, 1937

Ṛgveda-bhāṣya, Mādhava, Edited by C.K. Raja, Madras University Sanskrit Series -8,1935

*Ṛgveda-vyākhya,*Mādhava, Edited by C.K. Raja, Adyar Library, Madras, 1939

Ṛgveda-Saṁhitā with the commentary of Sāyaṇa, 4 Volumes Vaidika Saṁśodhana Maṇḍala, Poona, 1933-51

Ṛgveda Saṁhita with Ṛgartha-dīpikā, 4 Volumes, Edited by Lakshman Sarup, Motilal Banarsidass, Lahore , 1939-55

Aitareya-brāhmaṇa with Ṣaḍguruśiṣyakṛta Sukhapradāvṛtti sahita, Trivendrum 1942, reprint Delhi, 1991, 3 Volumes.

Aitareya-brāhmaṇa with the Commentary of Sāyaṇa, Edited by Sudhakara Malaviya, Tara Publications, Varanasi, 1980, 2 Volumes.

Bṛhaddevatā, Śaunaka, Edited and translated by R.K. Rai, Chaukhamba Sanskrit Sansthan, Varanasi, 1980

Nirukta, Yāska, Edited by V.K. Rajawade; Bhandarkar Oriental Research Institute, Poona, 1940

Yajurveda-Saṁhitā, S.D. Satavalekar, Edited, Svādhyaya Maṇḍala, Pardi, Vikram Samvat 2003

Samaveda Saṁhitā, S.D. Satavalekar, Svādhyaya Maṇḍala, Pardi, Vikram Saṁvat 2003

MODERN WORKS

Apte V.M., *The Student's English Sanskrit Dictionary,* Motilal Banarsidass, Delhi, 1974

Aufecht Theodor, *Die Hymnen des Rigveda,* Zwite Teil, Maṇḍala I- VI, Otto Harrassowitz, Wiesbaden, 1955

Benveniste E, *Problems Samantiques de la Reconstruction in word;* 10, New York, 1954

Bergaigne A., *la Religion de Vedique,* 3 Volume, Paris, 1881

Bhat M.S., *Vedic Tantrism,* (A Study of Ṛgvidhāna of Śaunaka with text and translation) Motilal Banarsidass, Delhi, 1987

Bhawe S.S., *The Soma Hymns of the Ṛgveda: A Fresh Inter-pretation,* M.S. University Research Series No. 3 and 5, Oriental Institute, Baroda, 1957-1960

Bloomfield M, A., *Vedic Concordance,* Harvard Oriental Series, Vol. ten, Harvard University Press, 1906

Coomaraswamy A.K., *The Ṛgveda as Landnāma-Bók,* London, 1935

Dhalla M.N., *Zoroastrian Theology,* New York, 1914

Eggeling J, *Śatapatha Brāhmaṇa,* (translated) 5 Volumes, Oxford, 1882-1900 (Sacred Books of the East, Vol. 20, 26, 41, 42, 43)

Dandekar R.N., *Vedic Bibliography,* Volumes I-IV (Vol. I. 2nd edition), Bhandarkar Oriental Research Institute, Poona, 1986, 1961, 1973. 1985

Geldner Karl Friedrich, *Der Rigveda,* Übersetzung and Erläutert, Erster Teil, Leipzig, 1951

Geldner Karl Friedrich and Pischel R., *Vedische Studien,* Leipzig, 1888

Deva Rājā Radhakānta, *Śabda kalpadruma,* 5 Volumes, Chaukhambha Sanskrit Series, Varanasi, 1969-70

Gonda J, *Aspects of Early Vaisnuism,* Utrecht, 1954, Motilal Banarsidass, Delhi, 1969

——, *Epithets in the Ṛgveda,* Amsterdam, 1959

——, *Four Studies in the Languages of the Veda,* The Hague, 1959

——, *Gods and Power in Veda,* S. Gravenhage, 1957

——, *Reflections on the numerals 'one' and 'two' in Ancient Indo-Europeon Languages,* N.V.A. Oosthoek, utrecht 1955

——, *Change and Continuity in Indian Religion,* London; The Hague, 1965

——, *Vision of the Vedic Poets,* The Hauge 1963

——, *Loka in the Veda,* Amsterdam, 1966

——, *Notes on names and the names of God in Ancient India,* Amsterdom, 1970

——, *World and Heaven in the Veda,* Amsterdom, 1966

——, *Dual Deites in the Religion of the Veda,* London, 1974

Goetze Albert, *Kleinasien Kultur Geschichte la de Alten Orients* IV, Munich, 1957, 2nd Edition.

Griffith R.T.H, *The Hymns of the Ṛgveda,* 2 Volumes (translated) Varanasi, 1963

——, *The Hymns of the Sāmaveda,* (translated) Chowkhambha Sanskrit Series, 28, Varanasi, 1963

Grassmann Hermann, *Rig-veda,* Überzetzt und mit Kritischen und Erläuternden Ammerkengen Verseinen, Erster Teil, F.A. Brockhaus, Leipzig, 1876

——, *Wörterbuch Zum Ṛgveda,* Wiesbaden 1964

Hillebrandt A, *Ritual Literatur,* Vedische opfer und Zauber, Strassburg 1897

Jackson A.V.W., *Avesta Grammar,* New York 1892

Johansson K.F, *Die Altindische Gottin Dhisana und Verwandtes Uppsala,* leipzig 1917

Kashikar C.G., *Bhāradvāja Śrauta Sūtra,* (Edited and translated) 2 Volumes, Poona 1964

Keith A.B., *The Vedas of the Black Yajus School,* entitled *Taittirīya Saṁhitā,* (Translated) 2 Volumes, Cambridge, 1914, (Harvard Oriental Series - 18,19)

——, *Rgveda Brāhmaṇa*, (= *Aitareya* and *Kauṣītaki Brāhmaṇas*) (Translated) Cambridge, 1929, (Harvard Oriental Series 25)

——, *Religion and Philosophy of Veda and Upaniṣads*, (first Indian Reprint), Delhi 1970 (Harvard Oriental Series -31,32)

——, *Vedic Index of Names and Subjects*, (I-II) London, 1912

Lindner B, *Altindische Nominallildeng*, Jenna, 1978

Lüders H., *Varuṇa*, Göttingen, 1951-59

Ludwig Alfred, *Der Rigveda*, (Mit Commentor und Einleitung) Leipzig, Prag, 1876

Macdonell, A.A, *Hymns from the Ṛgveda*, Selected and metrically translated, London, Oxford University Press Calcutta, 1922

——, *A, Vedic Grammar for Students*, Hindi translation, Dr Satya Vrat Shastri, Motilal Banarsidass, Delhi, 1971

——, *Bṛhaddevatā*, Harvard University Press (Edited), 1907

Mitra Rejendralal, *Bṛhaddevatā or an index to the Gods of the Ṛgveda* by Śaunaka, (Edited), Bibliotheca Indica, (Nos. 722, 760 and 819) (New Series), The Baptist Mission Press, Calcutta, 1893

Max Müller F, *India what Can teach Us*, Bombay, 1899

——, *Sacred Books of the East*, Vol 32, Dẹlhi, 1964

——, *Vedic Hymns* (Hymns to the Maruts, Rudra), Part I, Motilal Banarssidass, Delhi, 1964

——, *Ṛgveda-Saṁhitā*, (Hymns to Marut), London, 1969

Oldenberg Harmann, *Vedic Hymns*, Sacred Books of the East, Volume 46, Motilal Banarsidass, Delhi, 1964

——, *Ṛigveda textkritische und exegetische Noten*, Berlin, 1909

——, *Die religionen* des *Veda*, Berlin, 1923

Peter Peterson, *Hymns from the Rigveda* edited with Sāyaṇās commentary 3rd edition, revised and enlarged by S.R. Bhandarkar, BORI, Poona, 1924

Potdar KR, *Sacrifice in the Ṛgveda*, Bhartiya Vidya Bhawan Series, Bombay, 1953

——., *Āpri Hymns in the Ṛgveda*: A study and a theory, Journal of the University of Bombay Vol XIV, September 1945

Raja CK, *Ṛgveda-bhāṣya of Skandasvāmin,* (Edited) Madras University Sanskrit Series 8, 1939

——, . *Ṛgveda-Vyākhyā by Mādhava,* (Edited) Adyar Library Madras, 1939·

Renou Louis, Études Védiques ET Pāṇinéennes, Paris, 1954

Rosen Fridericus, *Rigveda-Saṁhitā,* Liber Primus, Sanskrit et latine; London, 1887

Sarup Lakshman, *The Nighaṇṭu and the Nirukta,* Motilal Banarsidass, Delhi, 1962

Ramgopal, *Vedic Vyākaraṇa,* National Publishing House, Delhi, 1969

Satavalekar SD, *Ṛgveda kā subodha-bhāṣya,* Svādhyāya Maṇḍala, Pardi, 1985

——, . *Rgveda Saṁhitā,* (Edited) Svādhyāya Maṇḍala, Aundh, 1939

——, *Maitrāyiṇī Saṁhitā,* Svādhyāya Maṇḍala, Aundh, 1942

——, *Atharvaveda Saṁhitā,* (Edited), Svādhyāya Maṇḍala, Aundh, 1943

——, *Śukla Yajurveda Saṁhitā,* (Edited) Svādhyāya Maṇḍala, Pardi, 1963

Shastri JagdishLal, *Śukla Yajurveda with commentary of Uvvaṭa and Mahīdhara* (Edited), Motilal Banarsidass, Delhi, 1970

——, *Upanisat-saṁgraha,* Motilal Banarsidass, Delhi, 1970

Sastri Kapali, *Ṛgveda-saṁhitā,* edited with Sanskrit Commentary entitled *Siddhañjana,* T.V. Sri Aurobindo Ashram, Pondicherry, 1950-51

Shastri C. Sankararama, *Aṣṭādhyāyī Sūtrapāṭha,* edited with Vārtikas, Gaṇas, Dhātupāṭha, Pāṇinīya-Śikṣā, Paribhāṣāpātha and sūtra Index, Introduction by Dr. Ratna Basu, Sharada Publishing house, Delhi, 1994

Singh Fateh, *The Vedic Etymology.* The Sanskrit Sadan, Kota, 1952

Sri Aurovindo, *Hymns to the Mystic fire*, Shri Aurovindo Ashram, Pondicherry, 1952

Saràsvati Kevalanand, *Mīmāṁsākoṣa*, (Edited) Prājña Phāṭhaśālā Maṇḍala, Wai, 1952

Suryakanta, *A Practical Vedic Dictionary*, Oxford University Press, Delhi, 1981

Tarkavācaspati Tārānātha, *Vācaspatyama*, 6 Volumes, Chaukhambha Sanskrit Series, Varanasi, 1967

Velankar HD, *Ṛgveda Maṇḍala* VI, University of Bombay, 1963

Ṛk-sūkta-Vaijanti, Vaidika Saṁsodhana Maṇḍala, Poona, 1965

——, .. *Ṛgveda Maṇḍala II*, University of Bombay, 1966

——, . *Ṛgveda Maṇḍala III*, University of Bombay, 1968

——, *Word Economy in the Ṛgvedic Intrepretation*, ABORI, Pune, 1965

Vishva Bandh'u, *Ṛgveda-bhāṣya of Udgīthācārya*, (Edited), Lahore, 1935

——, . *Ṛgveda with Commentary of Skandasvamin, Udagīṭṭha Veṅkatamādhava and Mudgala*, (Edited) Vishvesvaranand Vaidik Research Institute, Hoshiarpur, 1963

——, *Vedic Padānukrama Kośa*, A Vedic word concordance, 5 Volumes subdivided in 16 parts, Vishvesvaranand Vaidik Research Institute, Hoshiarpur, 1942

Verma Siddheshvar, *Etymology of Yāska*, Vishvesvaranand Vaidik Research Institute, (V.I. Seris -5), Hoshiarpur, 1953

Venkatsubiah A, *Vedic Studies*, Vol. I, Mysore, 1932

Wackernagel Jakob and Debrunner Albert, *Altindische Grammatik*, Vanden Hoeck and Ruprecht, Göttingen, 1954

Whitiney W.D, *Sanskrit Grammar*, Delhi, 1962

William Monier, *Sanskrit English Dictionary*, Oxford University Press, 1963

* * *

MANTRA INDEX

World Index

* * *